"Happy Coloring!"

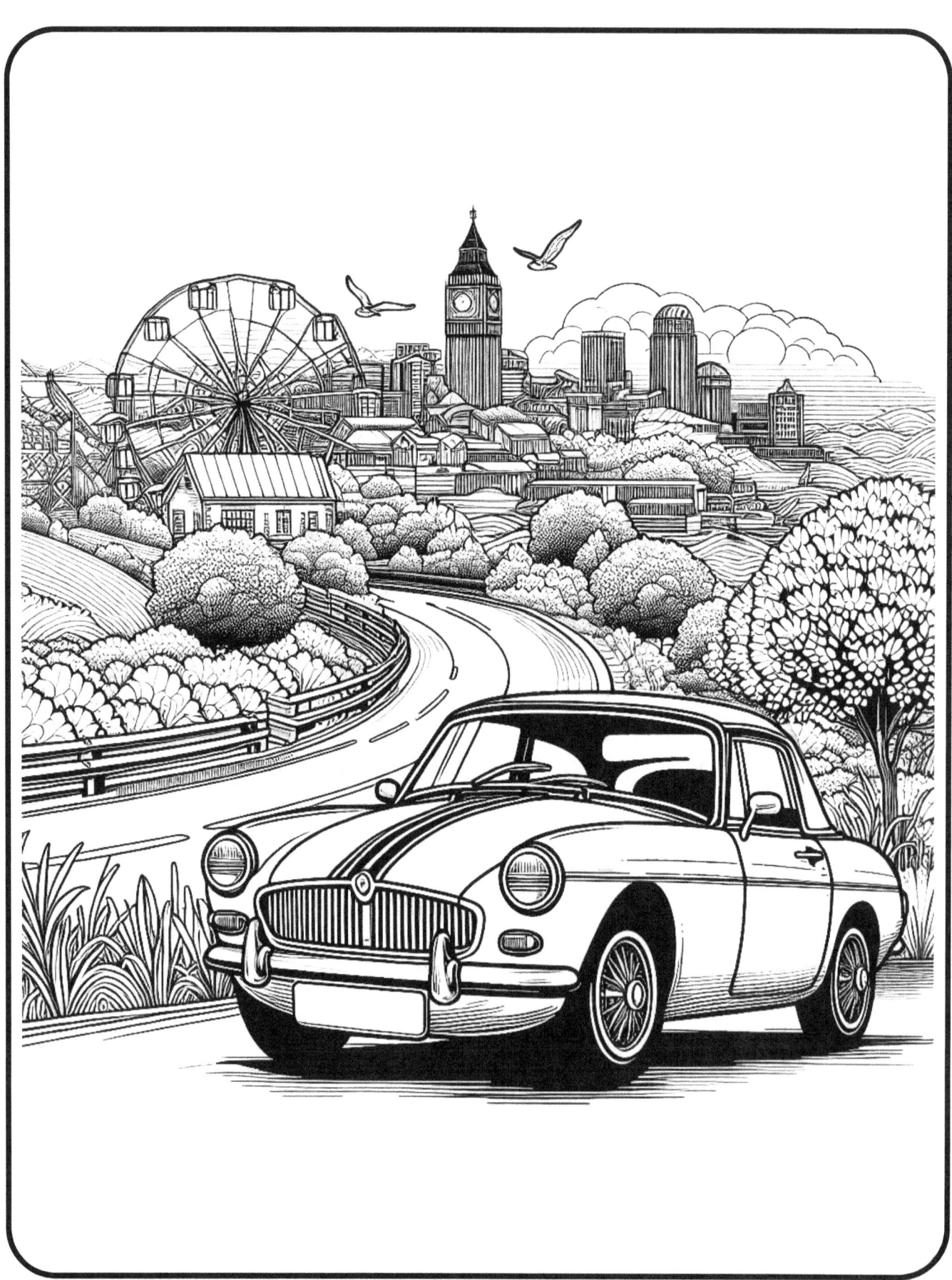

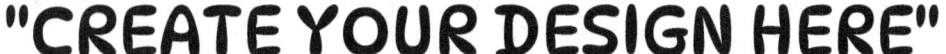

"CREATE YOUR DESIGN HERE"

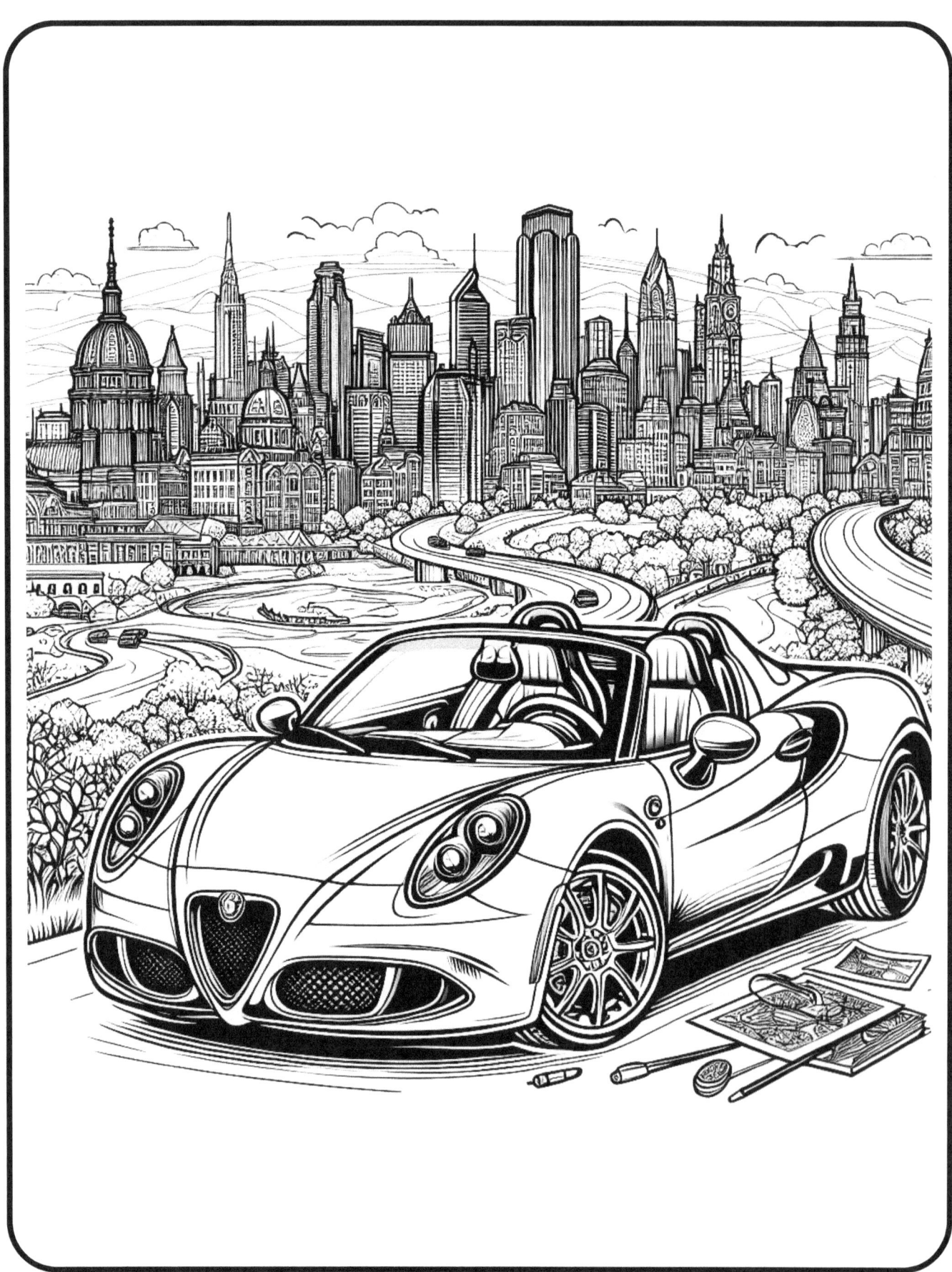

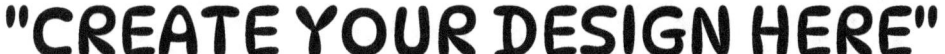

"CREATE YOUR DESIGN HERE"

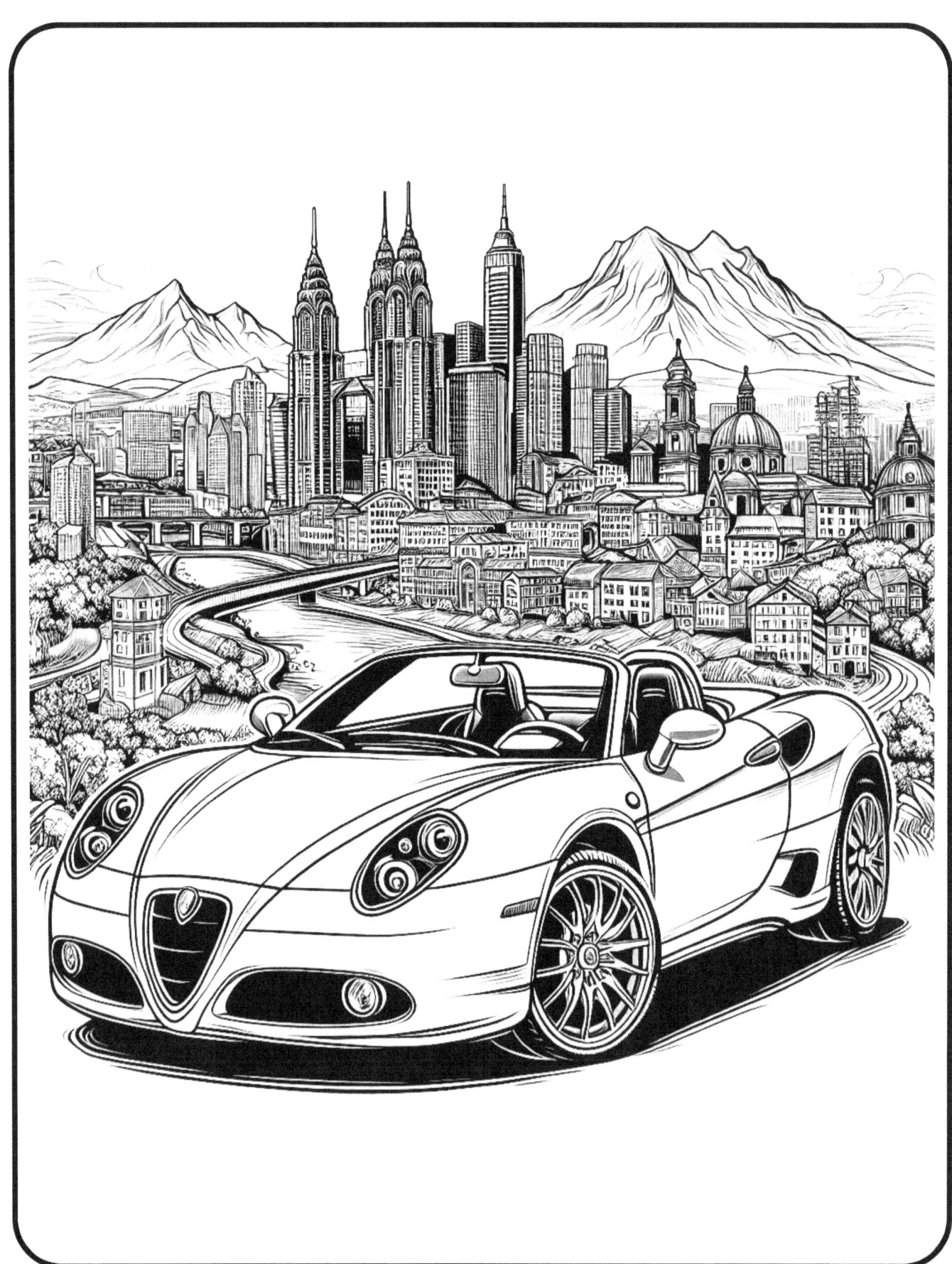

"CREATE YOUR DESIGN HERE"

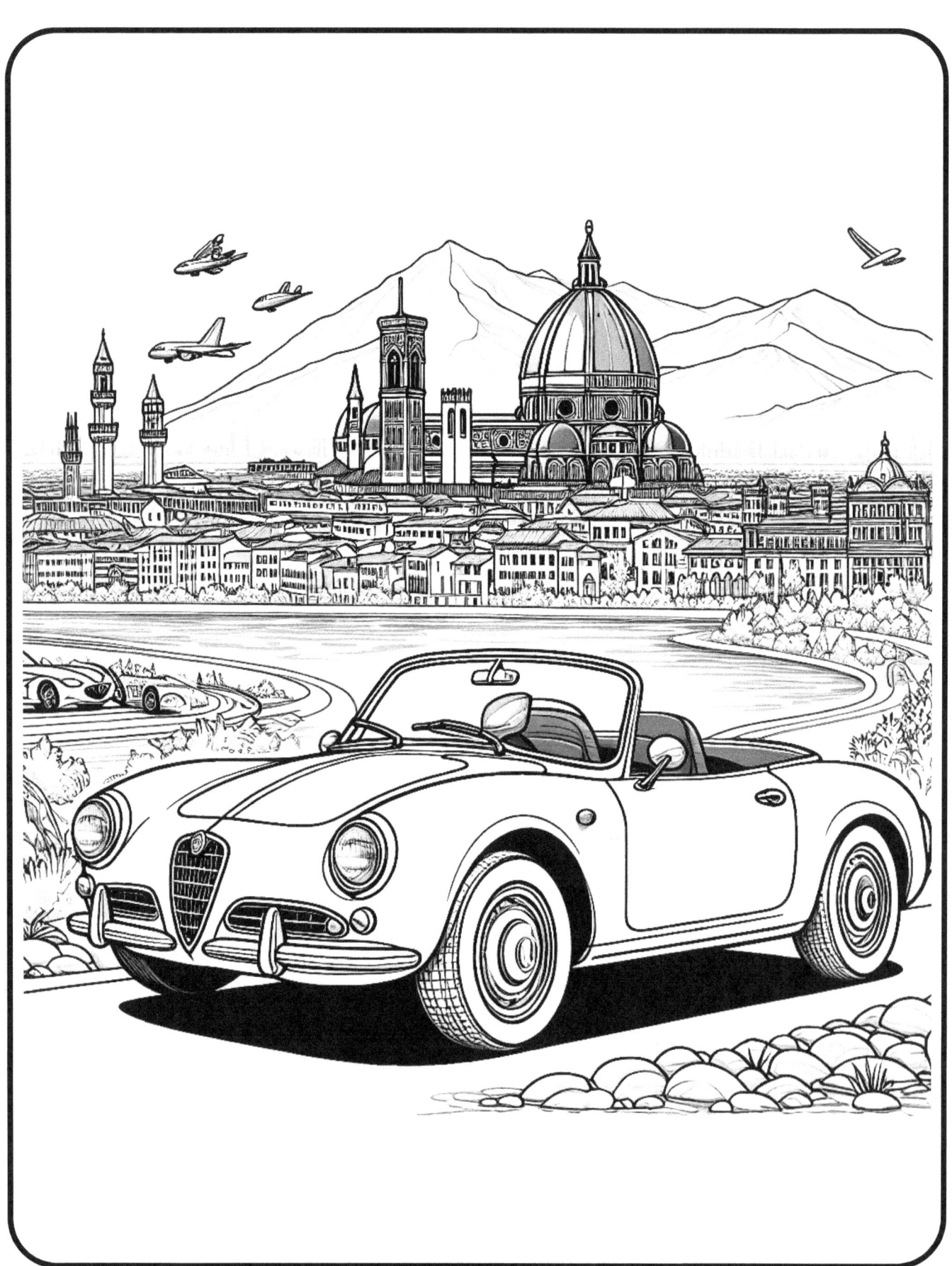

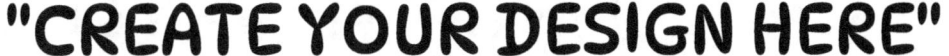
"CREATE YOUR DESIGN HERE"

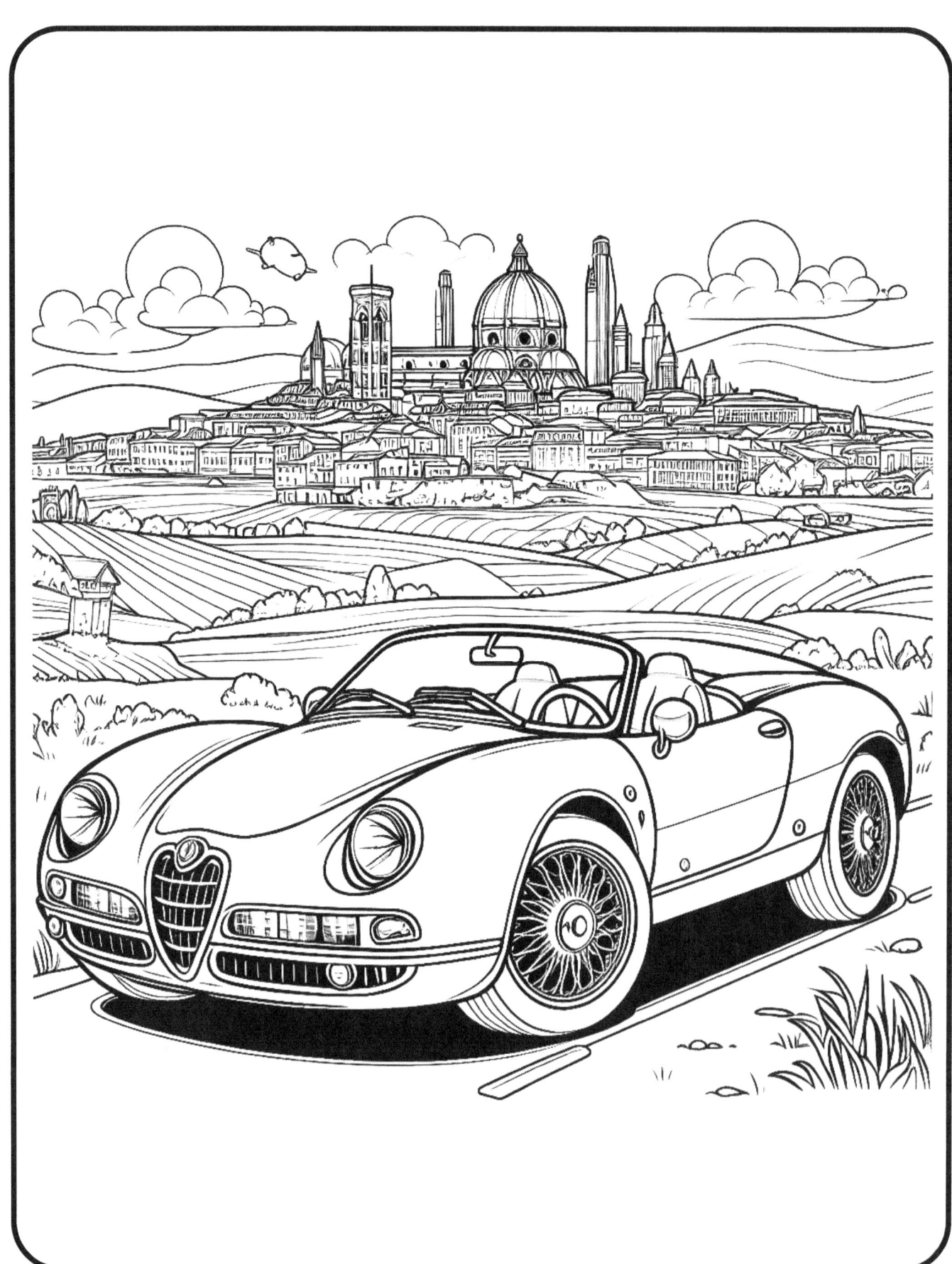

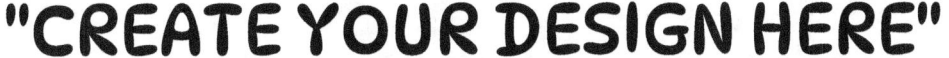

"CREATE YOUR DESIGN HERE"

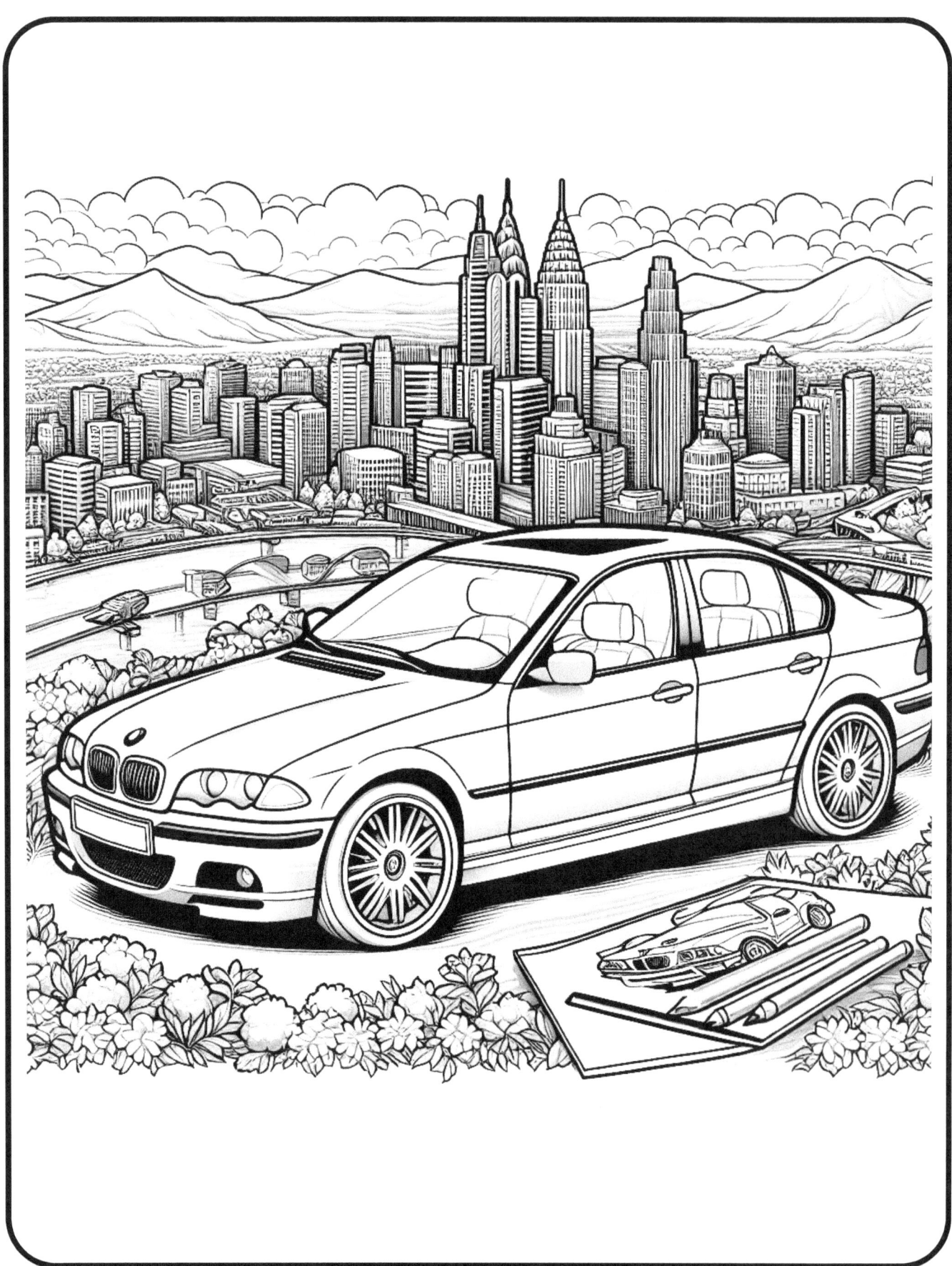

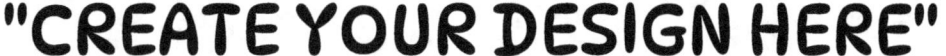
"CREATE YOUR DESIGN HERE"

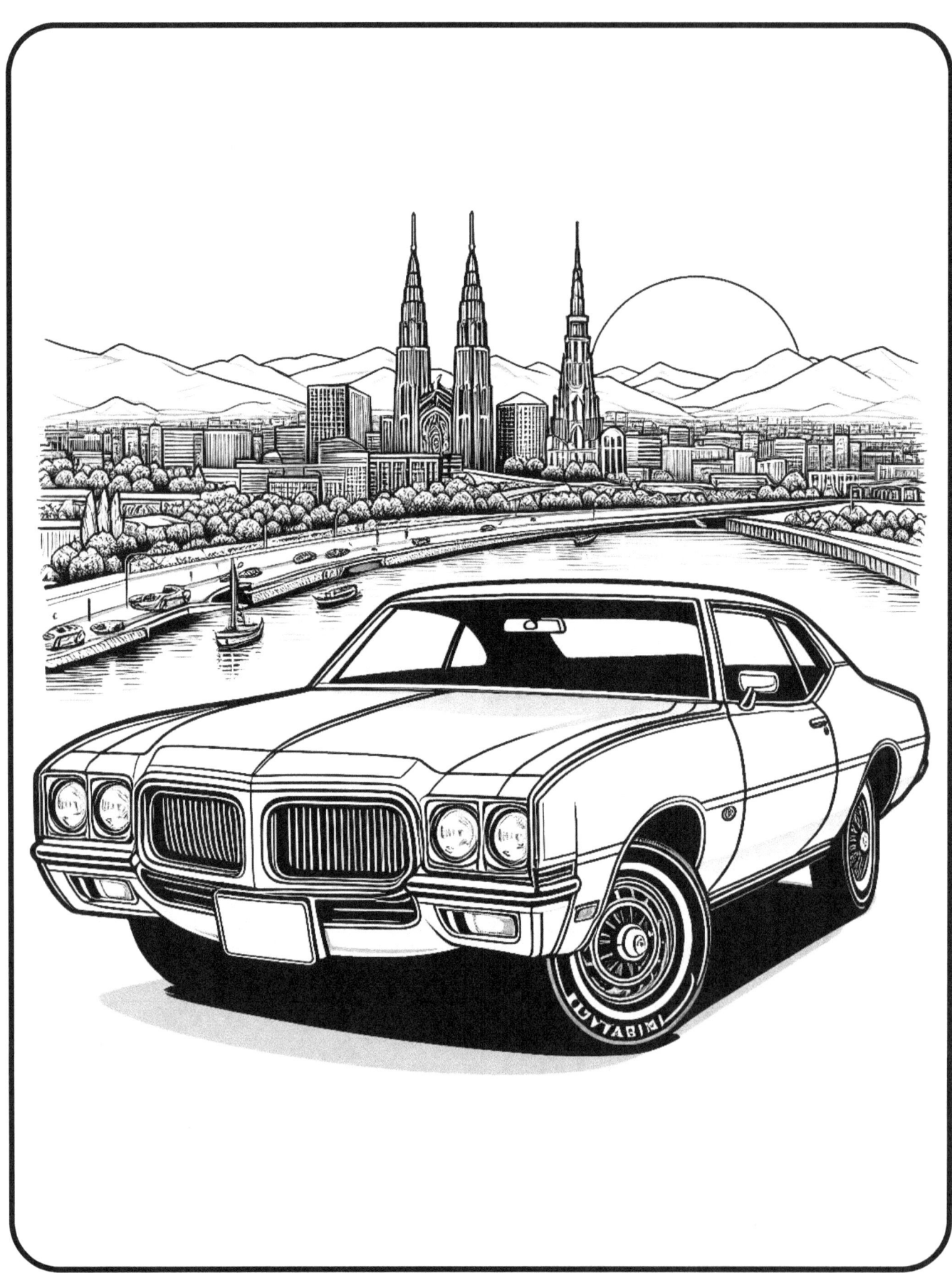

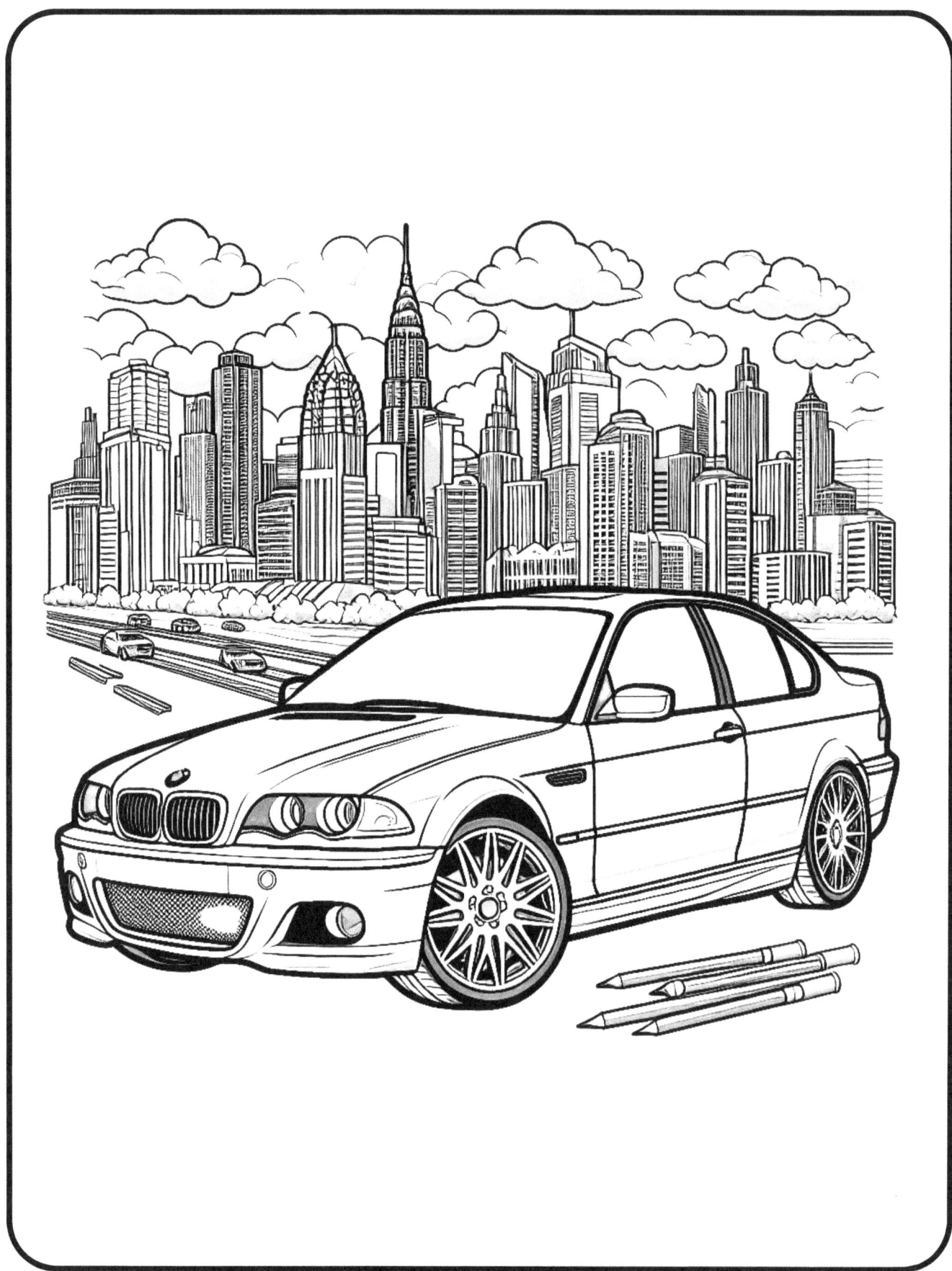

"CREATE YOUR DESIGN HERE"

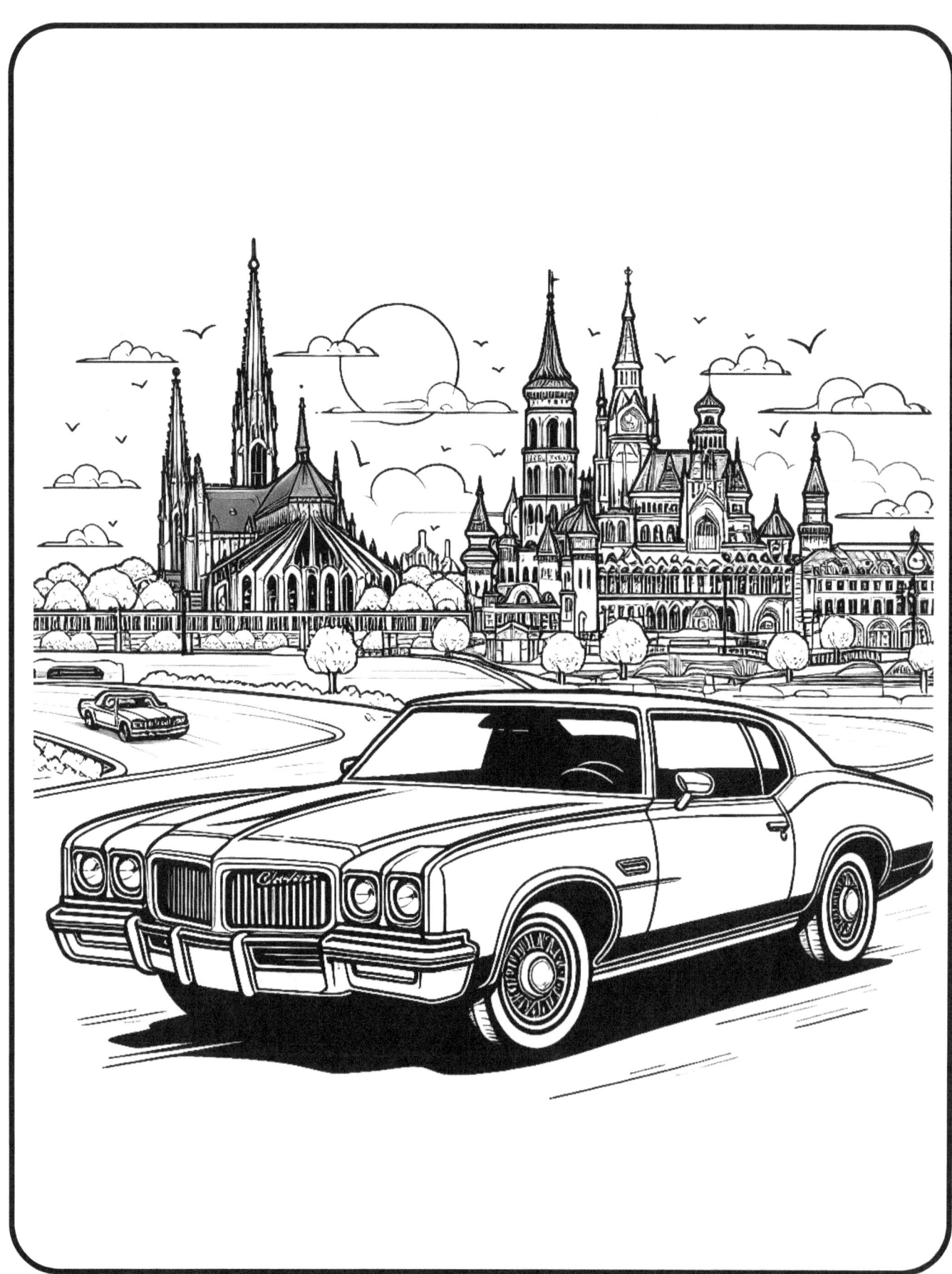

"CREATE YOUR DESIGN HERE"

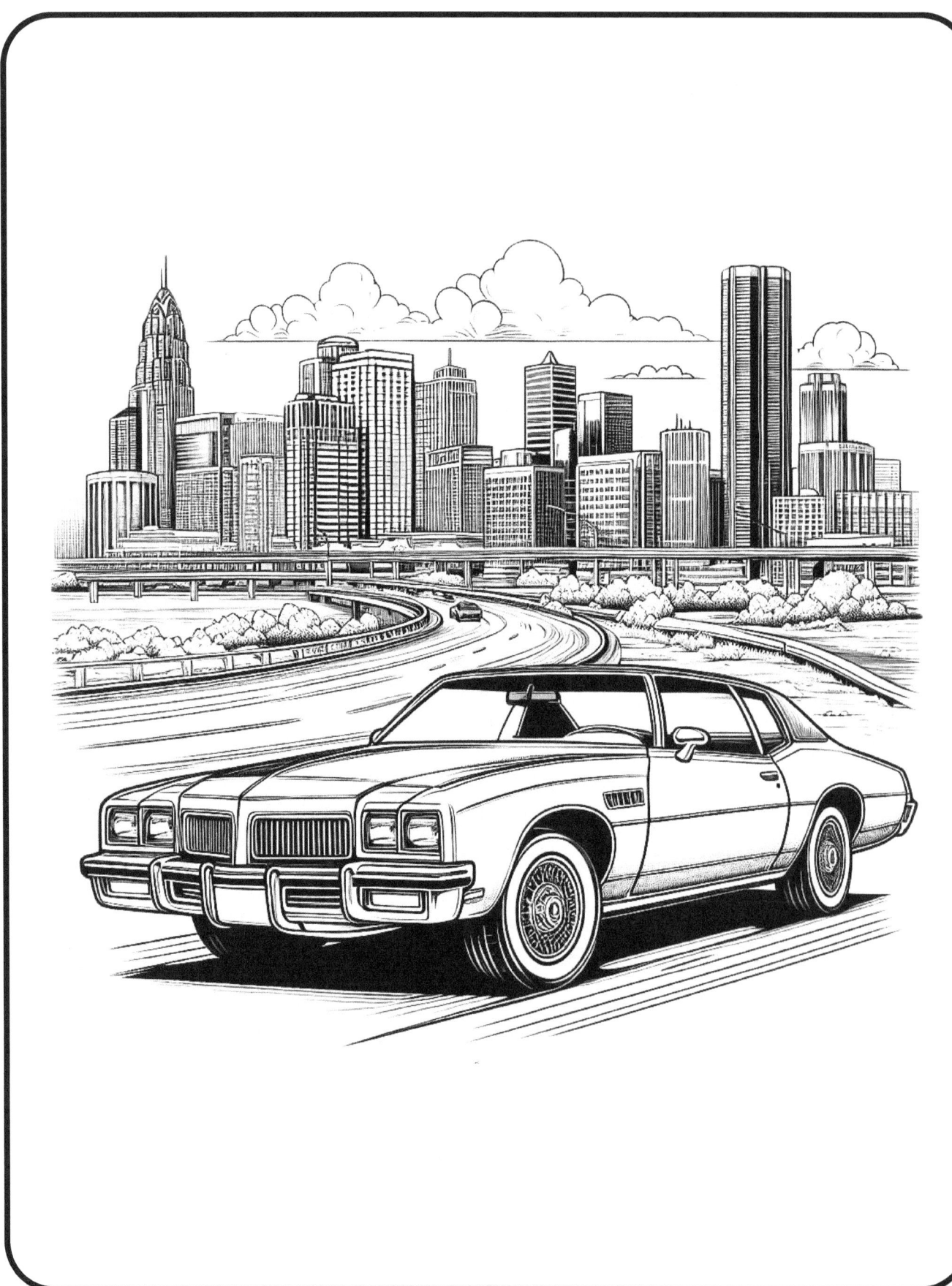

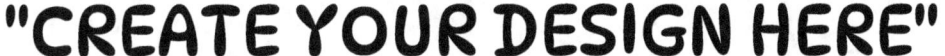

"CREATE YOUR DESIGN HERE"

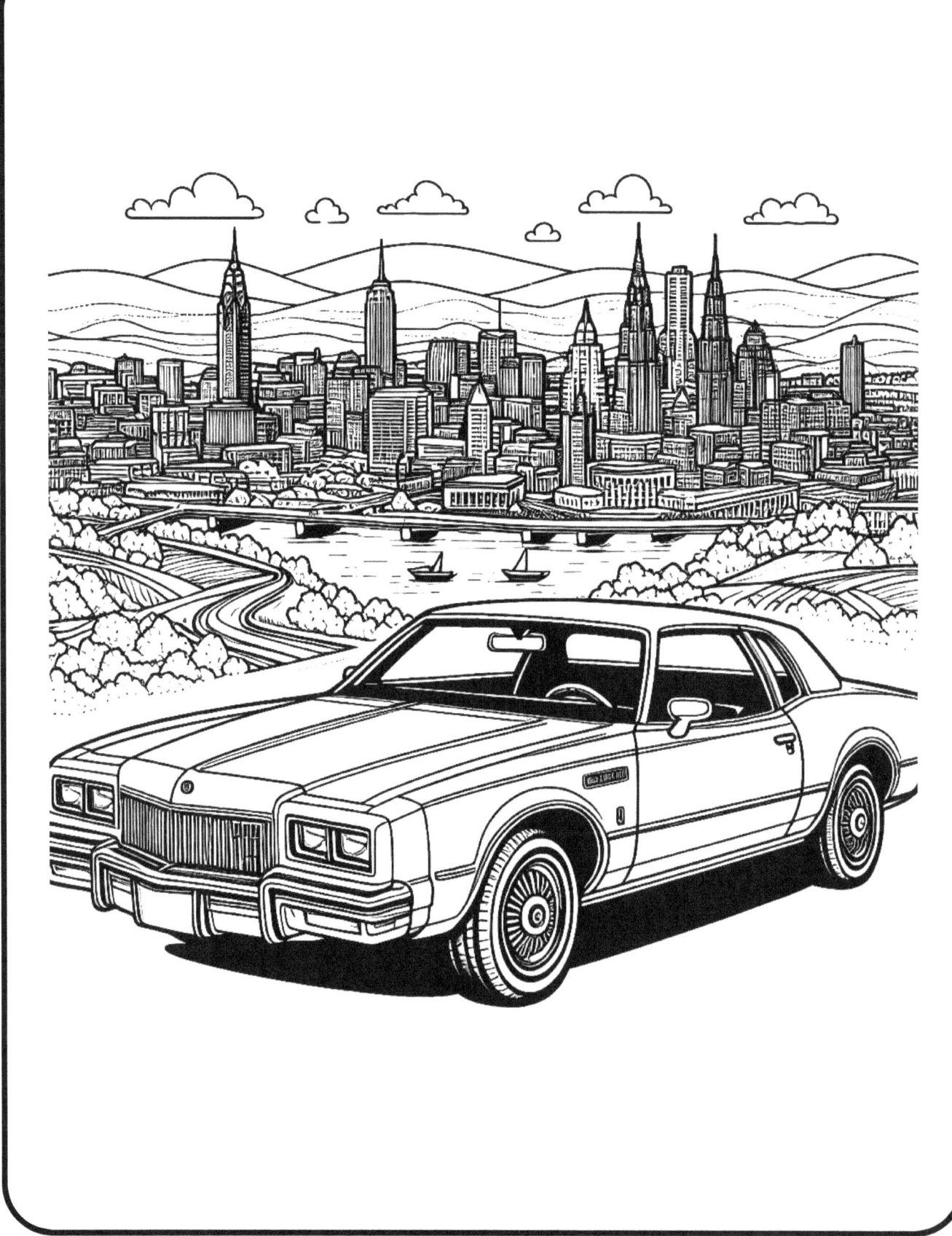

"CREATE YOUR DESIGN HERE"

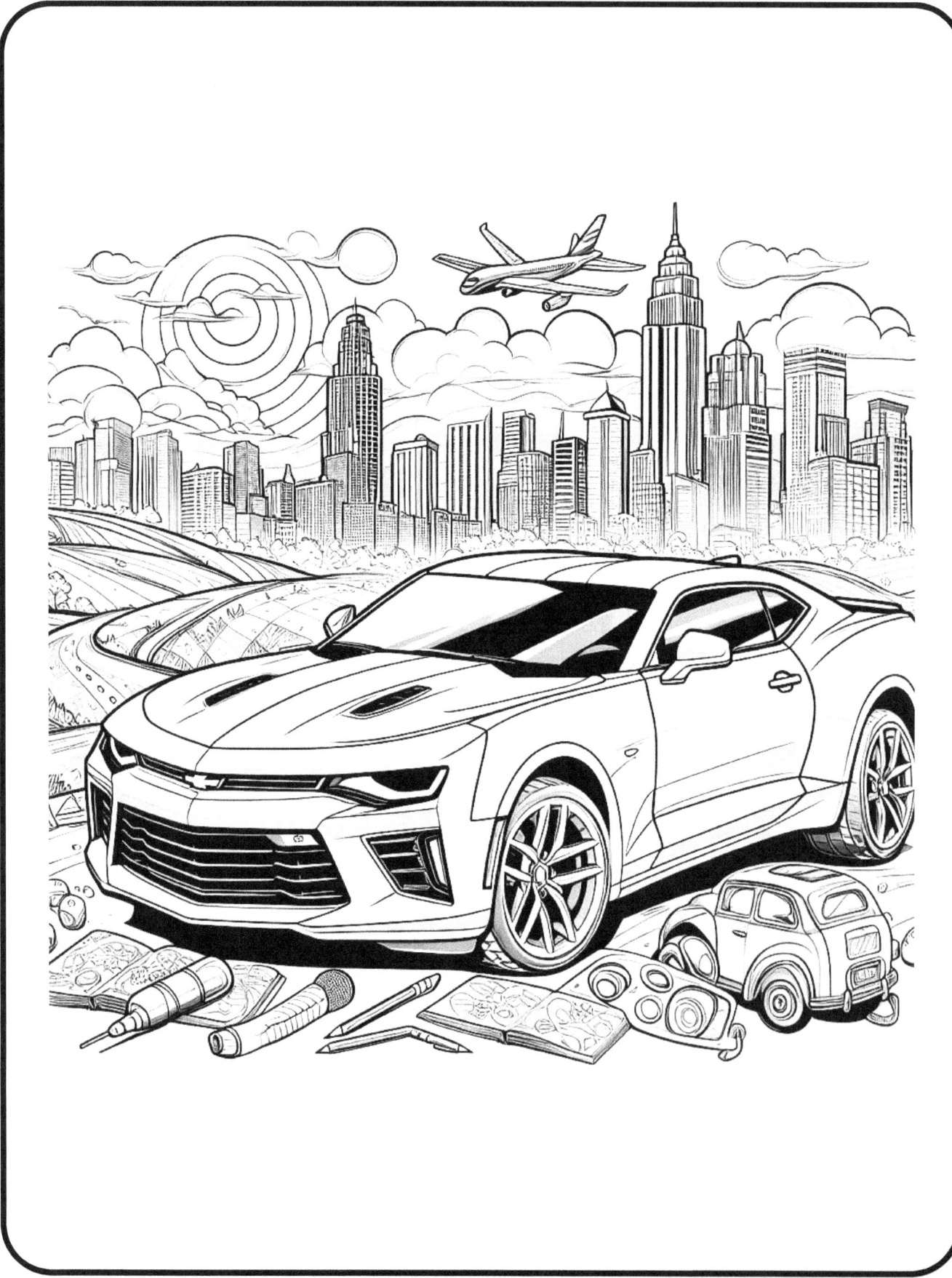

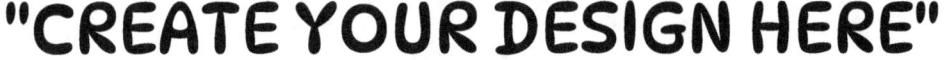
"CREATE YOUR DESIGN HERE"

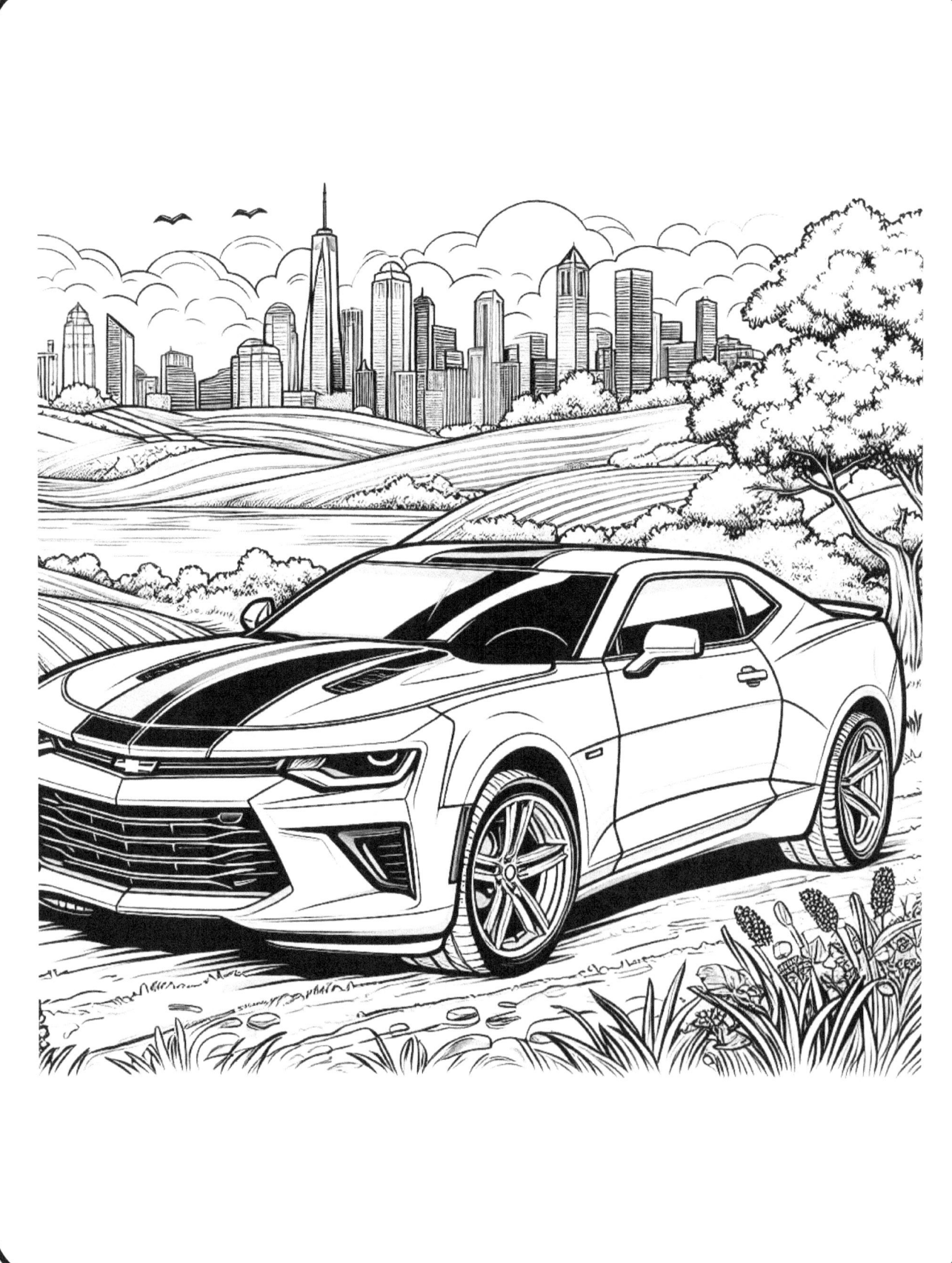

"CREATE YOUR DESIGN HERE"

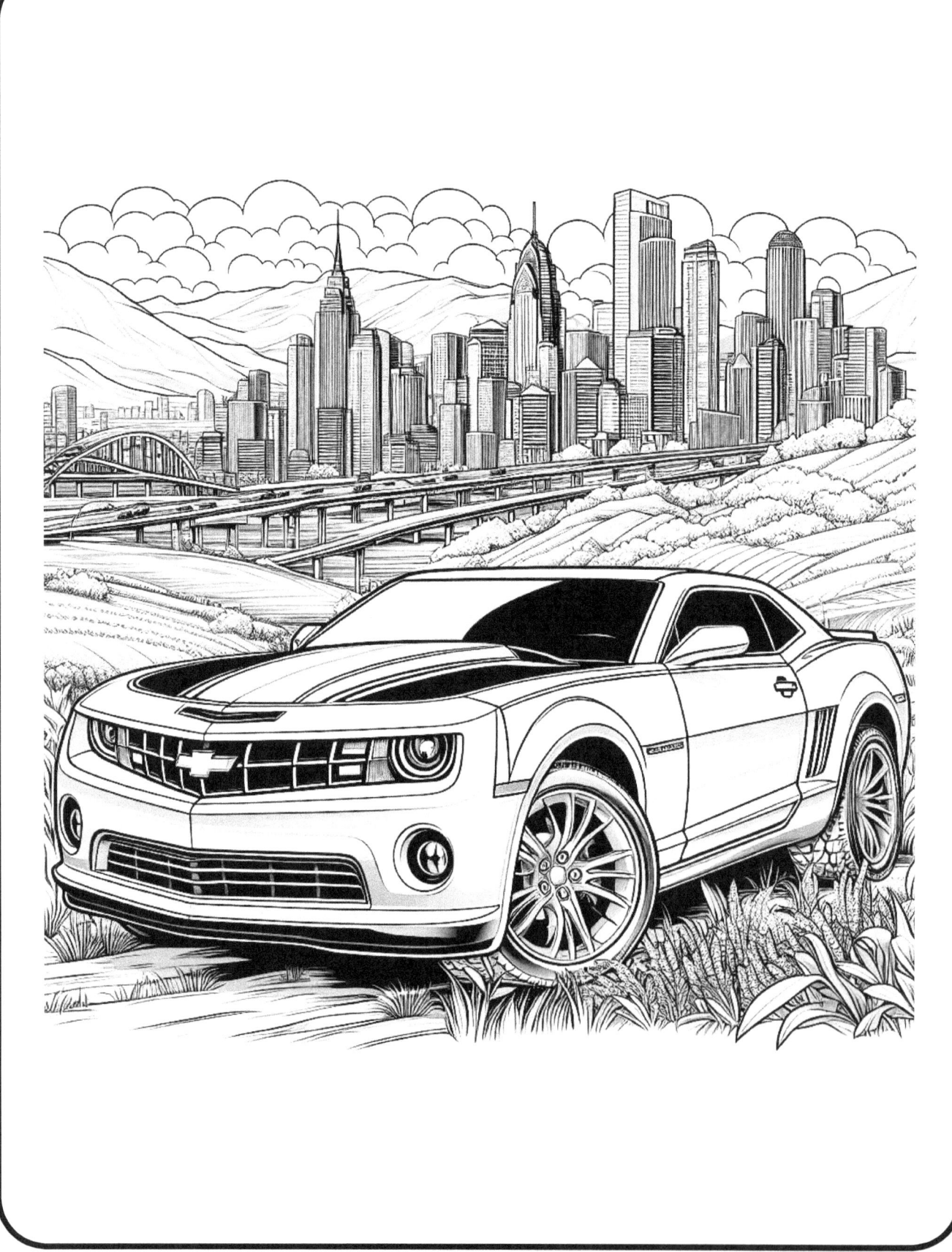

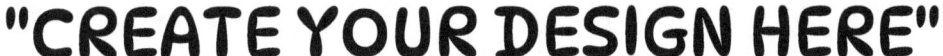

"CREATE YOUR DESIGN HERE"

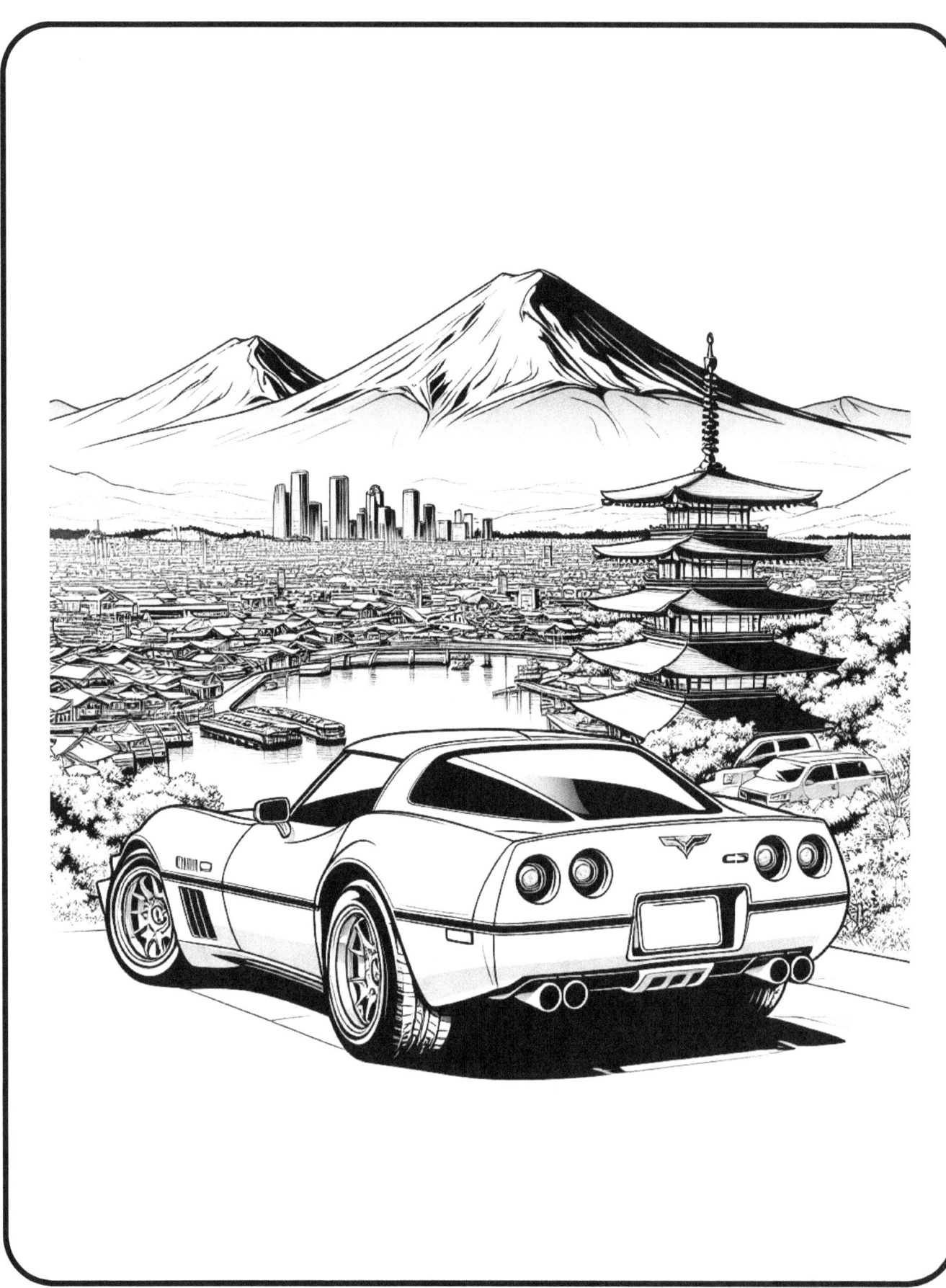

"CREATE YOUR DESIGN HERE"

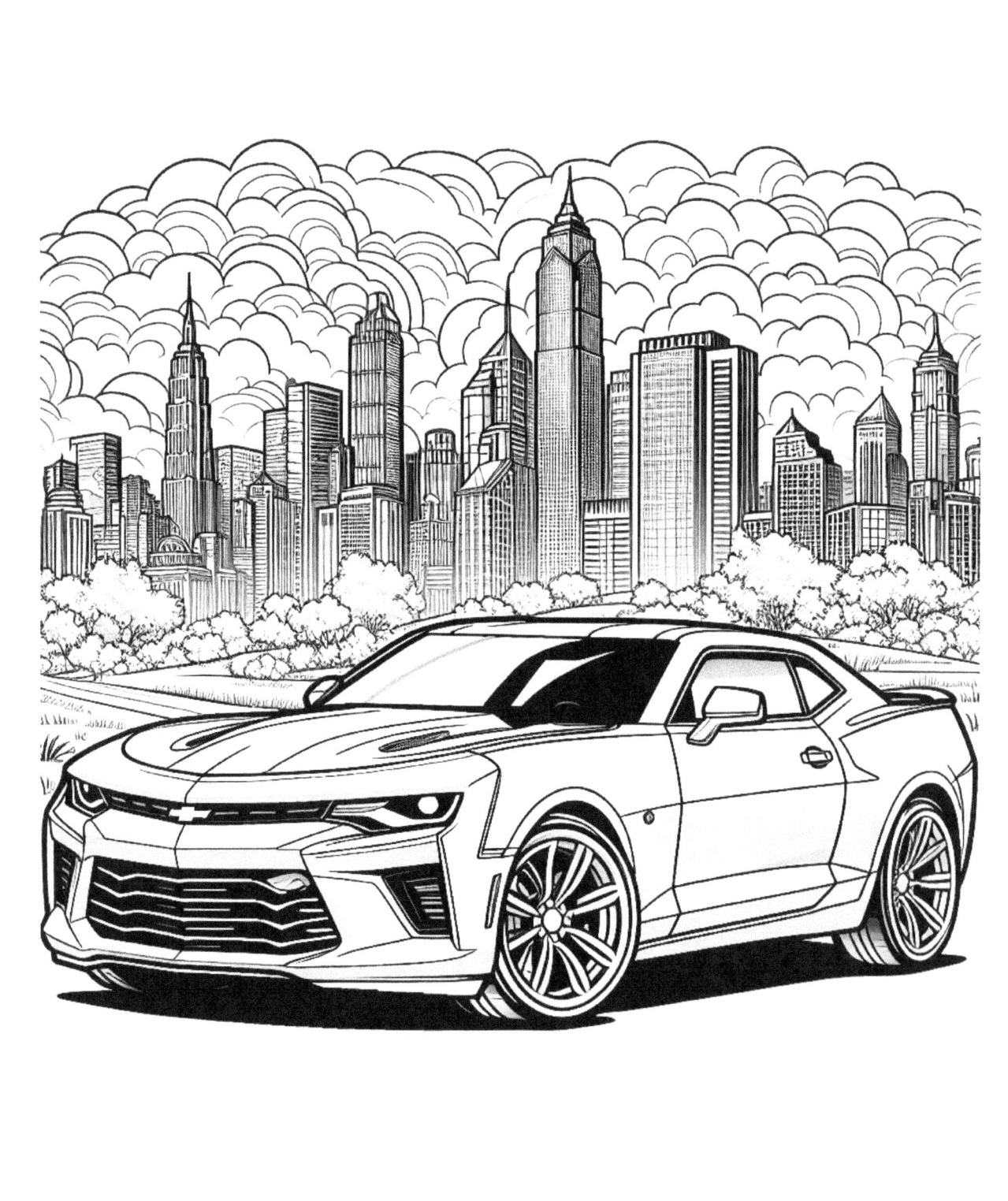

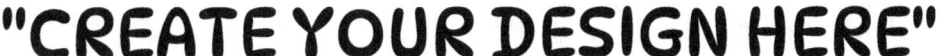

"CREATE YOUR DESIGN HERE"

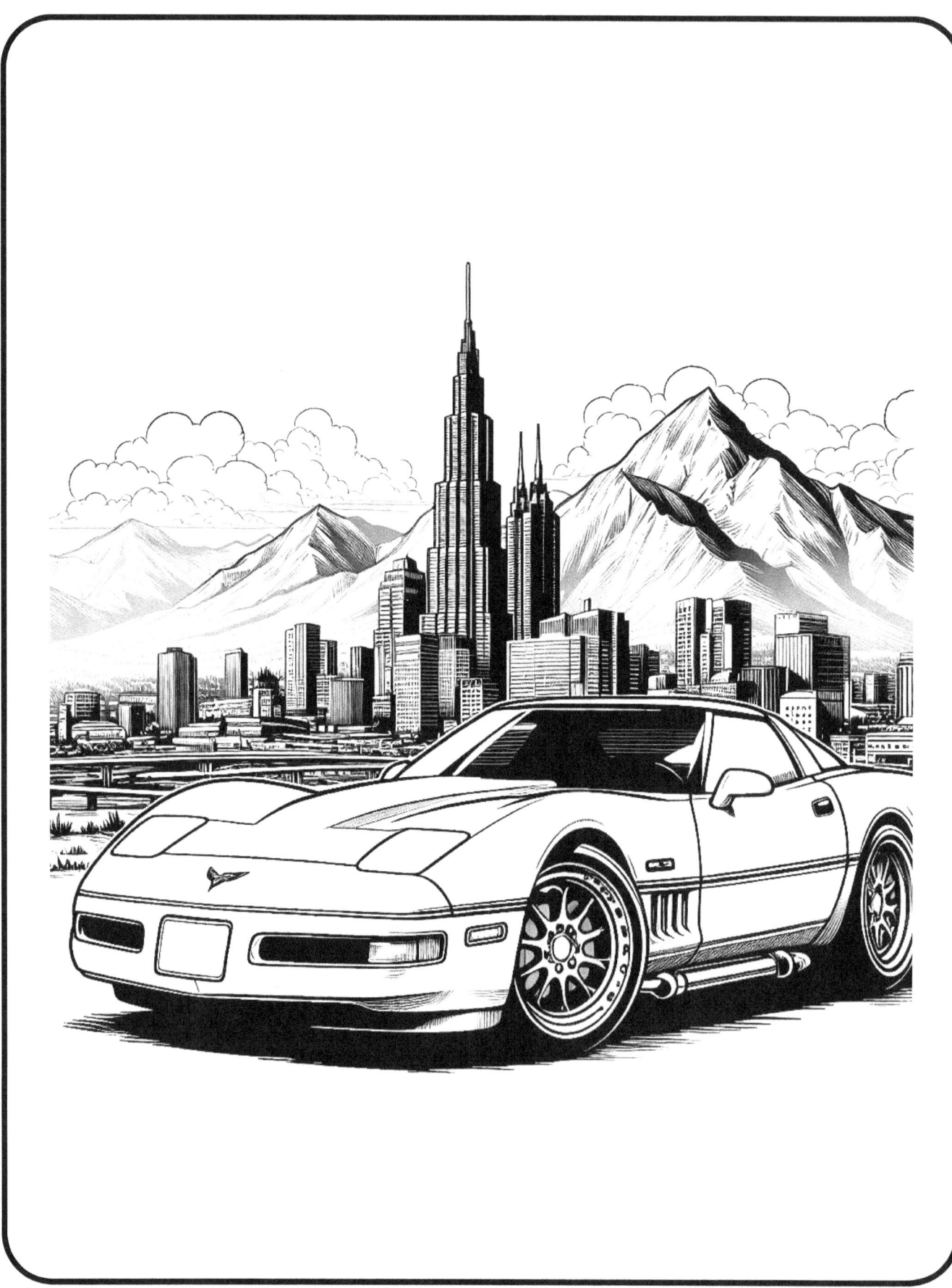

"CREATE YOUR DESIGN HERE"

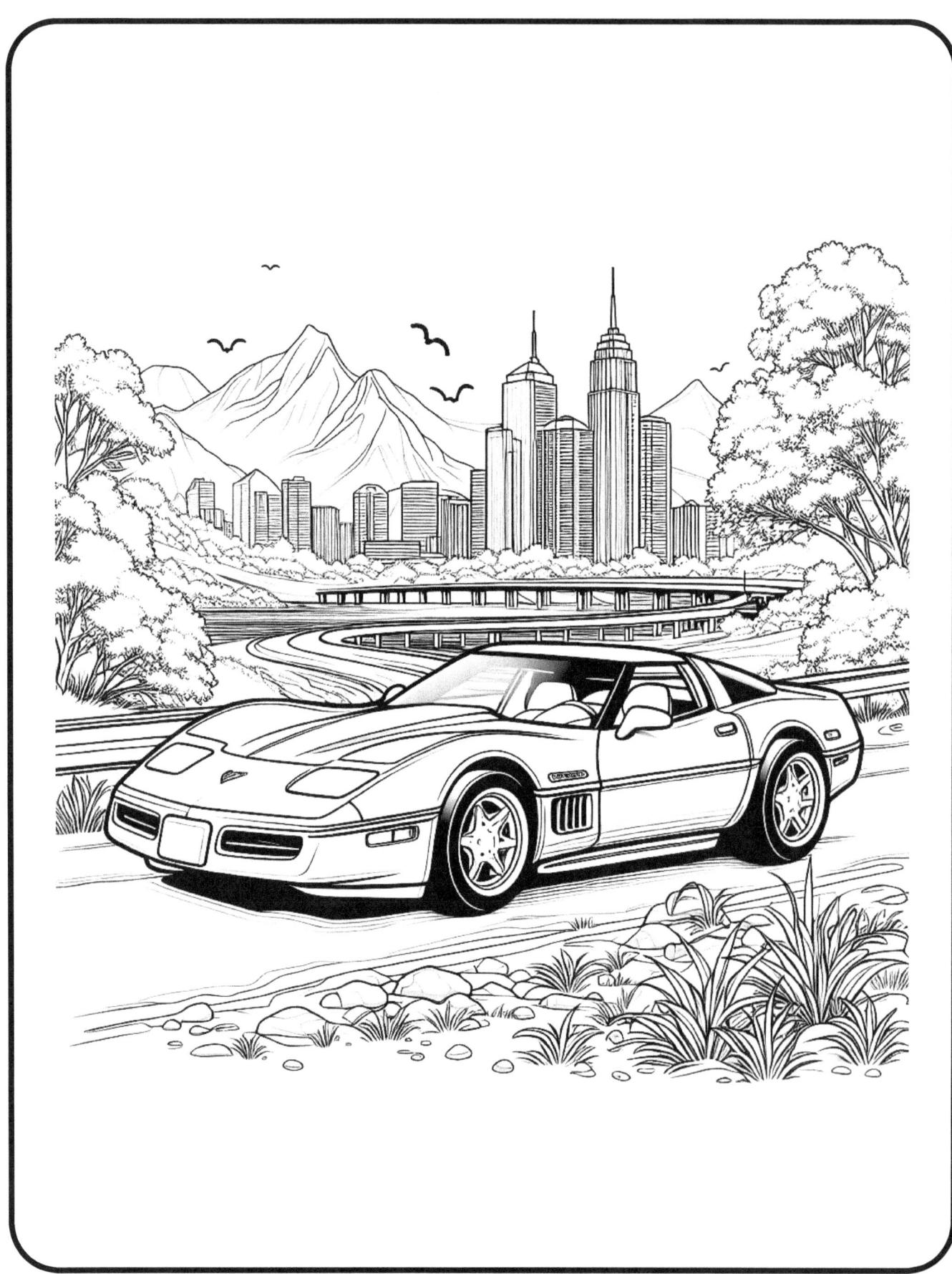

"CREATE YOUR DESIGN HERE"

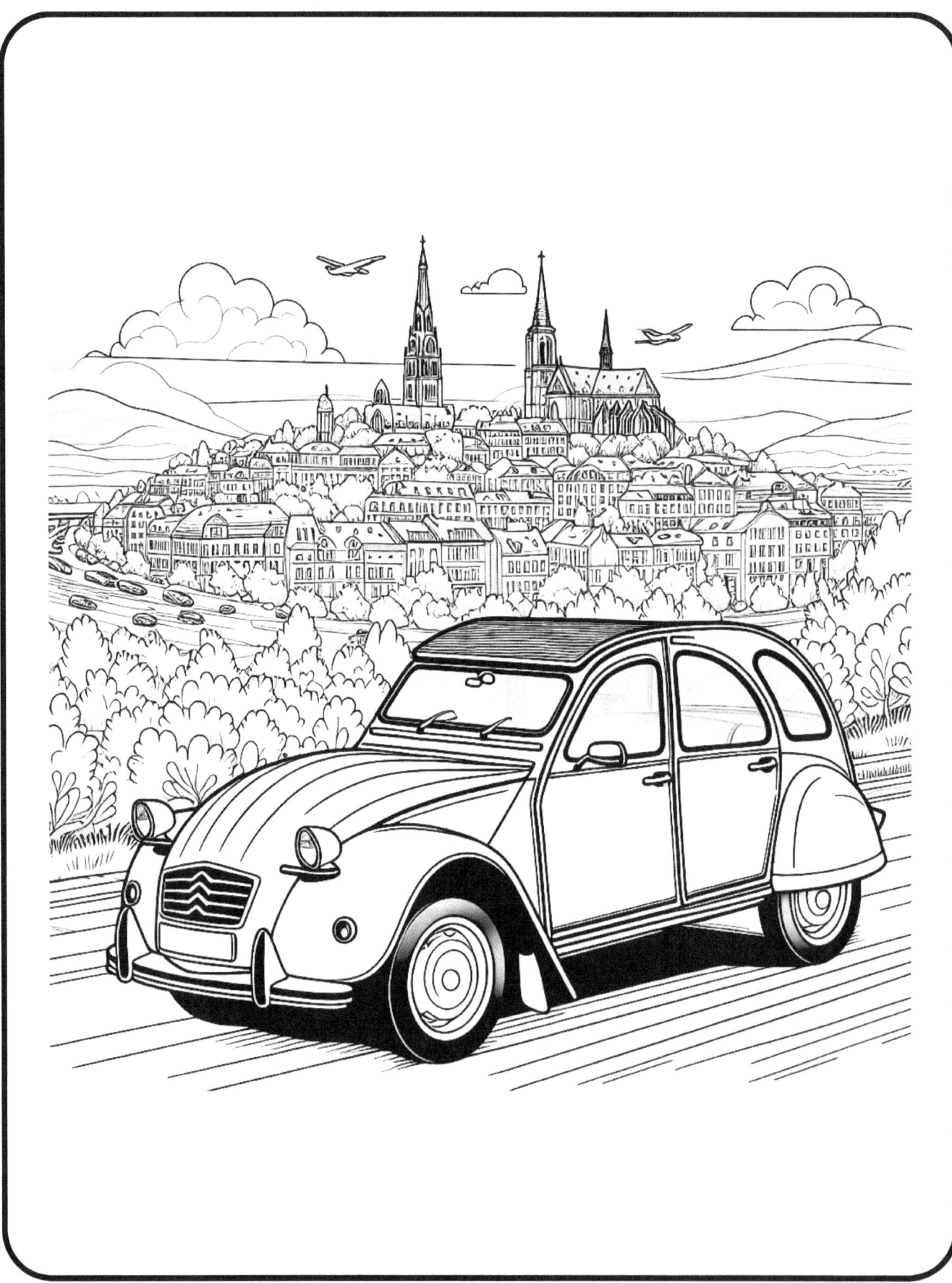

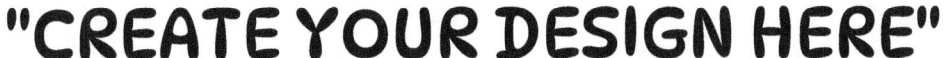

"CREATE YOUR DESIGN HERE"

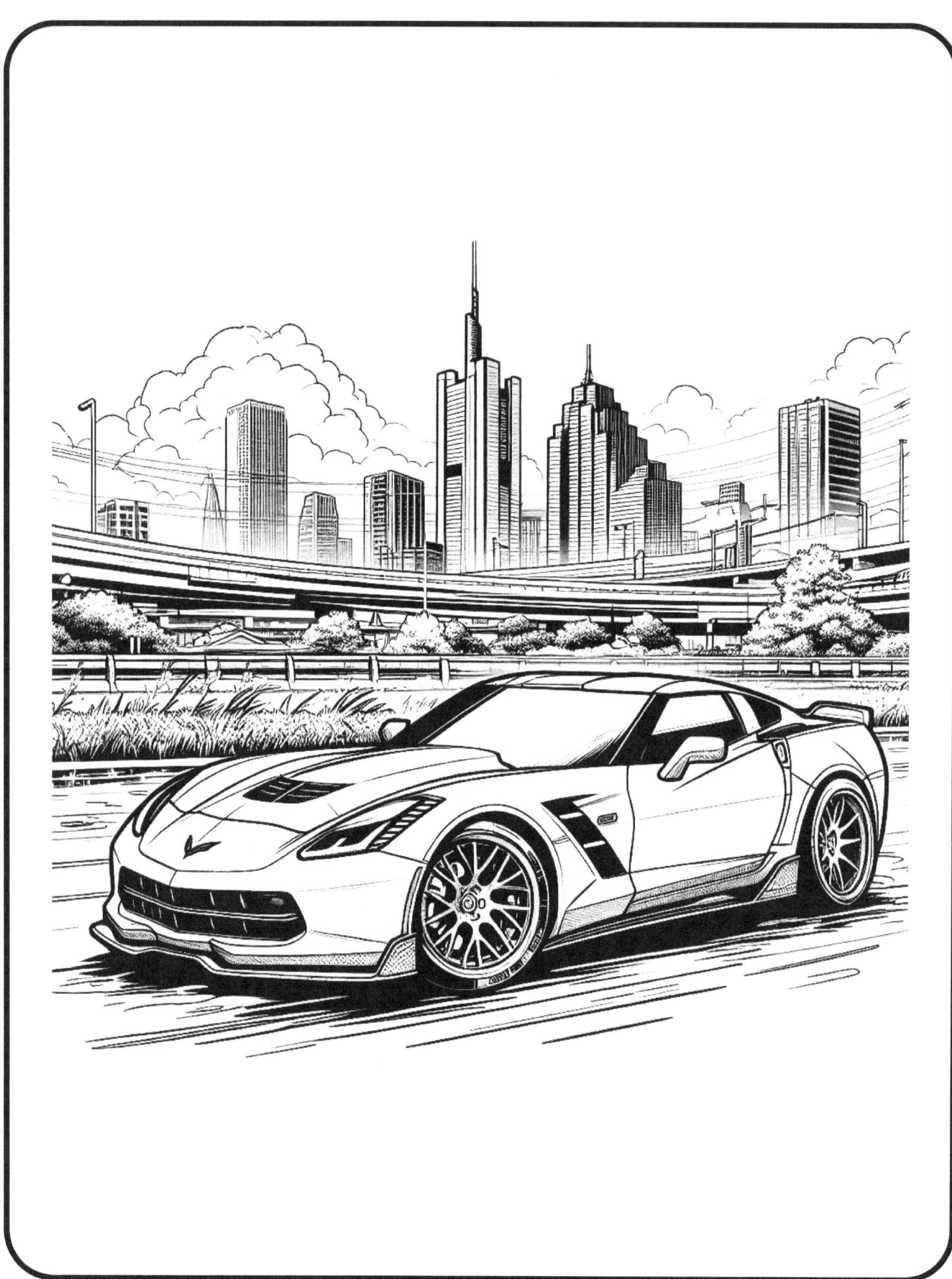

"CREATE YOUR DESIGN HERE"

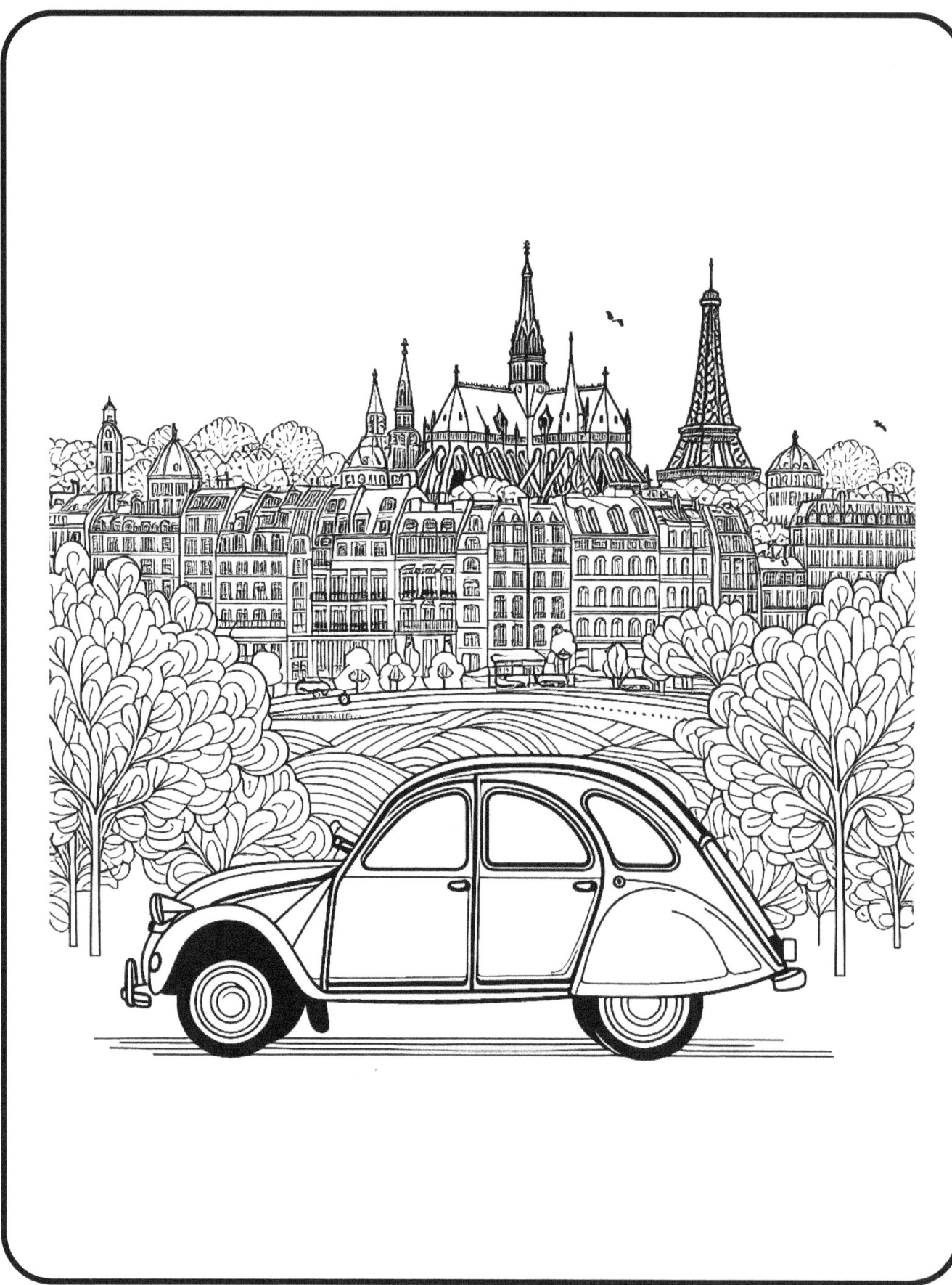

"CREATE YOUR DESIGN HERE"

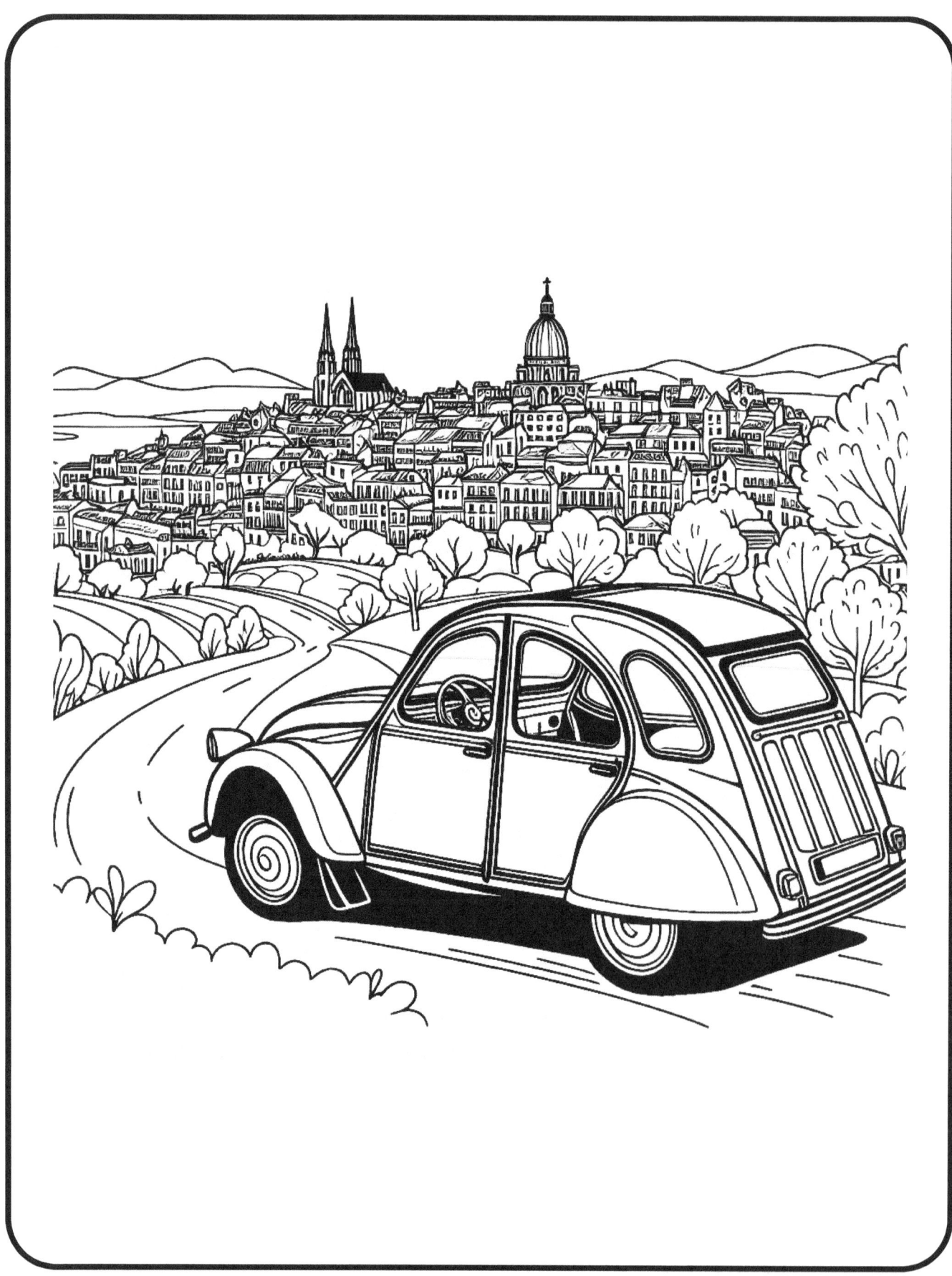

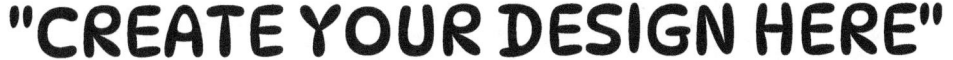

"CREATE YOUR DESIGN HERE"

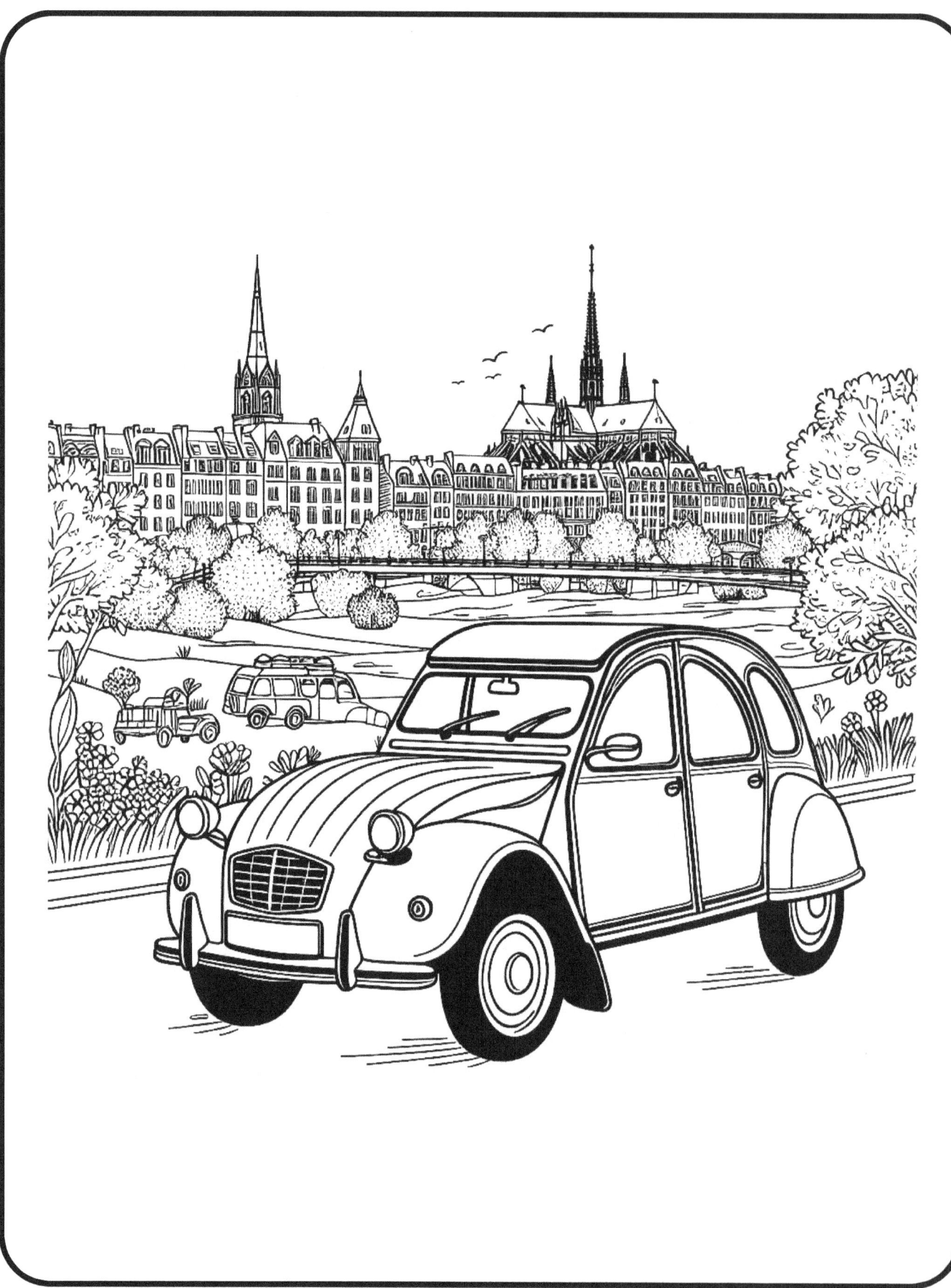

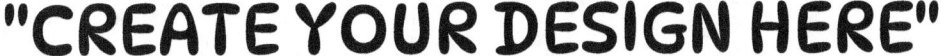

"CREATE YOUR DESIGN HERE"

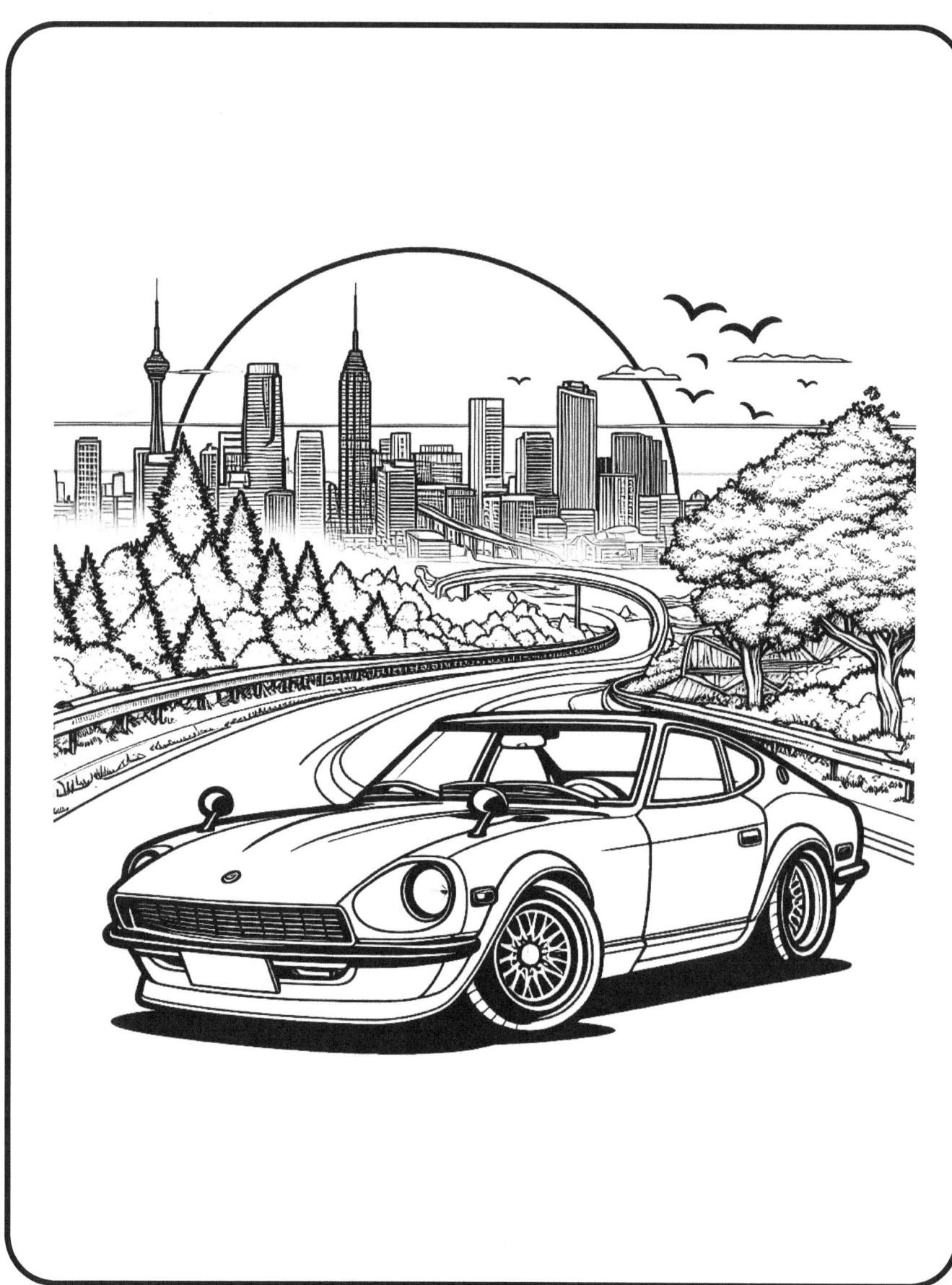

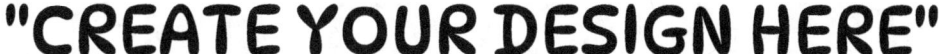
"CREATE YOUR DESIGN HERE"

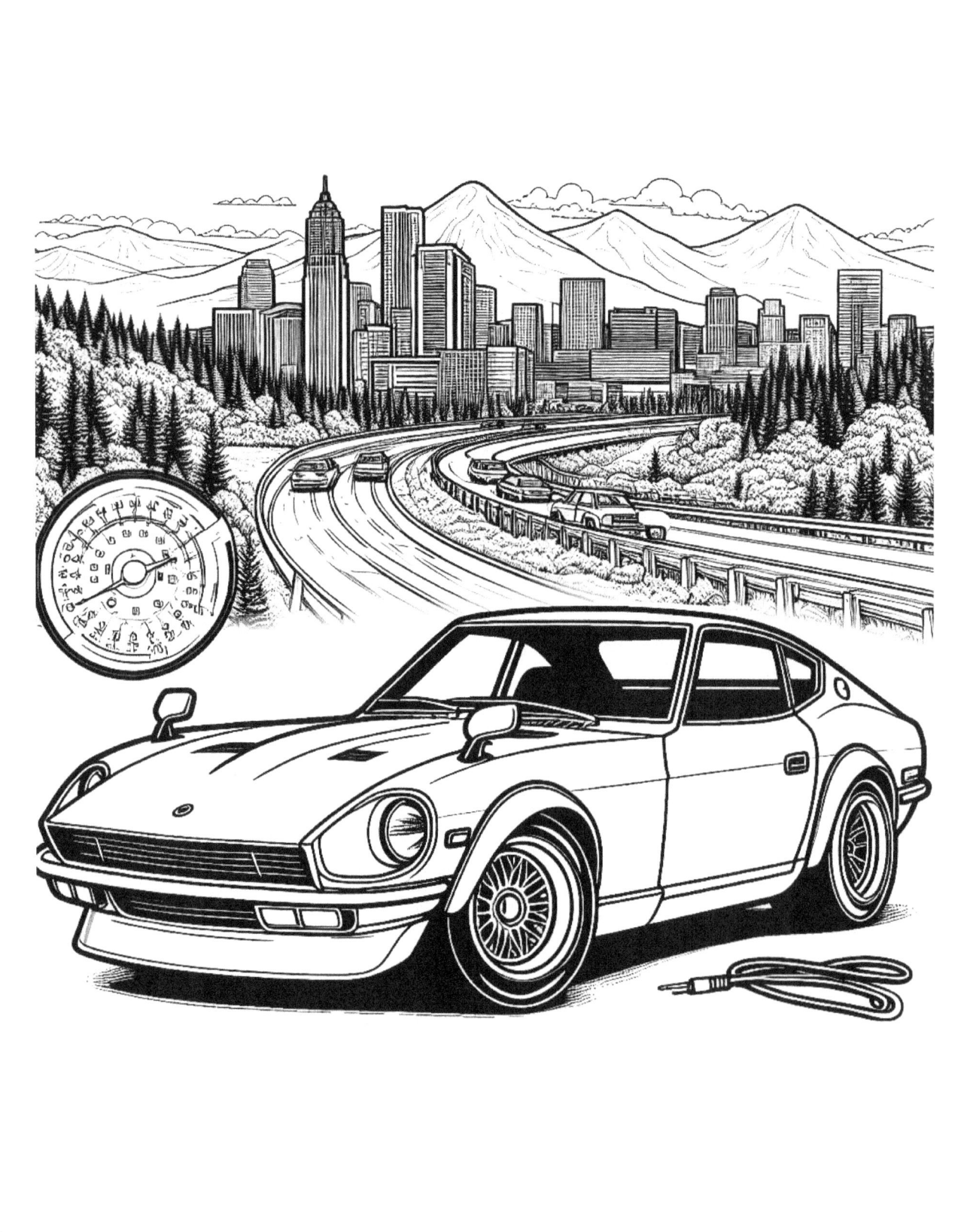

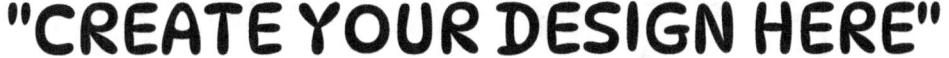

"CREATE YOUR DESIGN HERE"

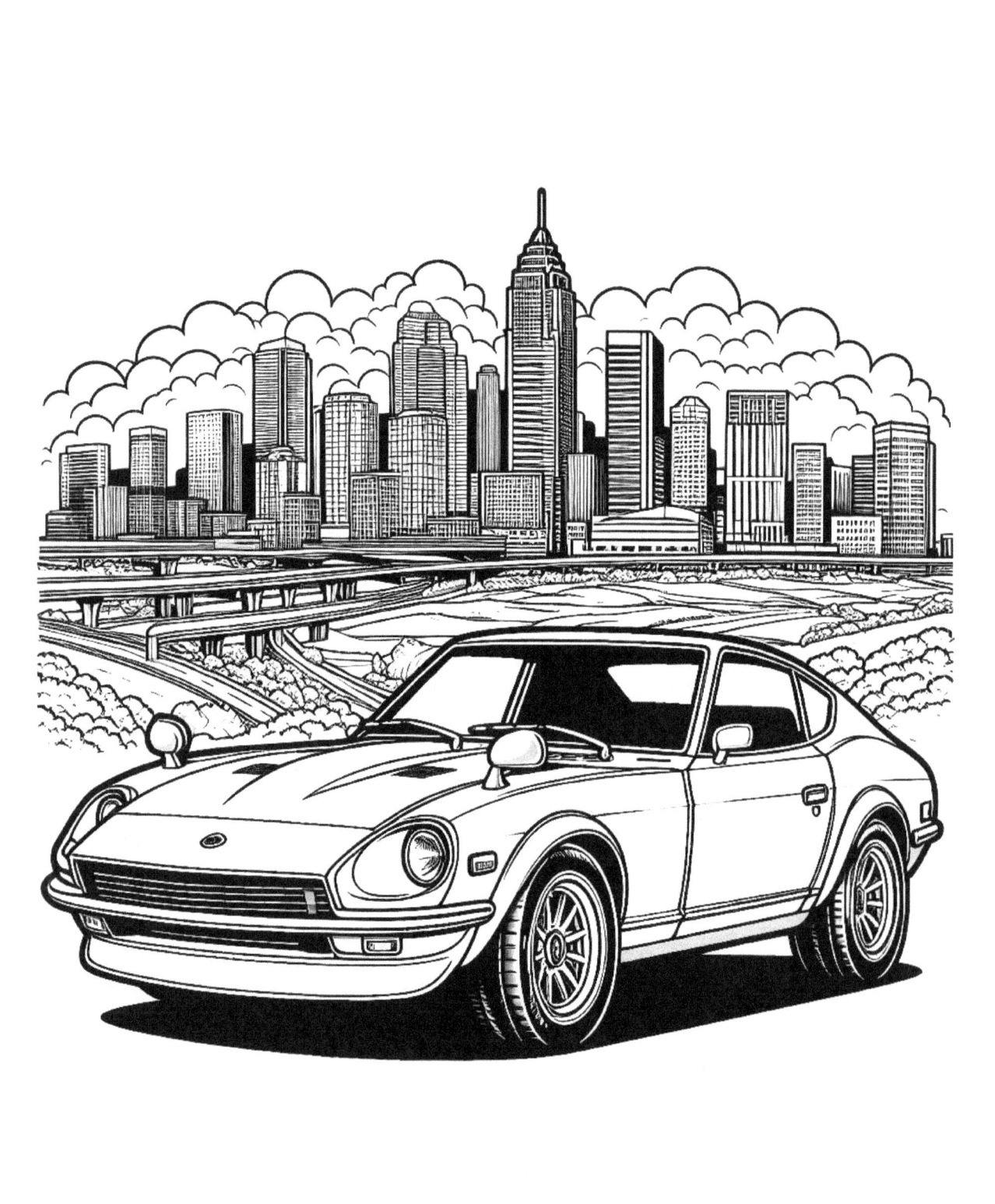

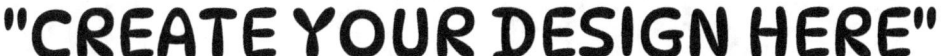
"CREATE YOUR DESIGN HERE"

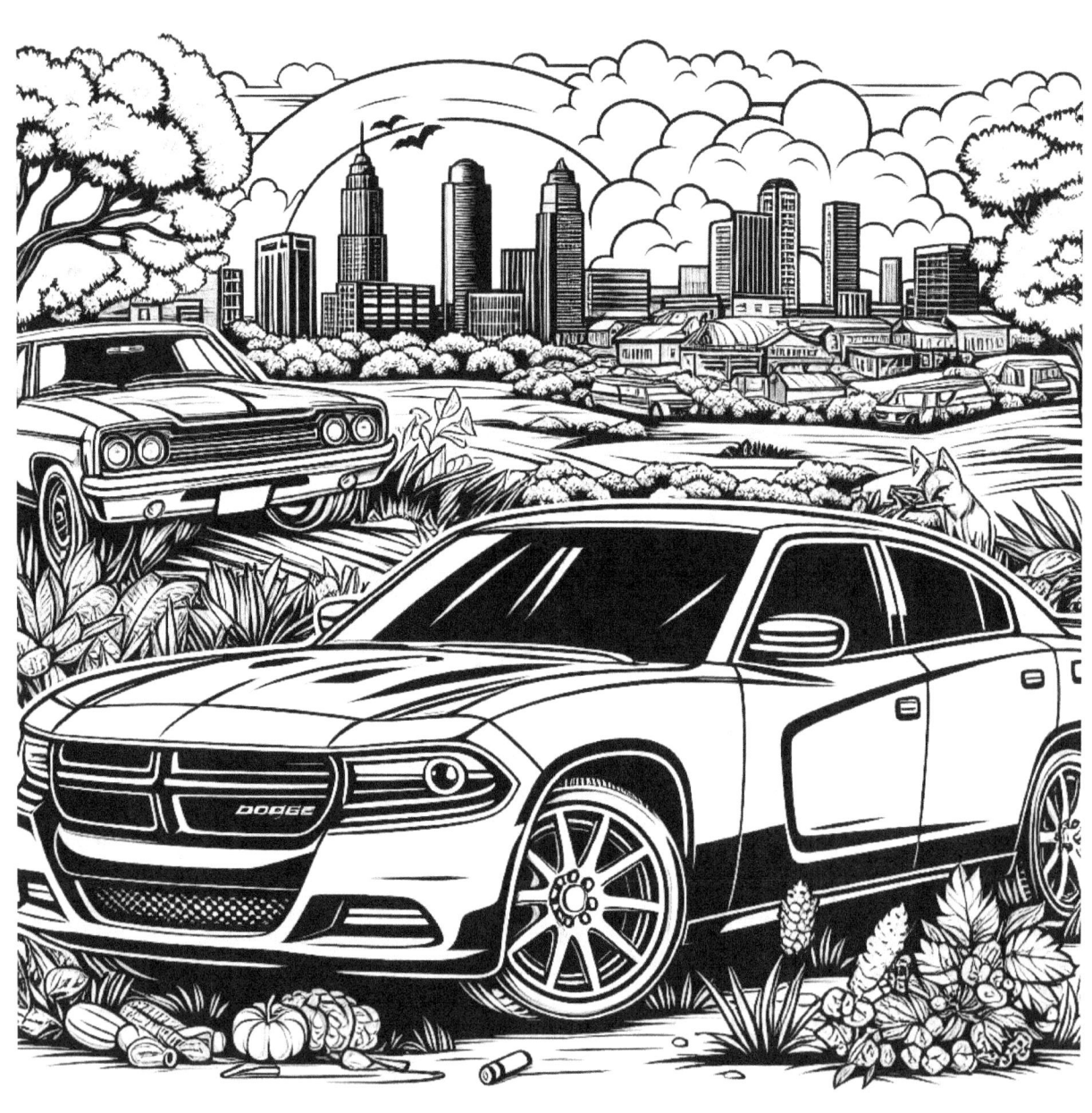

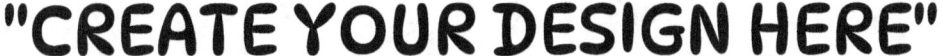

"CREATE YOUR DESIGN HERE"

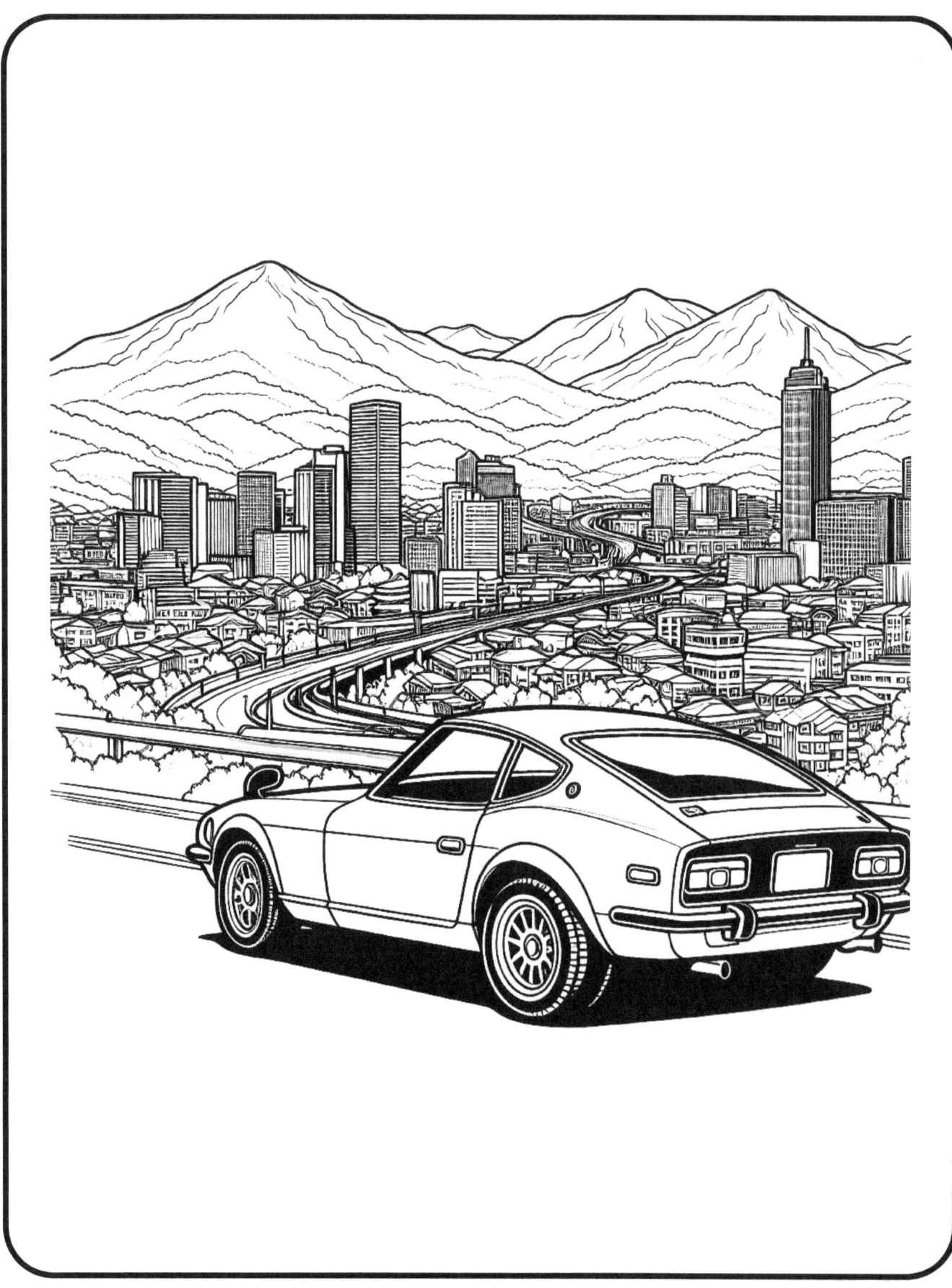

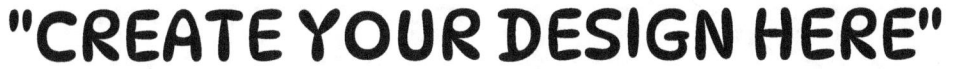

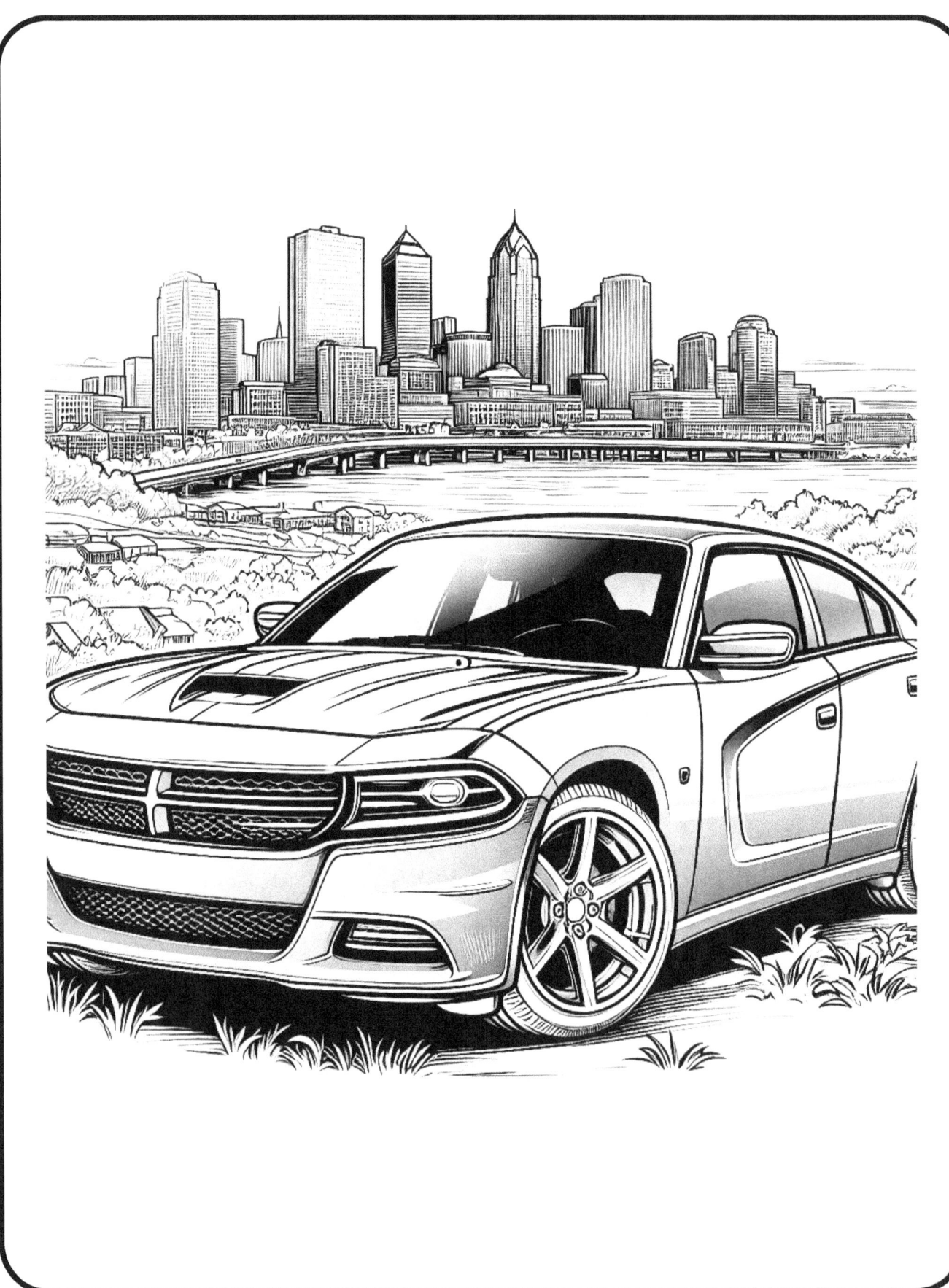

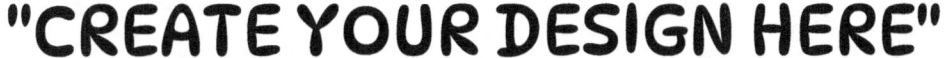
"CREATE YOUR DESIGN HERE"

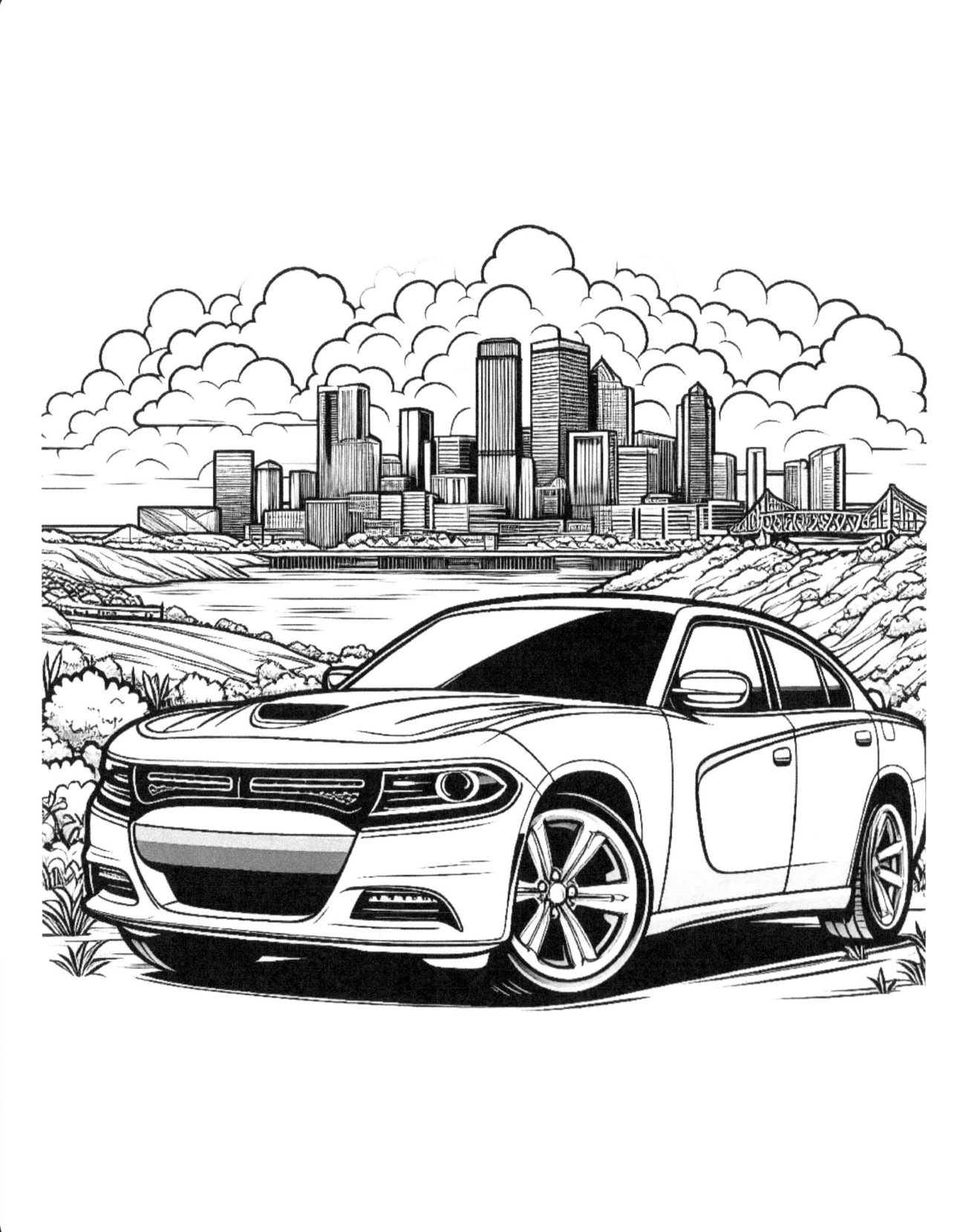

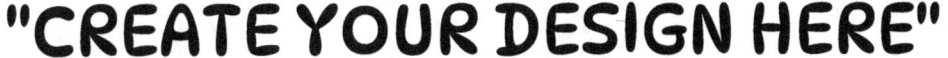

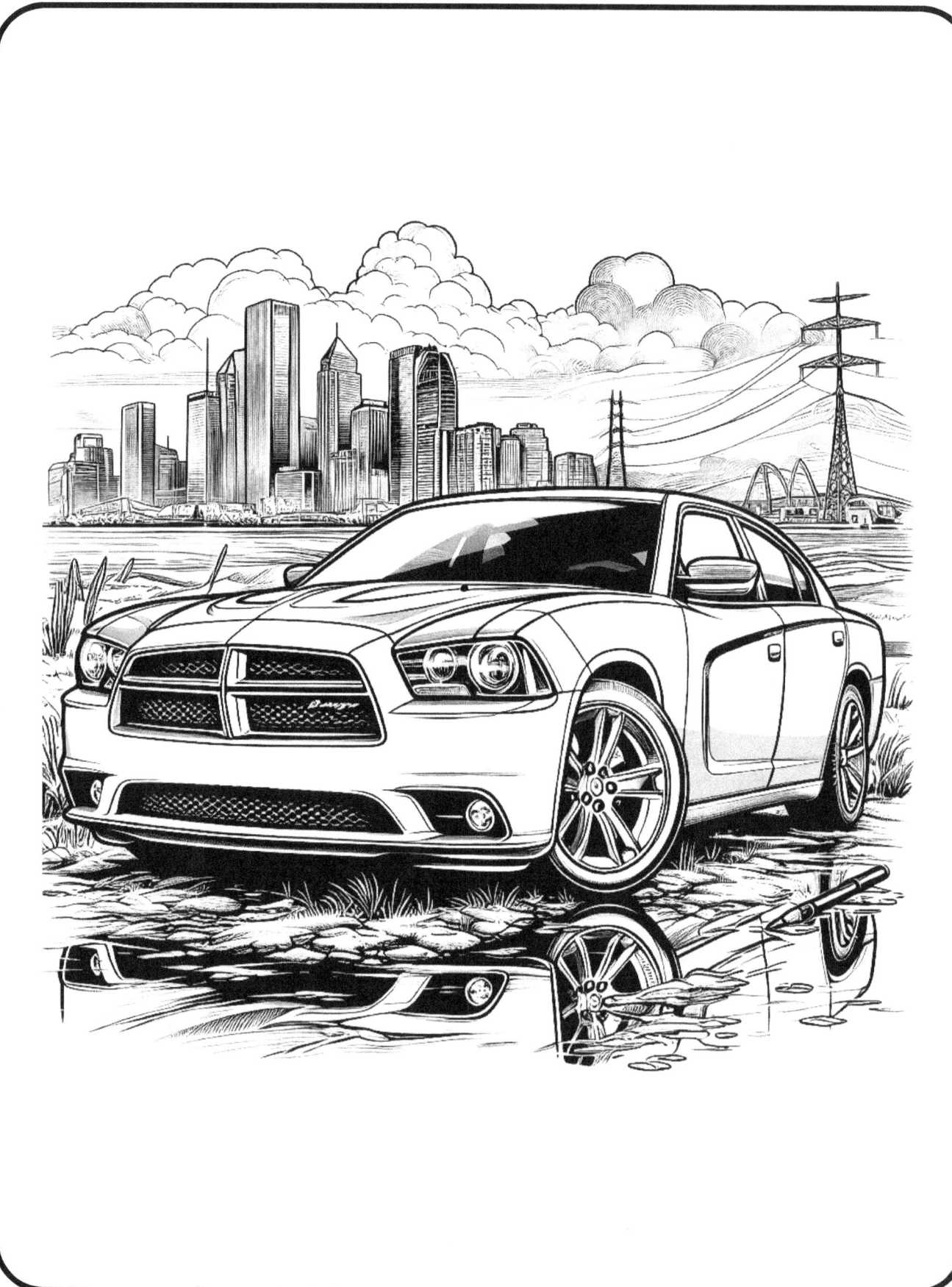

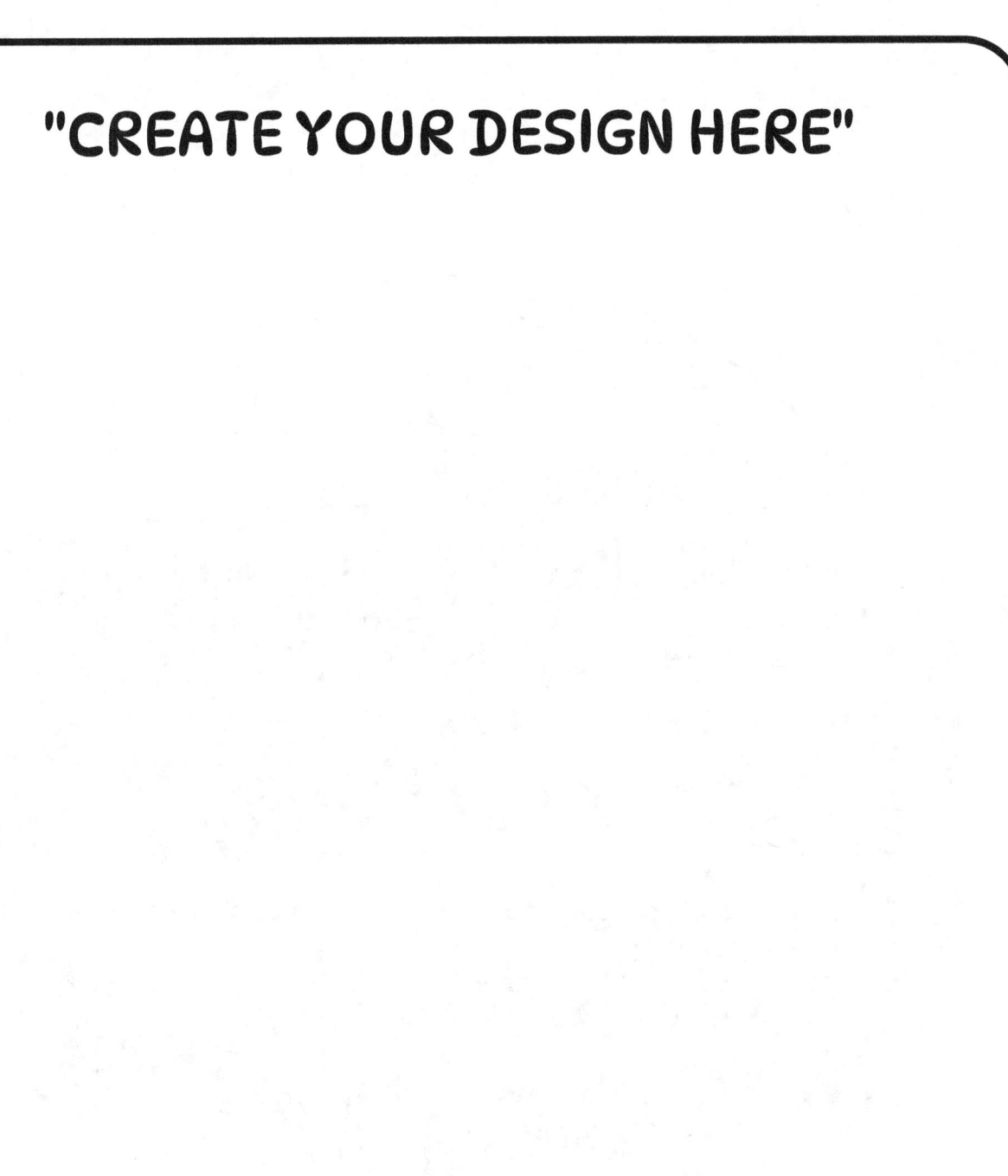

"CREATE YOUR DESIGN HERE"

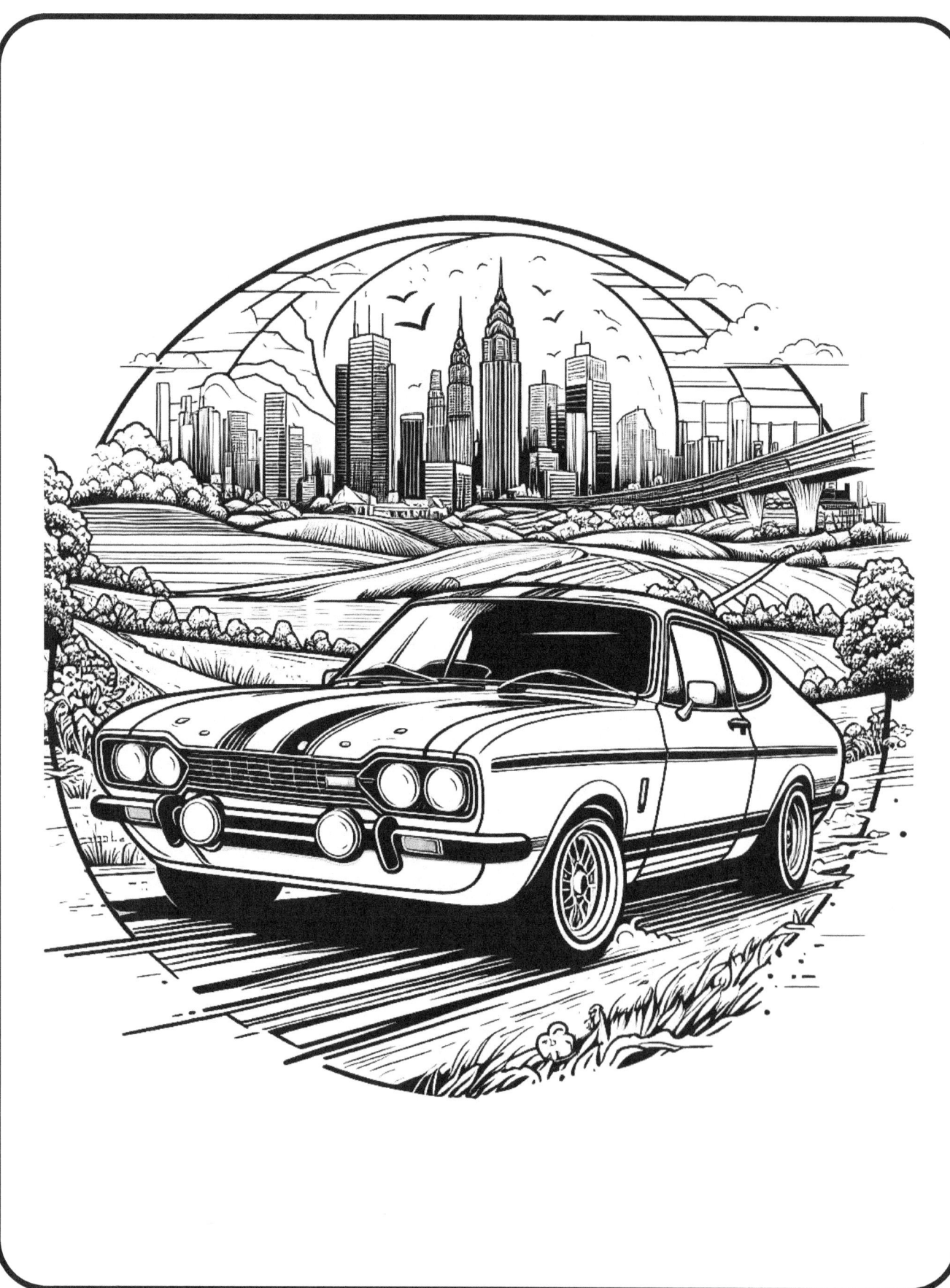

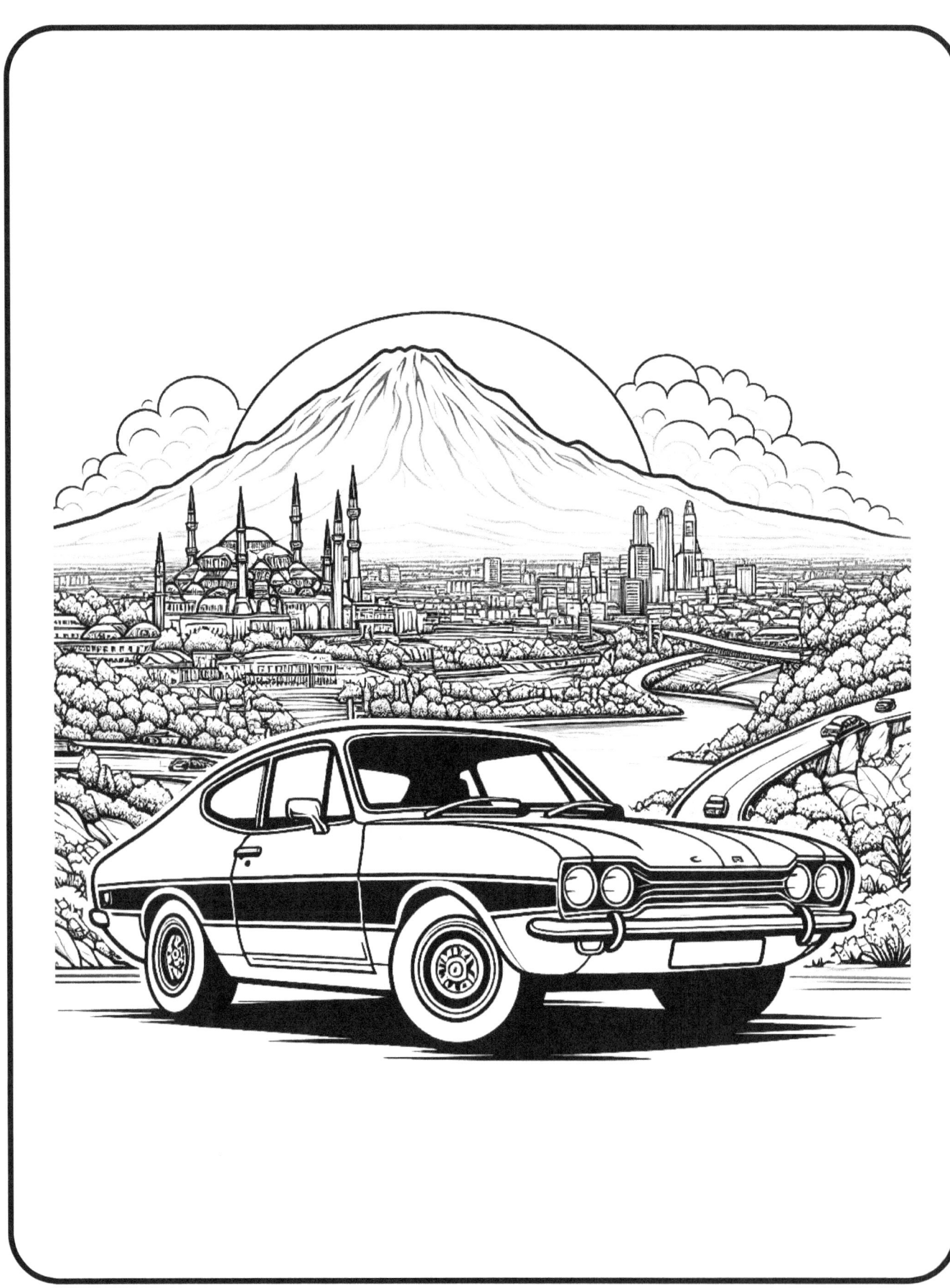

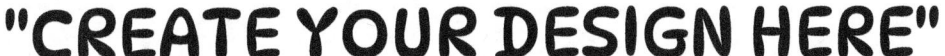

"CREATE YOUR DESIGN HERE"

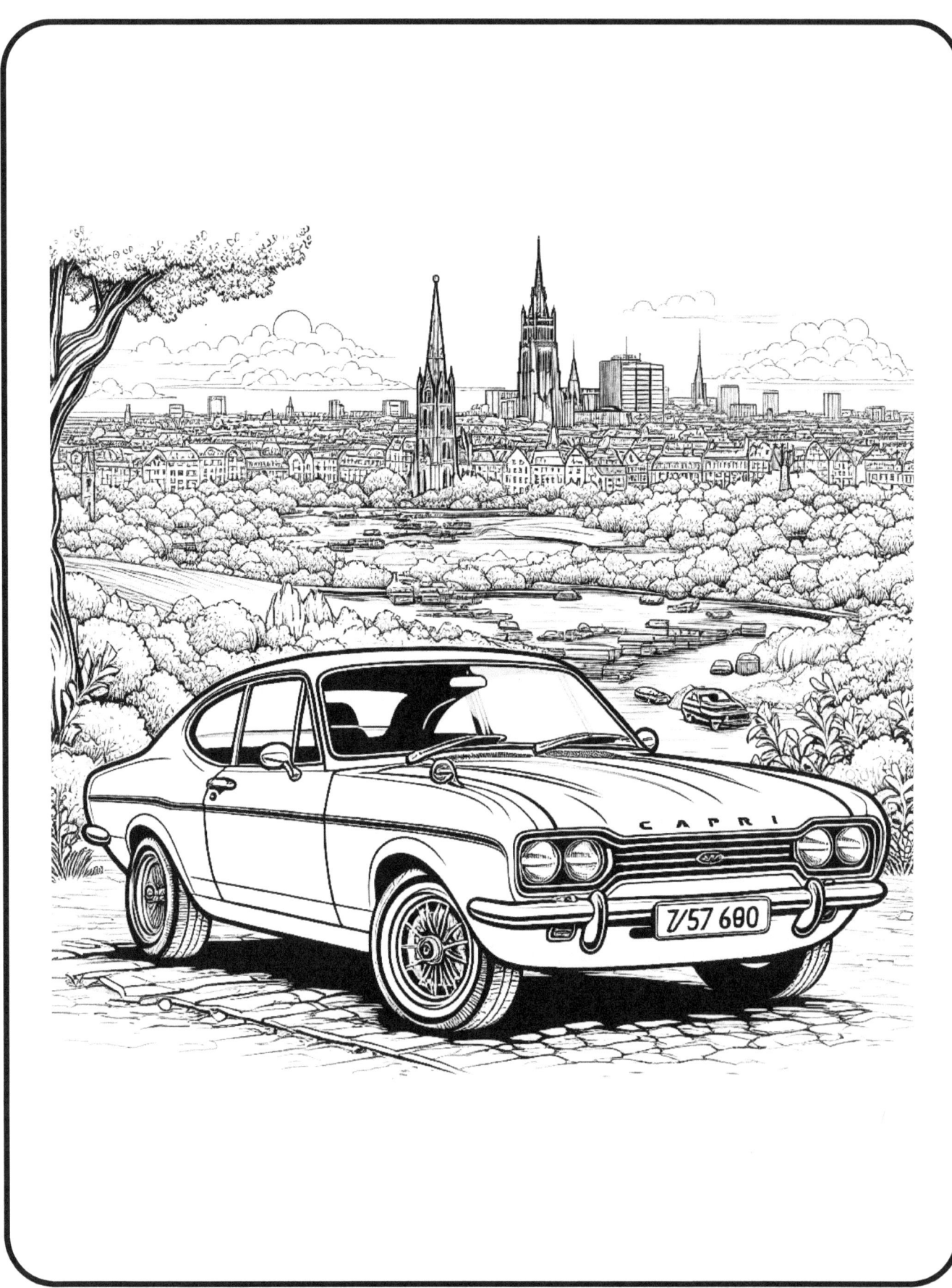

"CREATE YOUR DESIGN HERE"

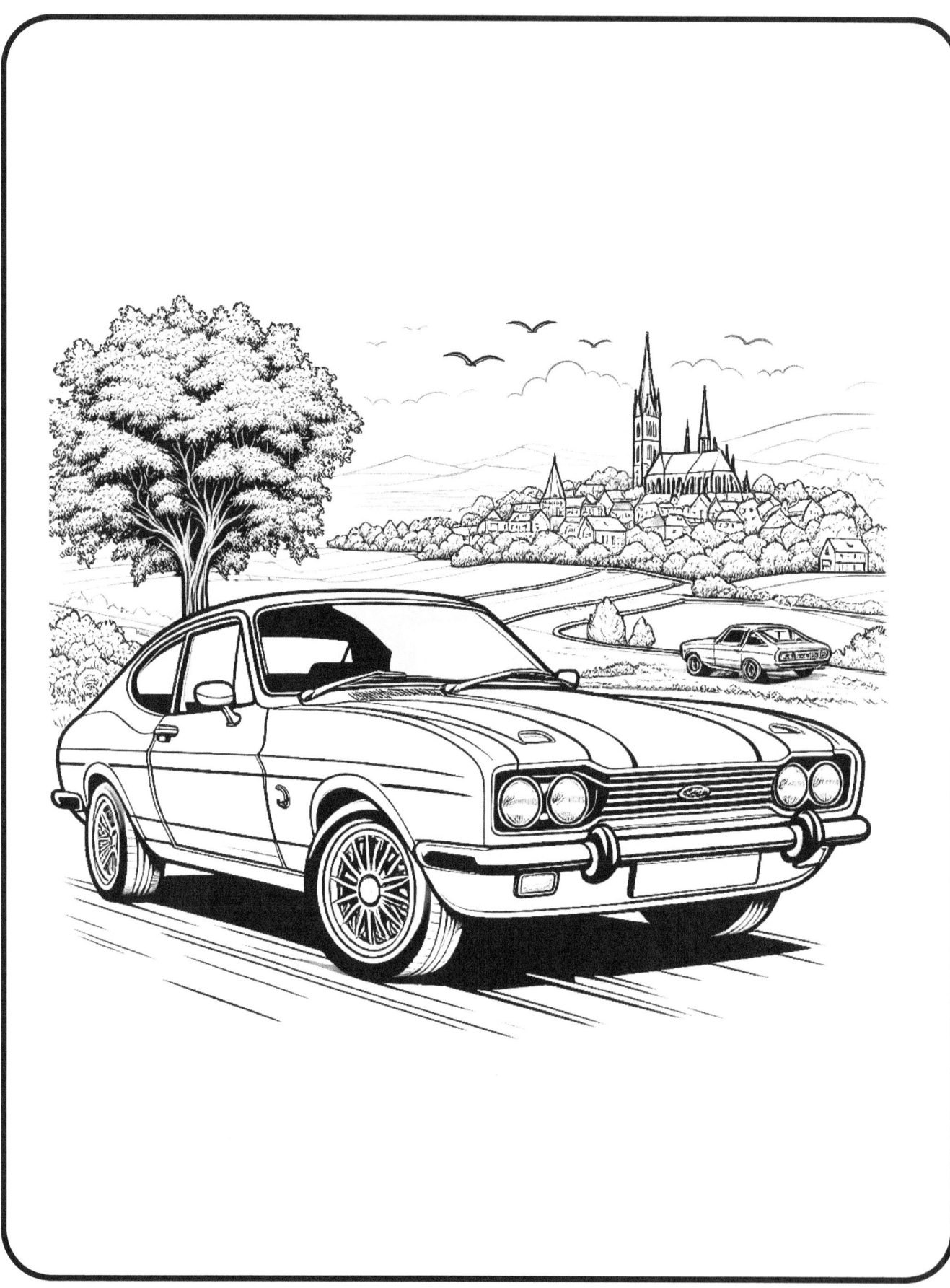

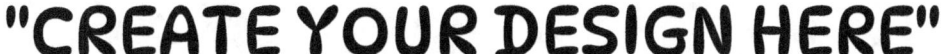

"CREATE YOUR DESIGN HERE"

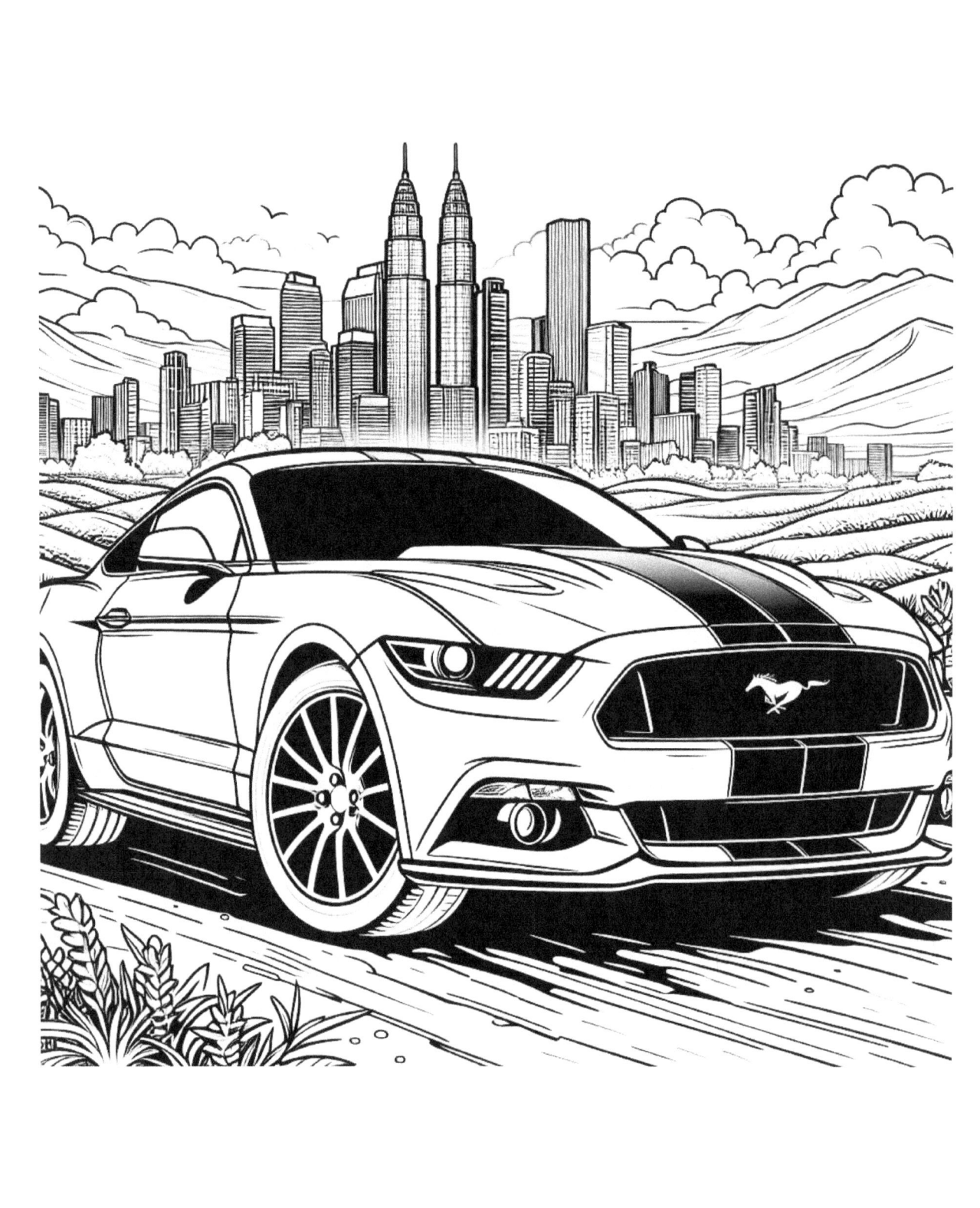

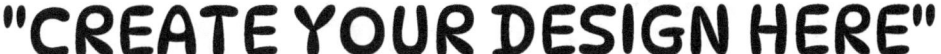

"CREATE YOUR DESIGN HERE"

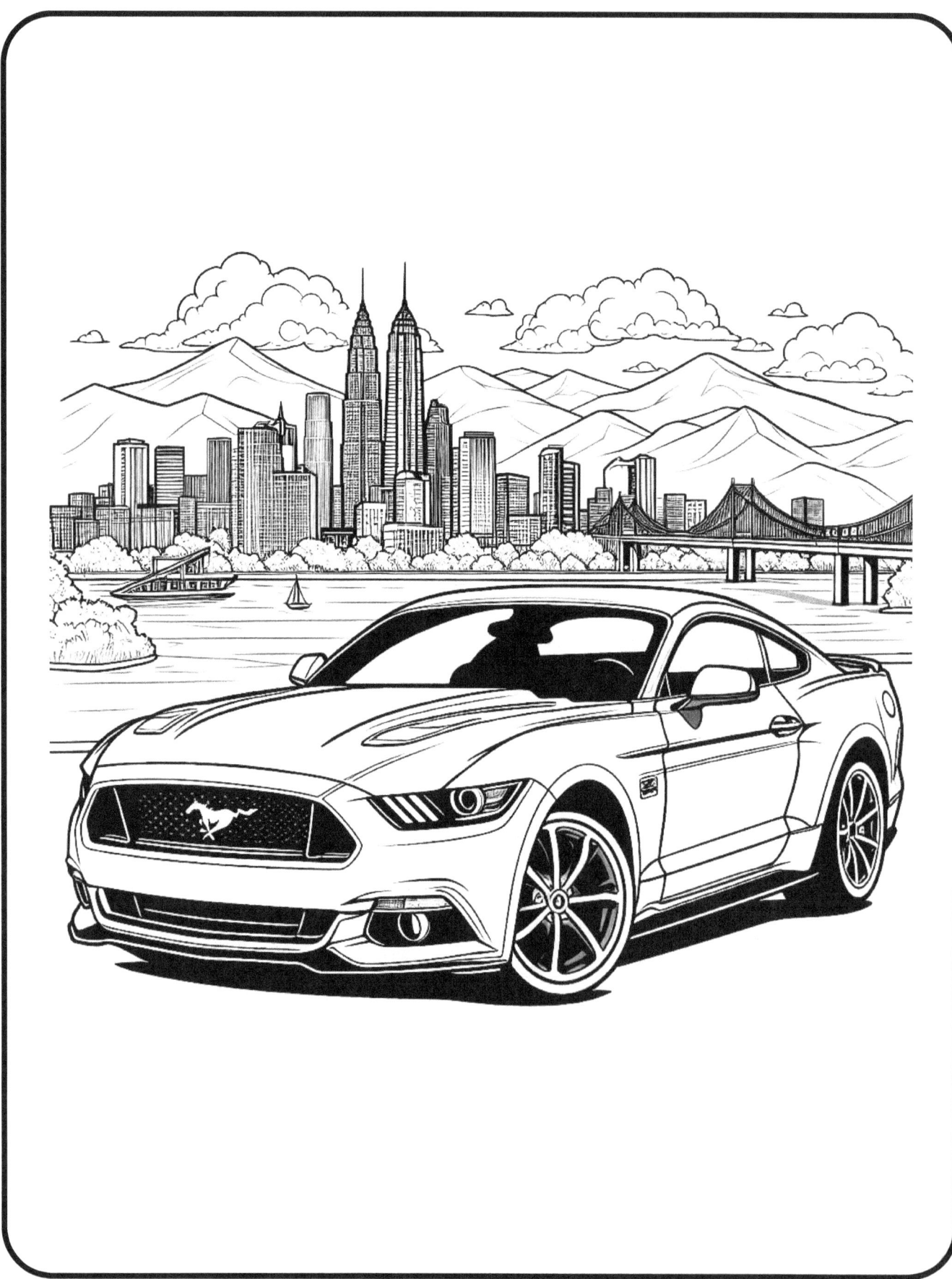

"CREATE YOUR DESIGN HERE"

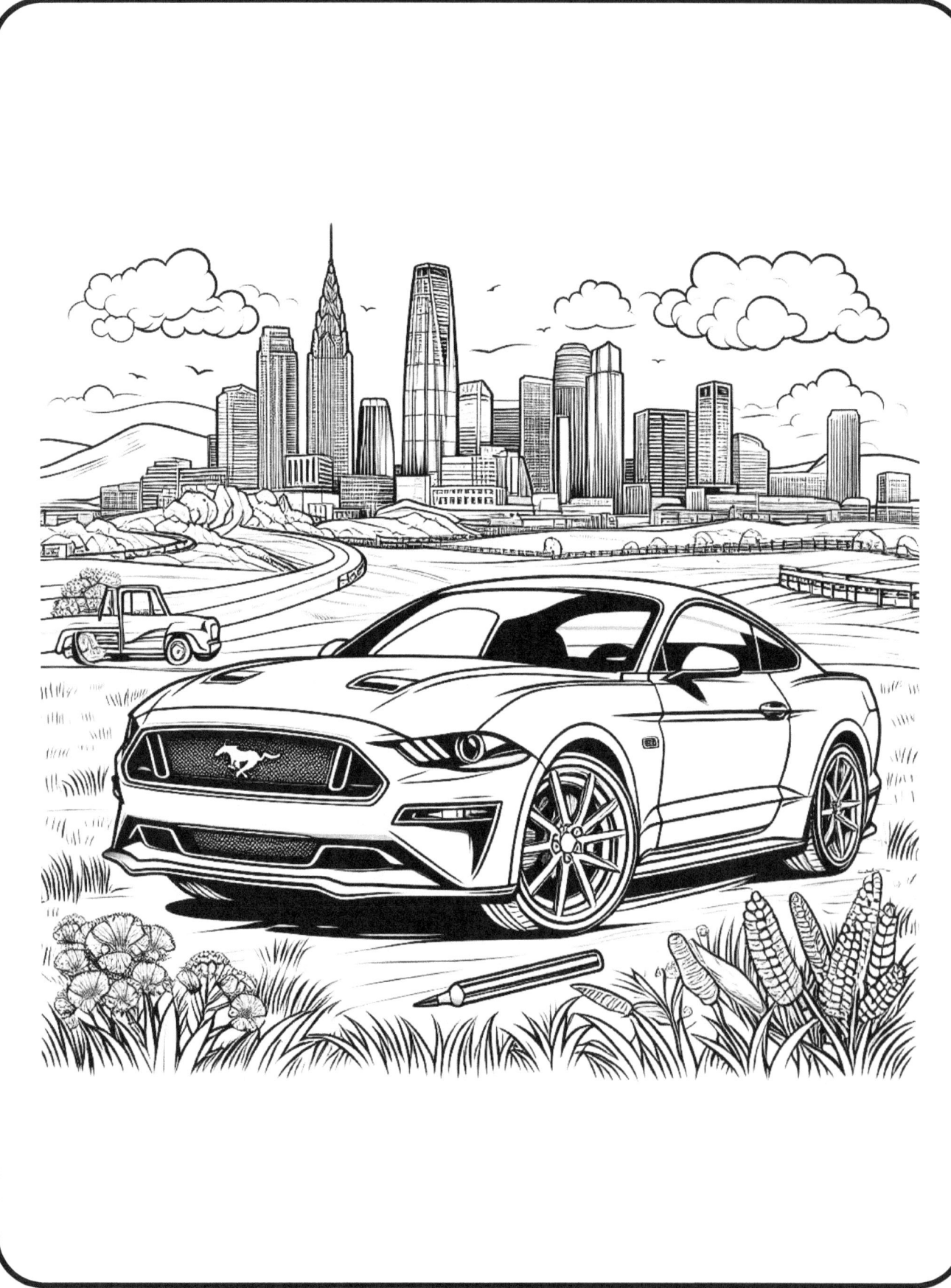

"CREATE YOUR DESIGN HERE"

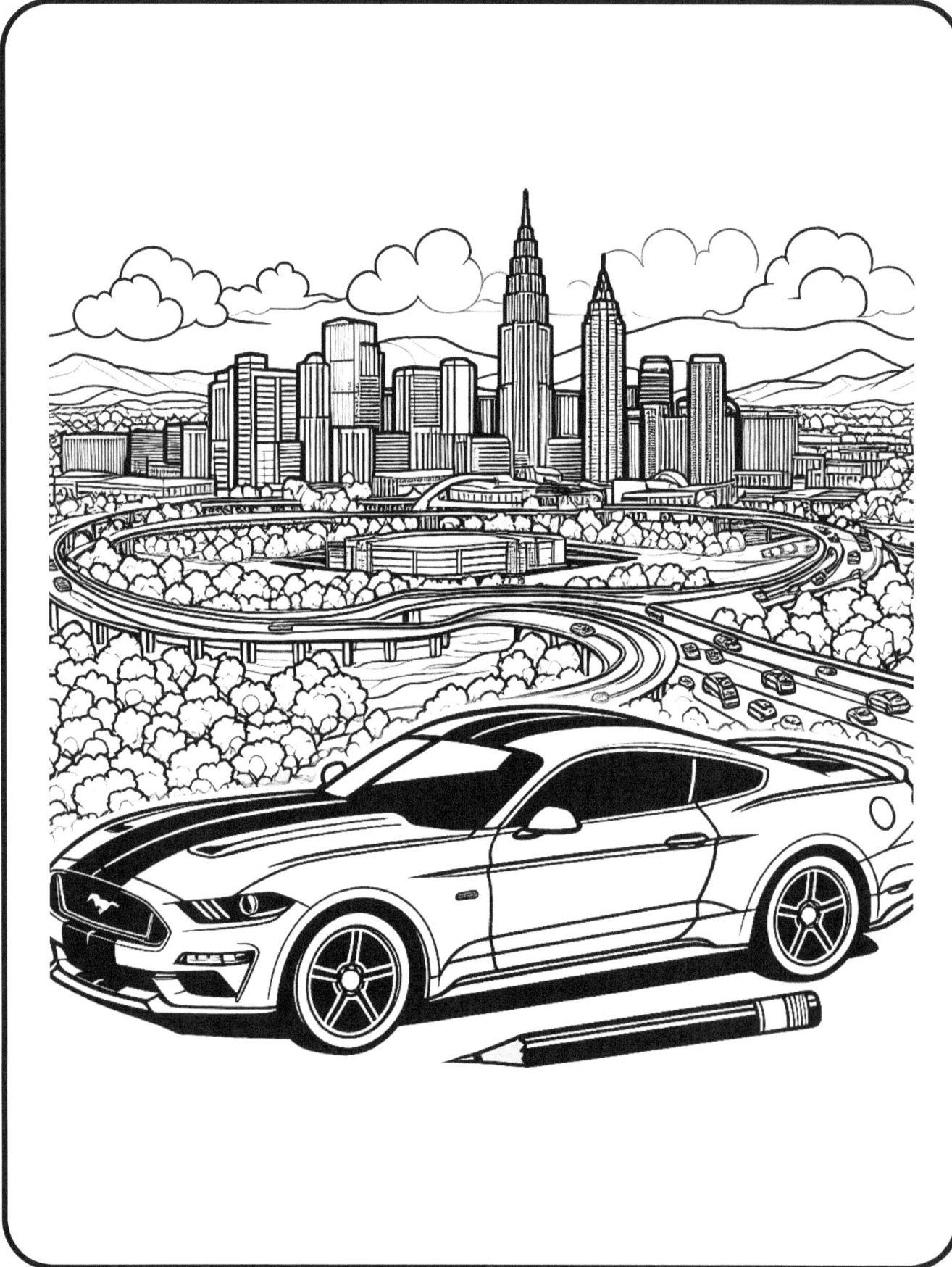

"CREATE YOUR DESIGN HERE"

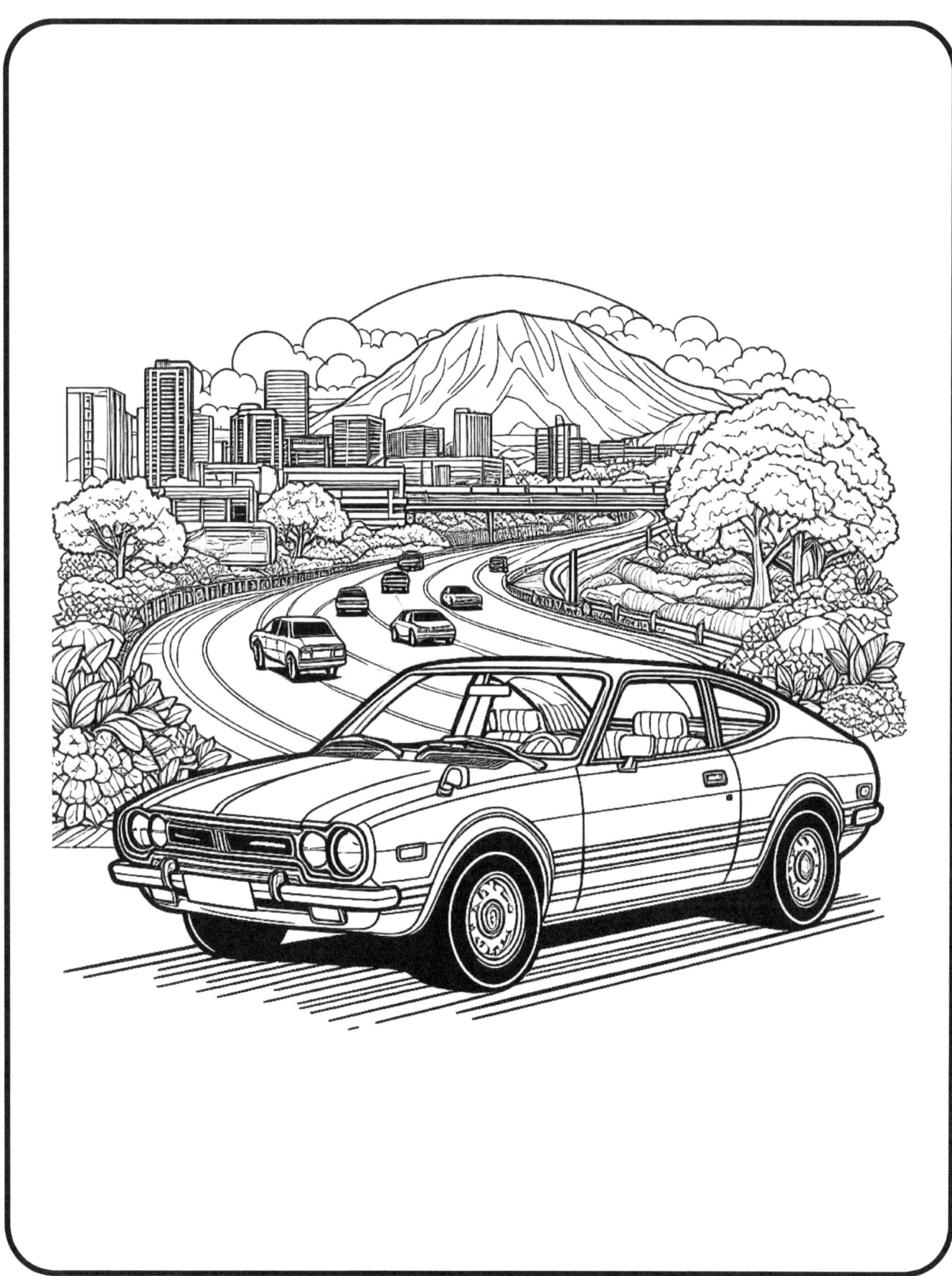

"CREATE YOUR DESIGN HERE"

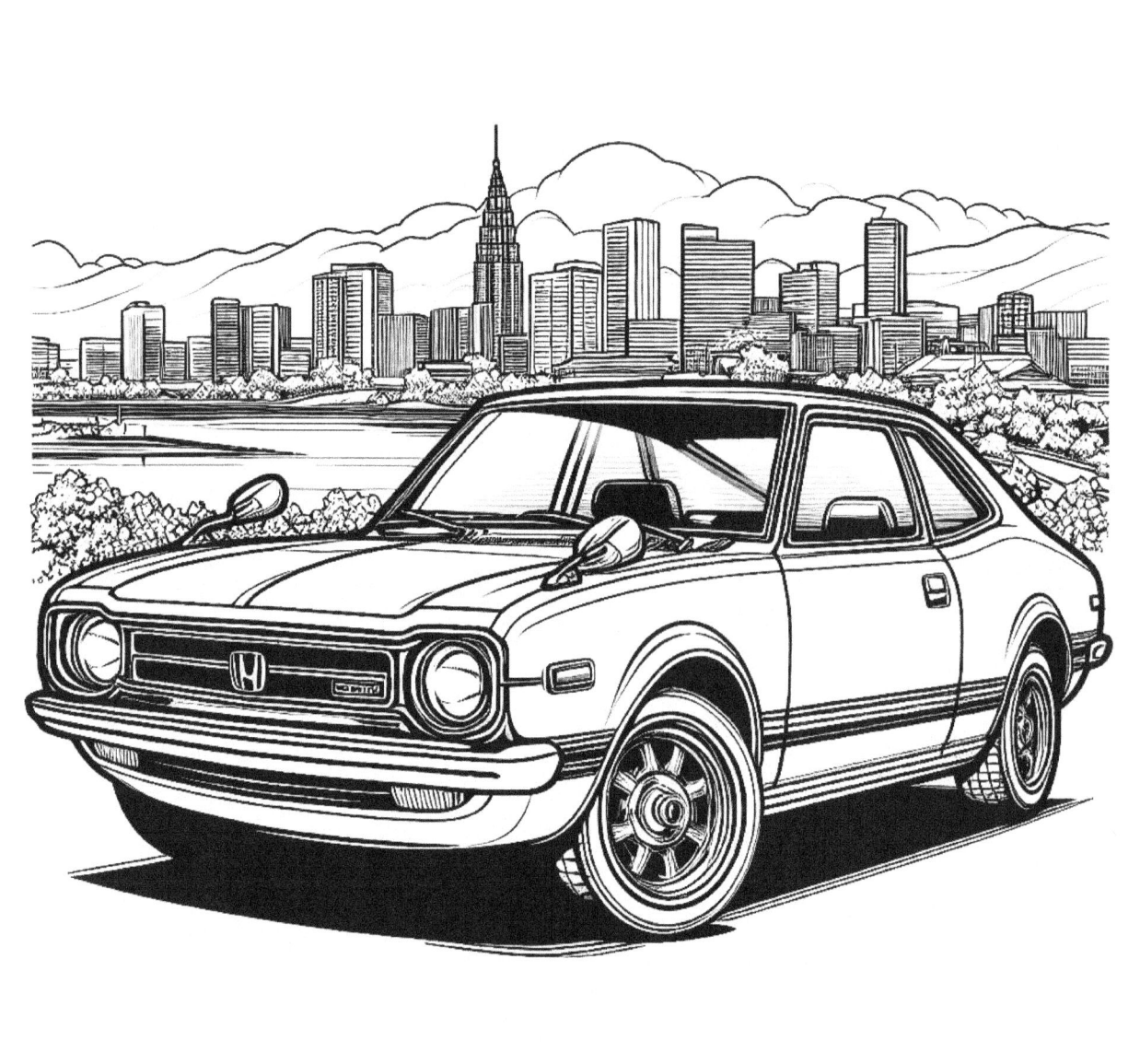

"CREATE YOUR DESIGN HERE"

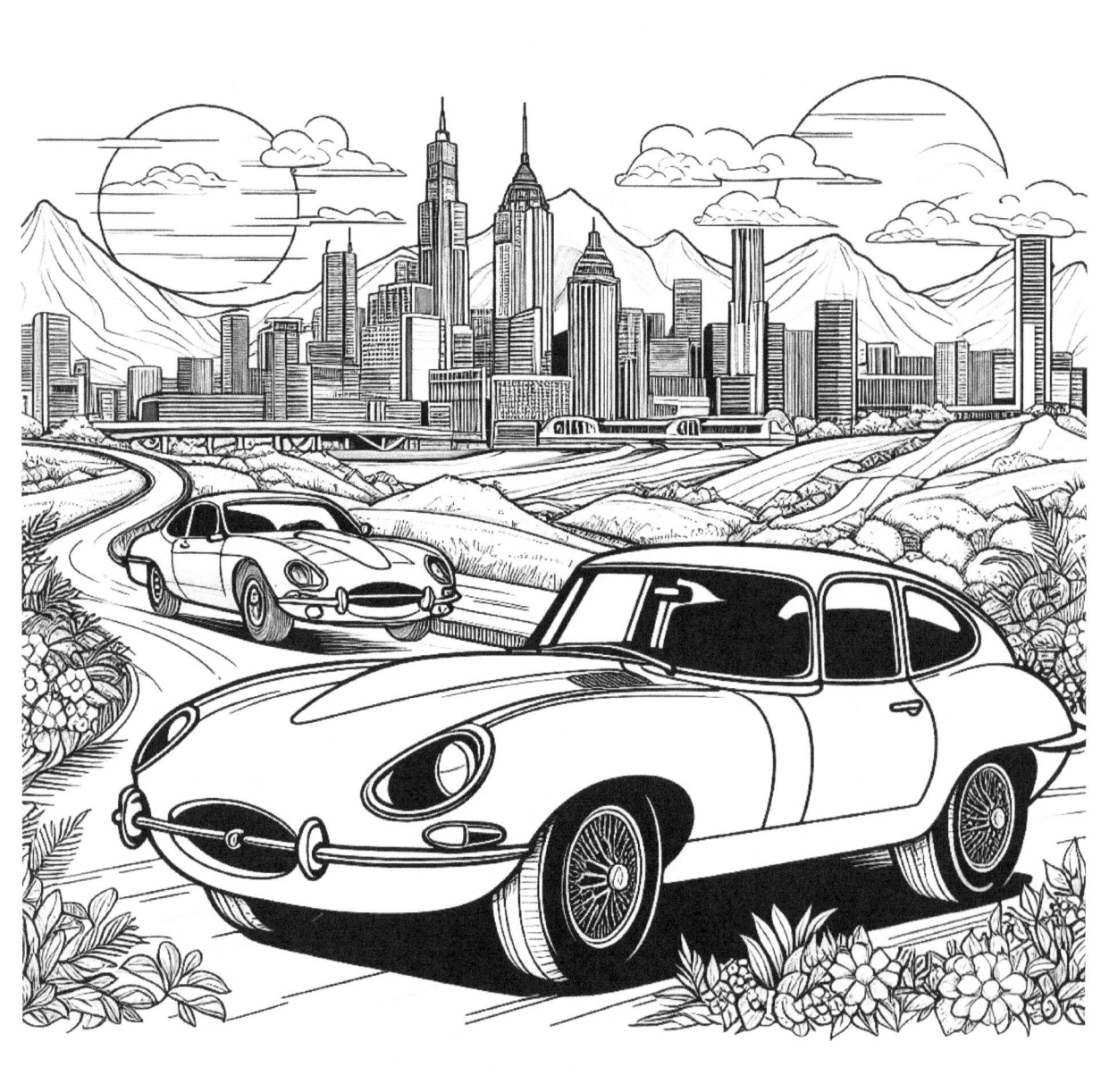

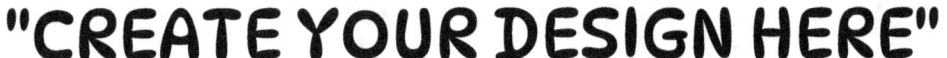

"CREATE YOUR DESIGN HERE"

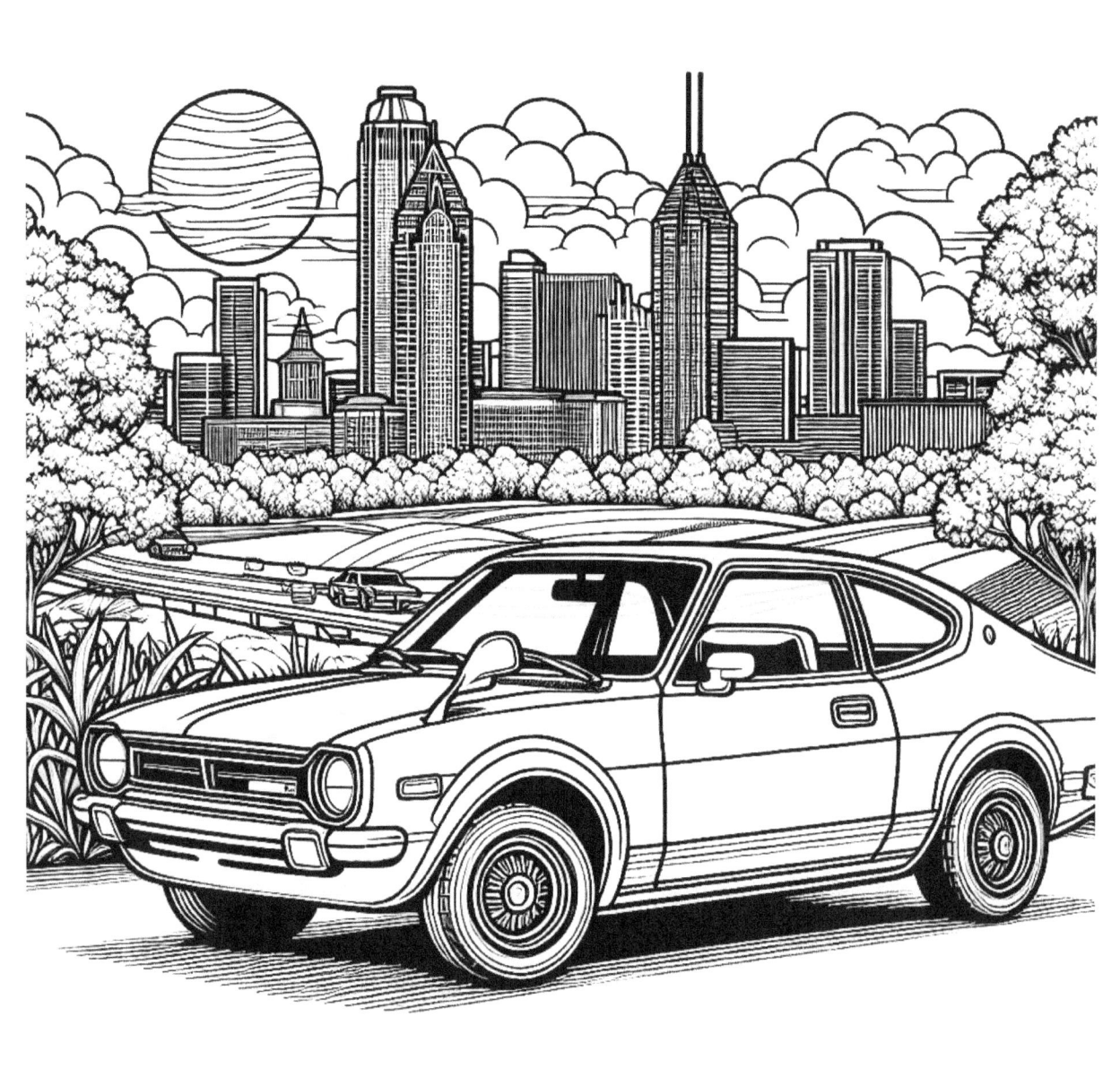

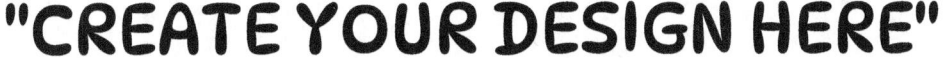

"CREATE YOUR DESIGN HERE"

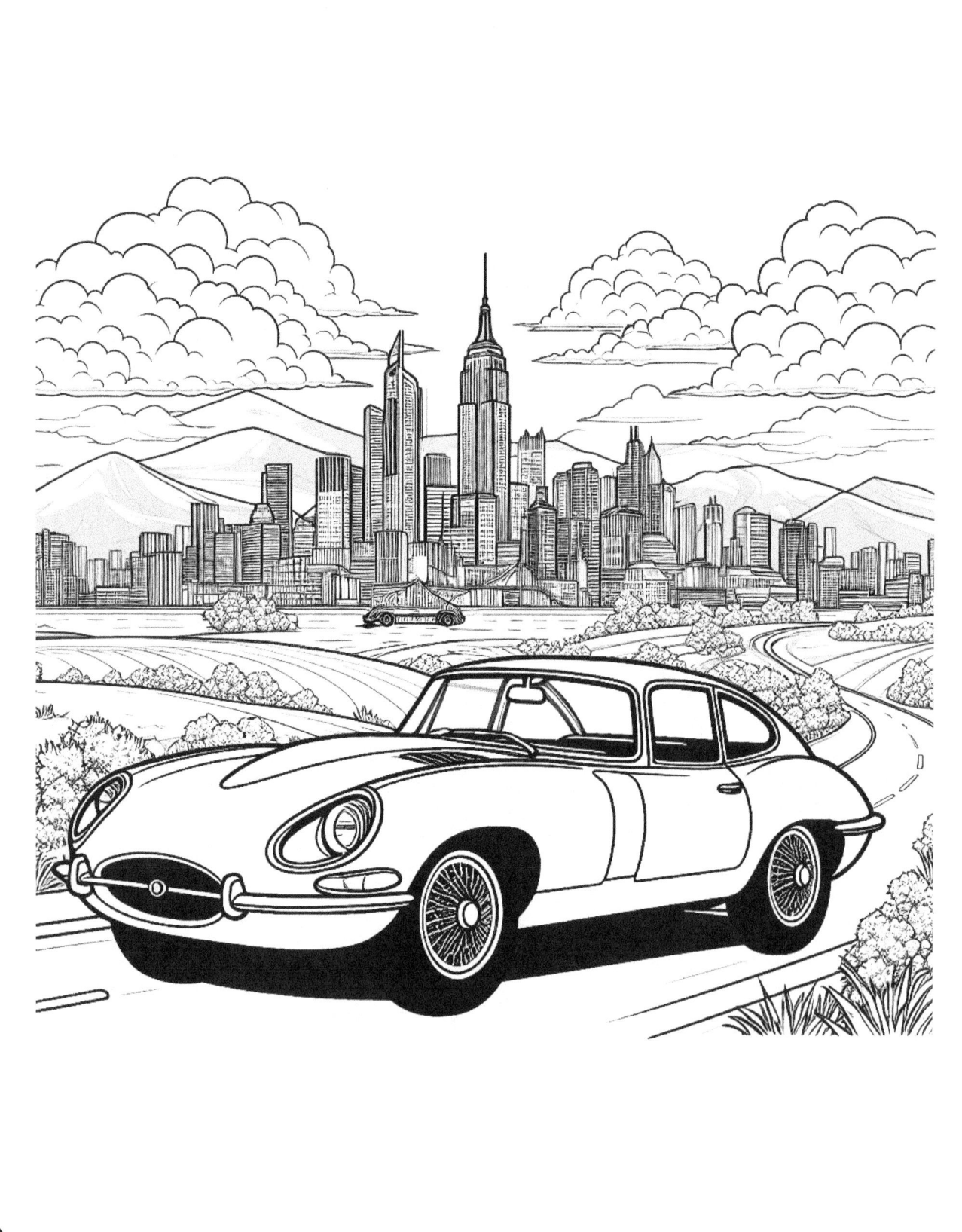

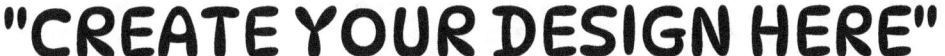
"CREATE YOUR DESIGN HERE"

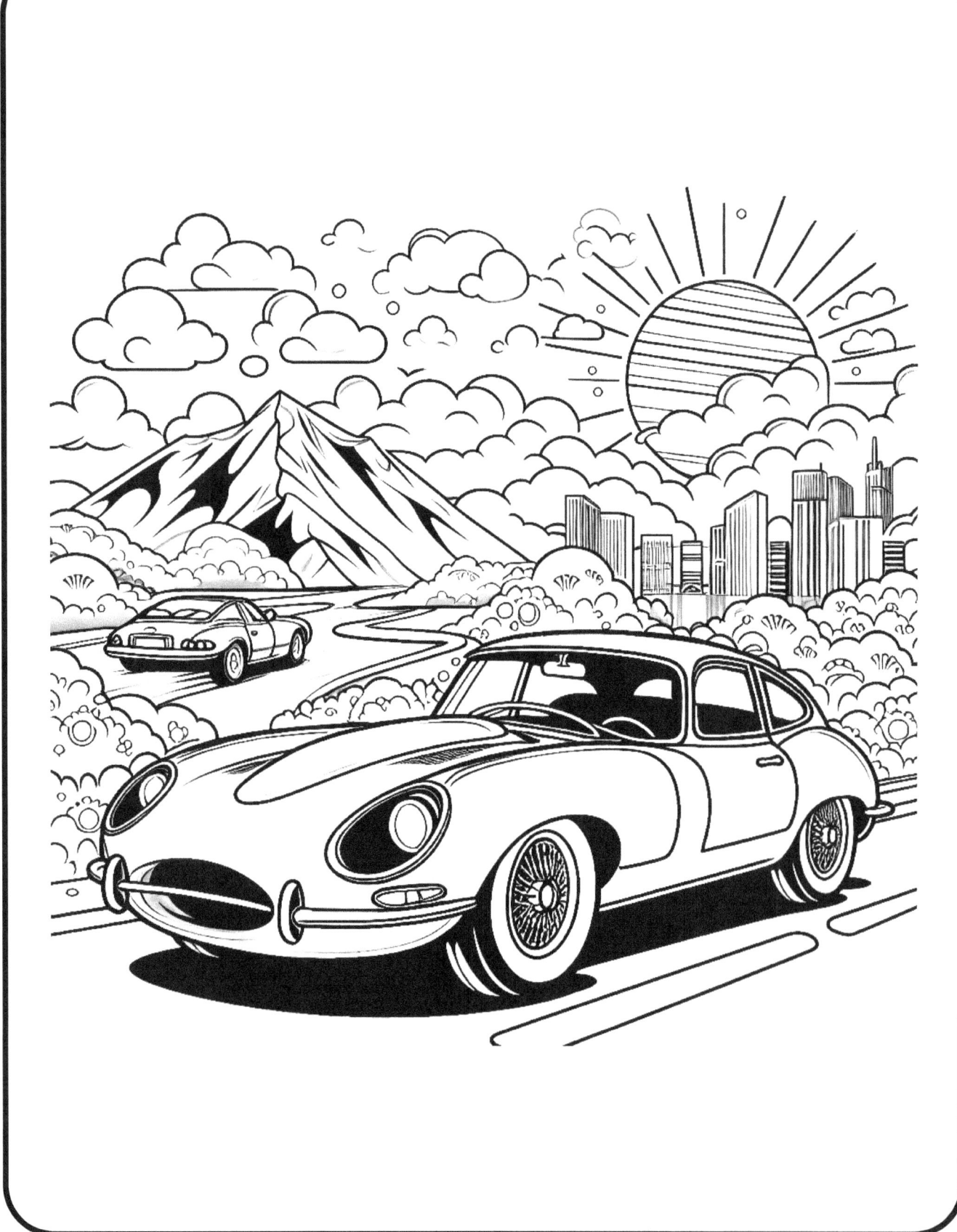

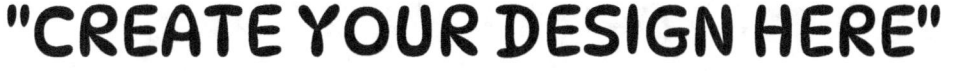
"CREATE YOUR DESIGN HERE"

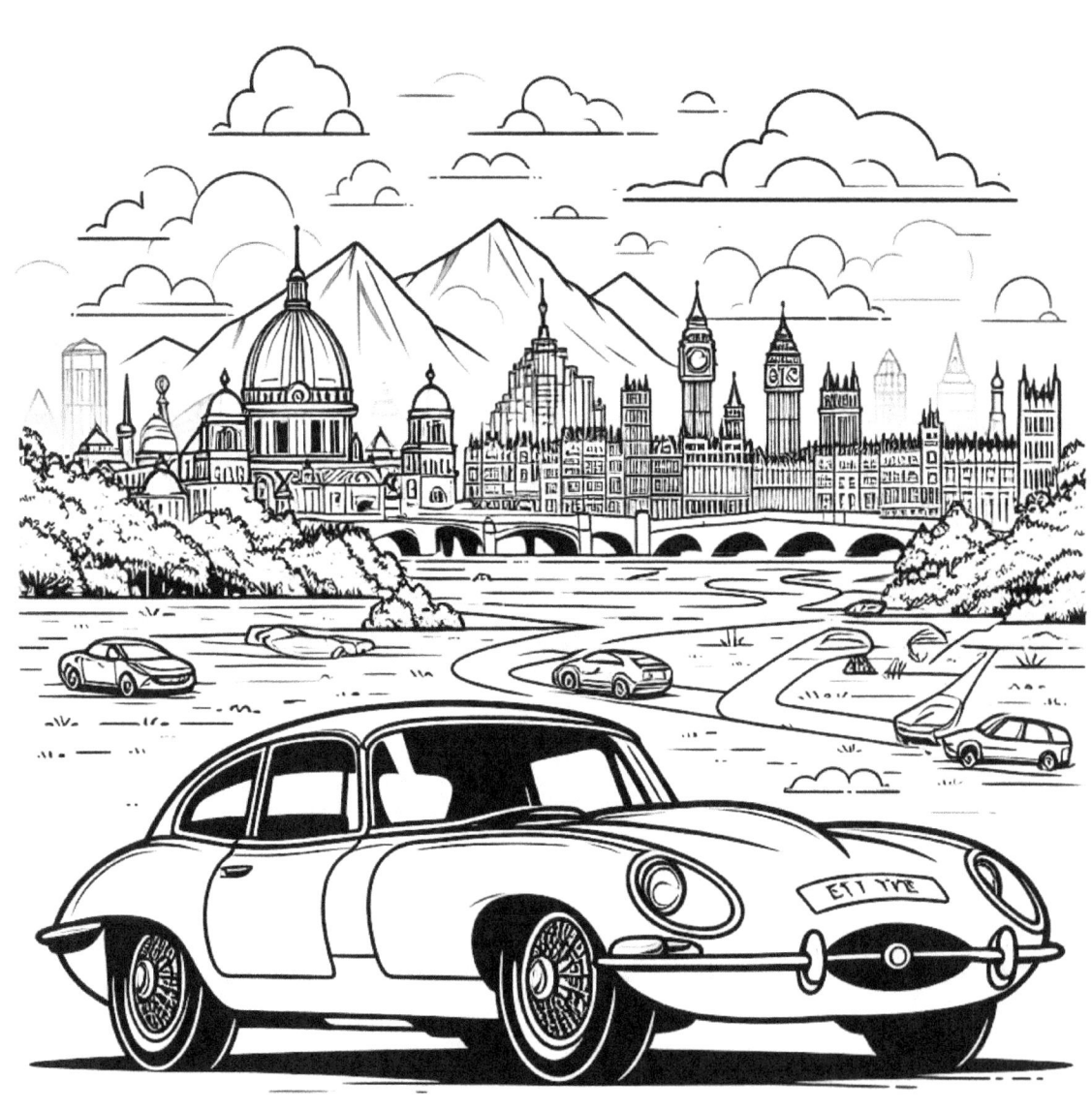

"CREATE YOUR DESIGN HERE"

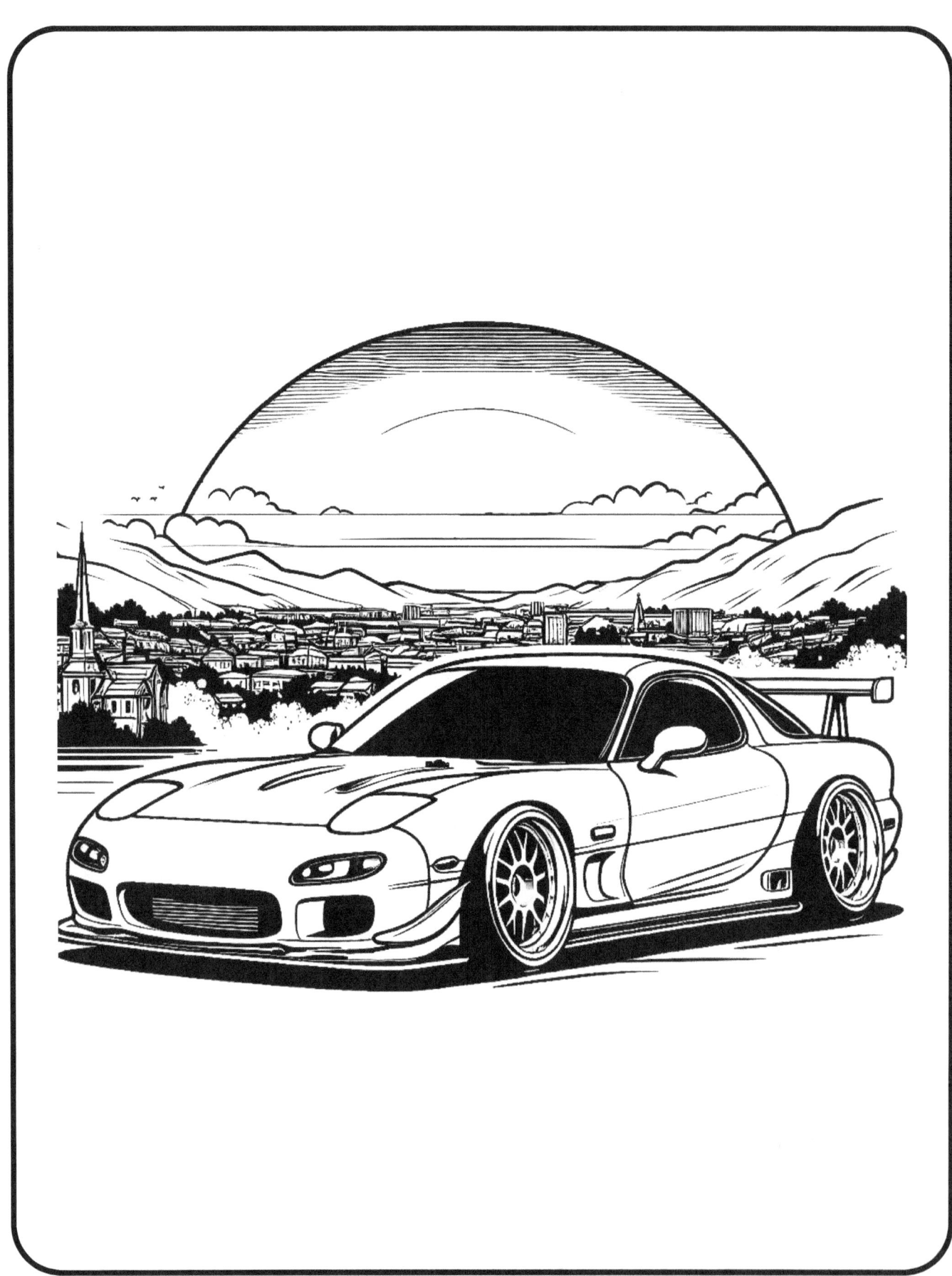

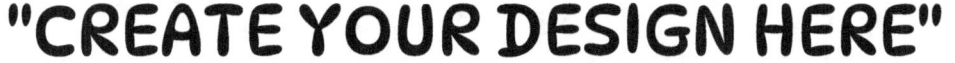
"CREATE YOUR DESIGN HERE"

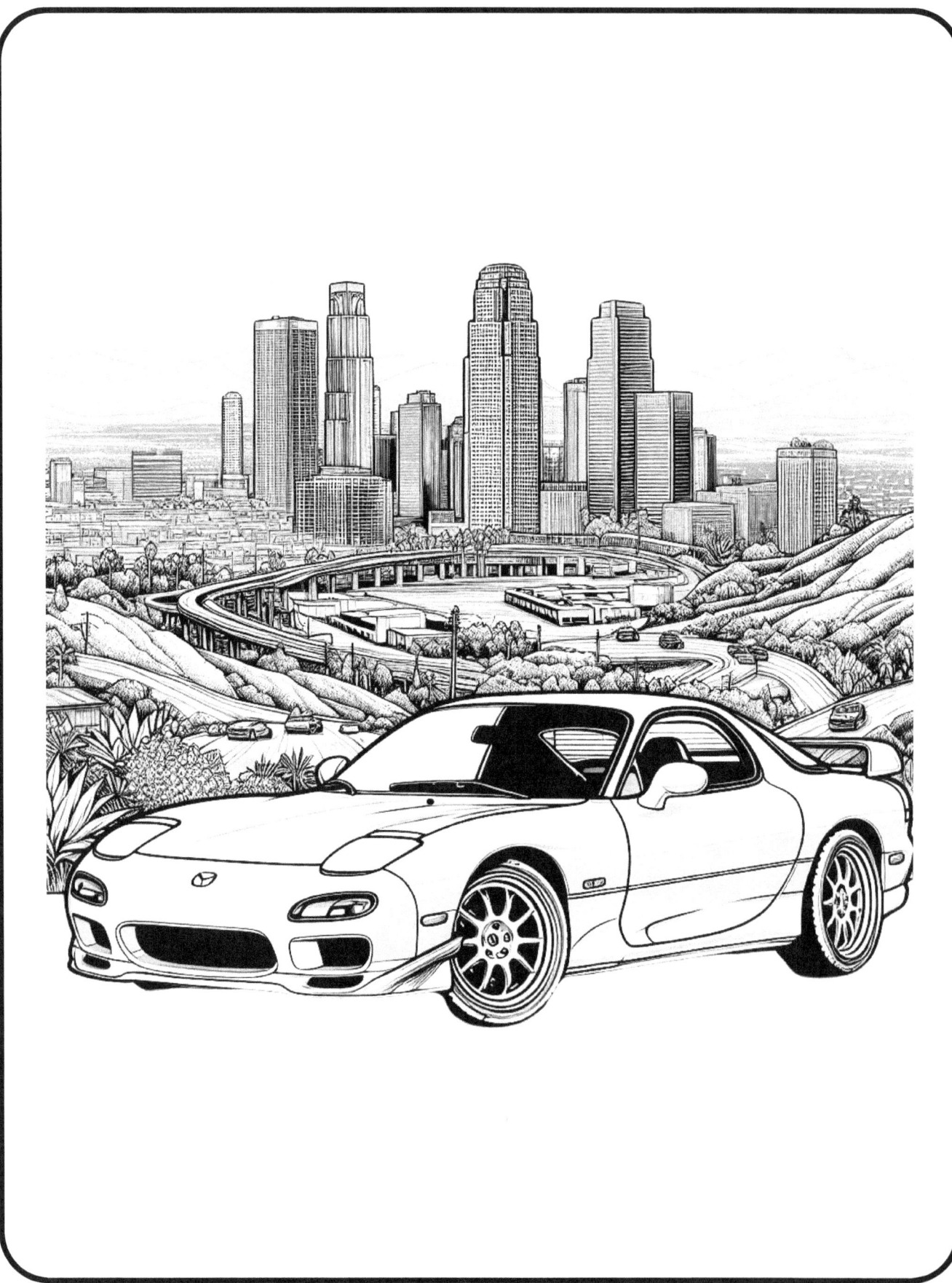

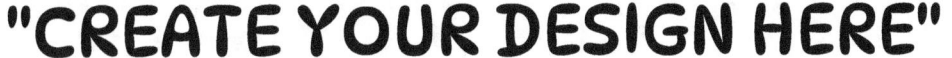

"CREATE YOUR DESIGN HERE"

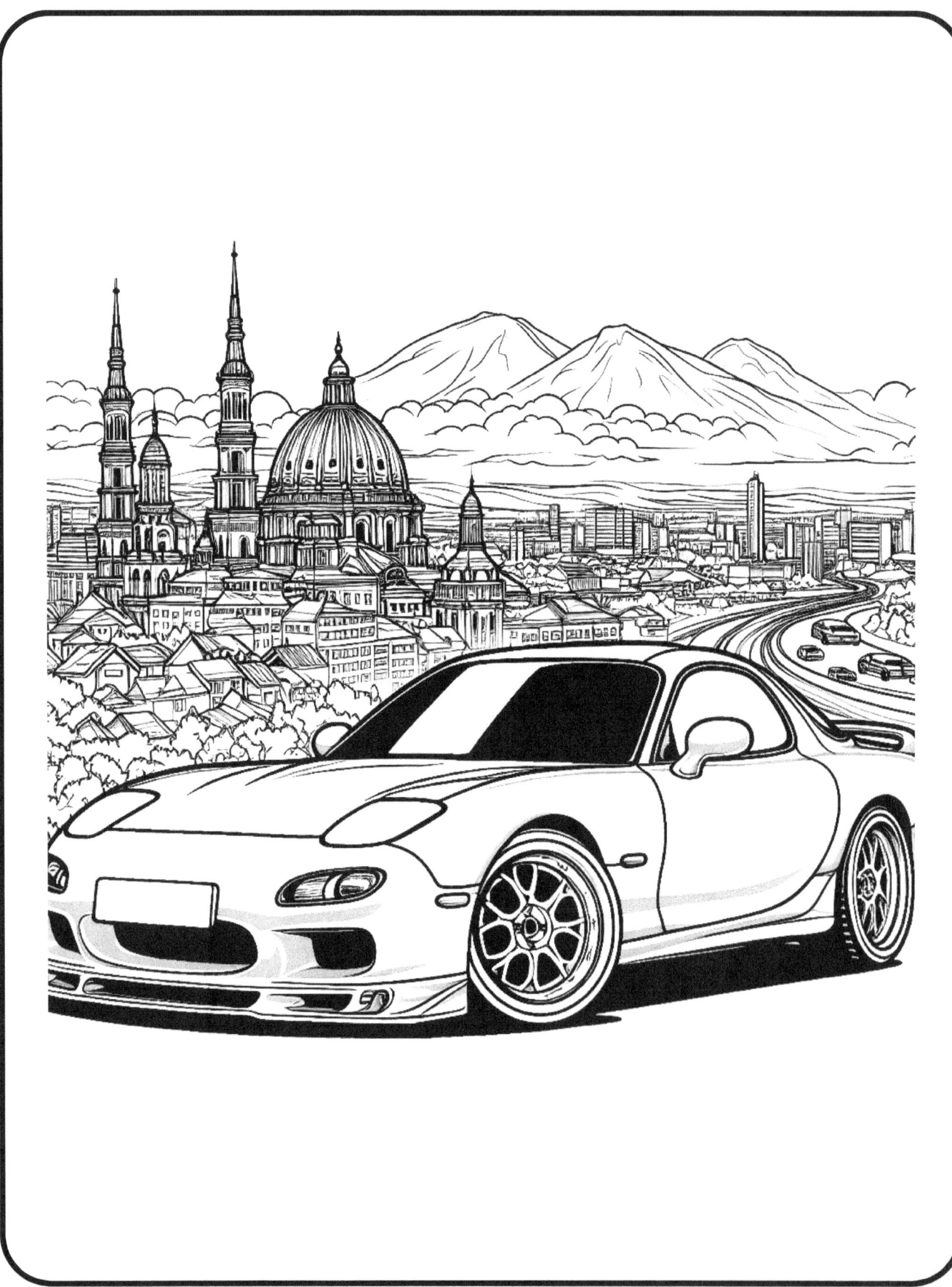

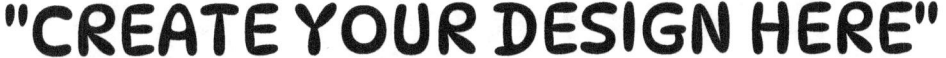

"CREATE YOUR DESIGN HERE"

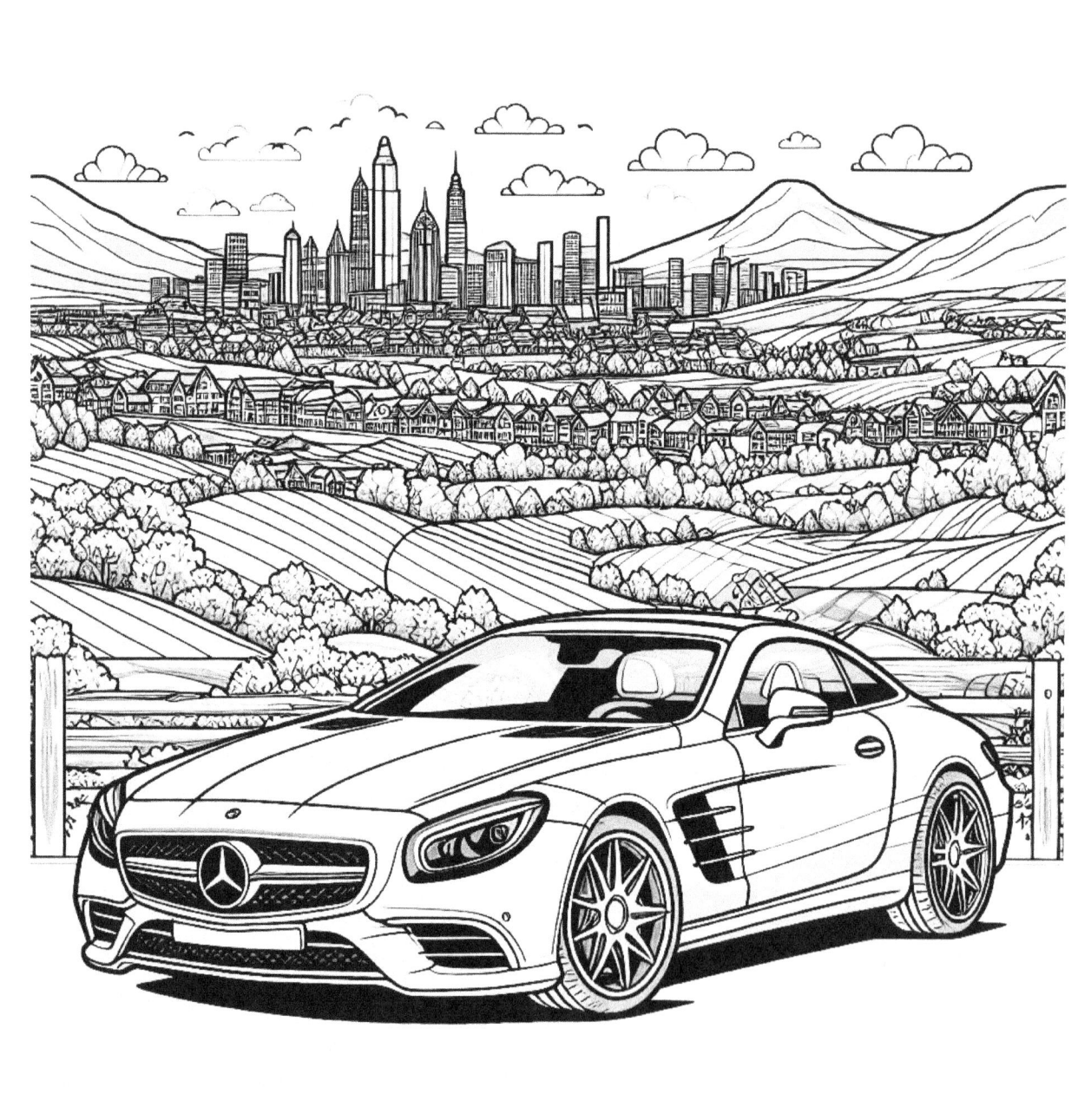

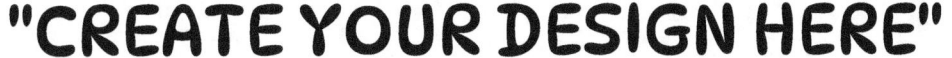

"CREATE YOUR DESIGN HERE"

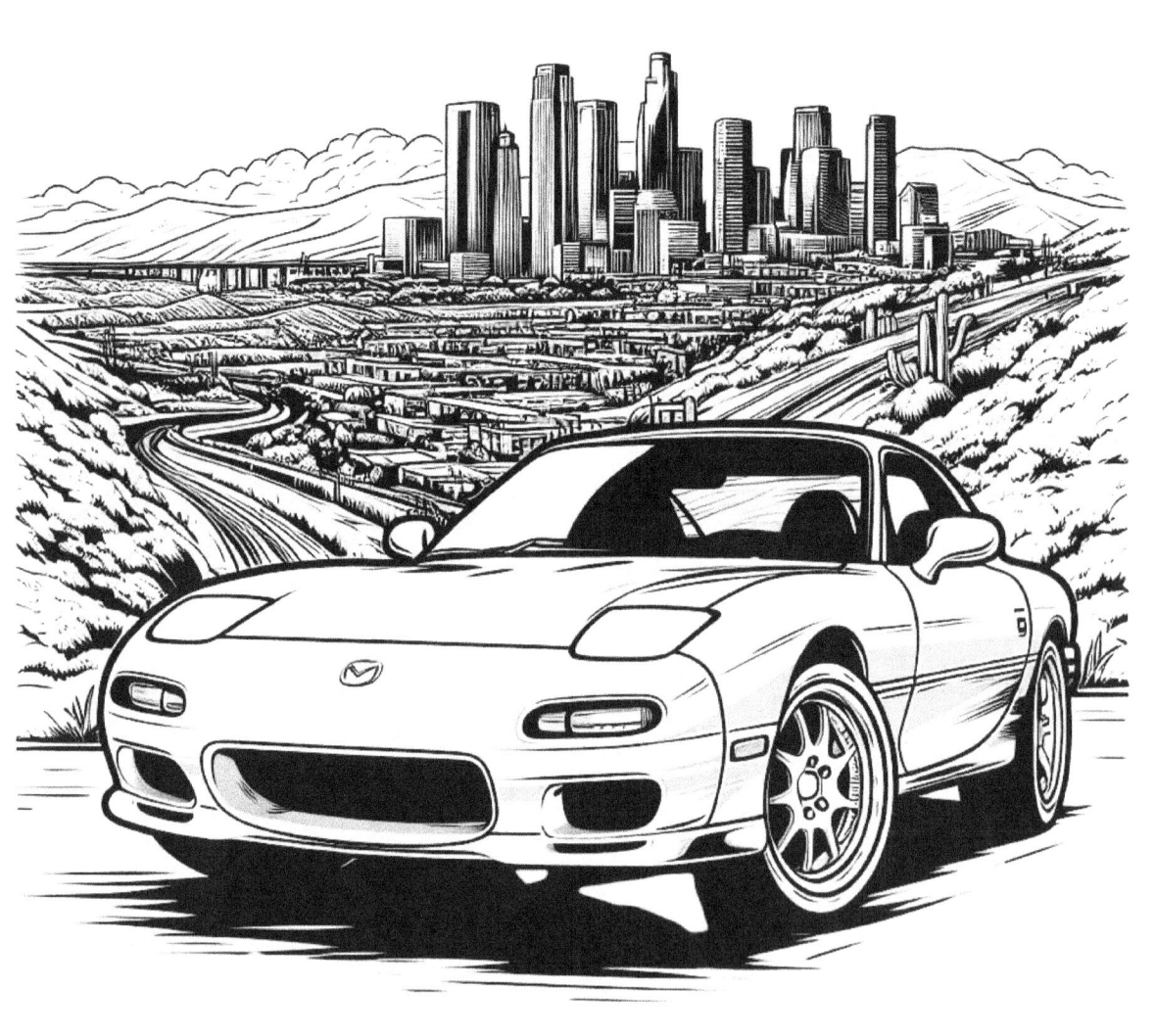

"CREATE YOUR DESIGN HERE"

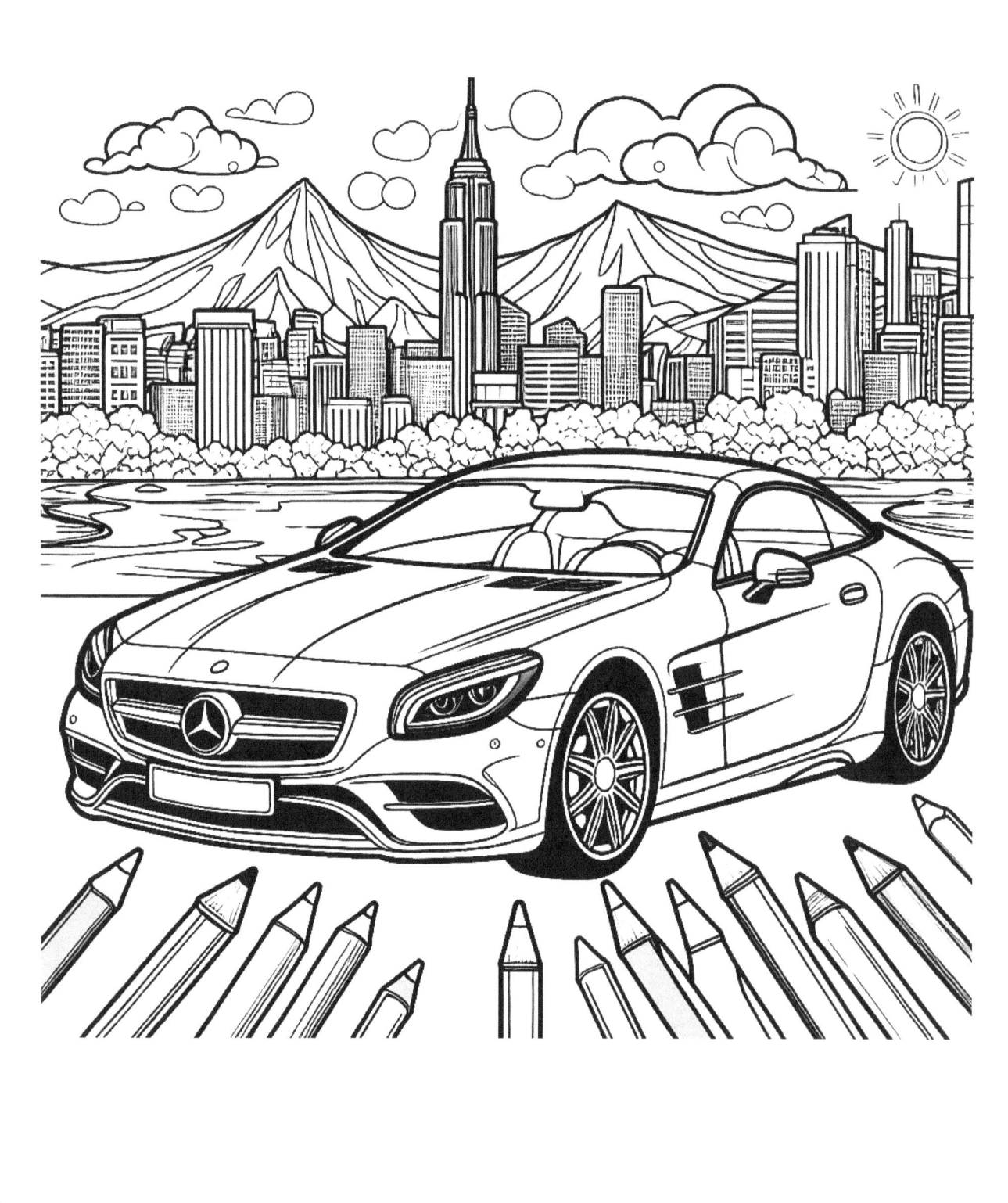

"CREATE YOUR DESIGN HERE"

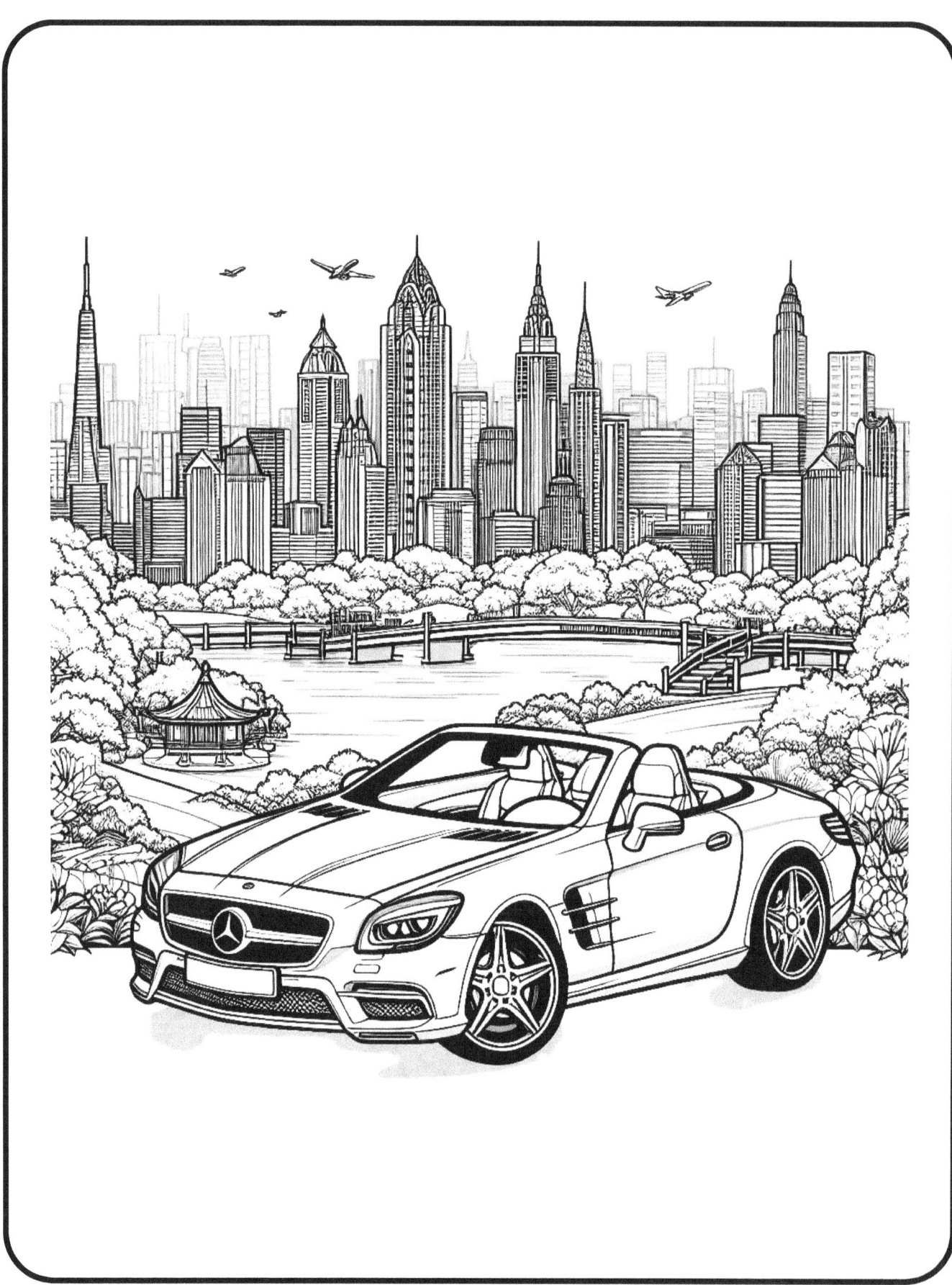

"CREATE YOUR DESIGN HERE"

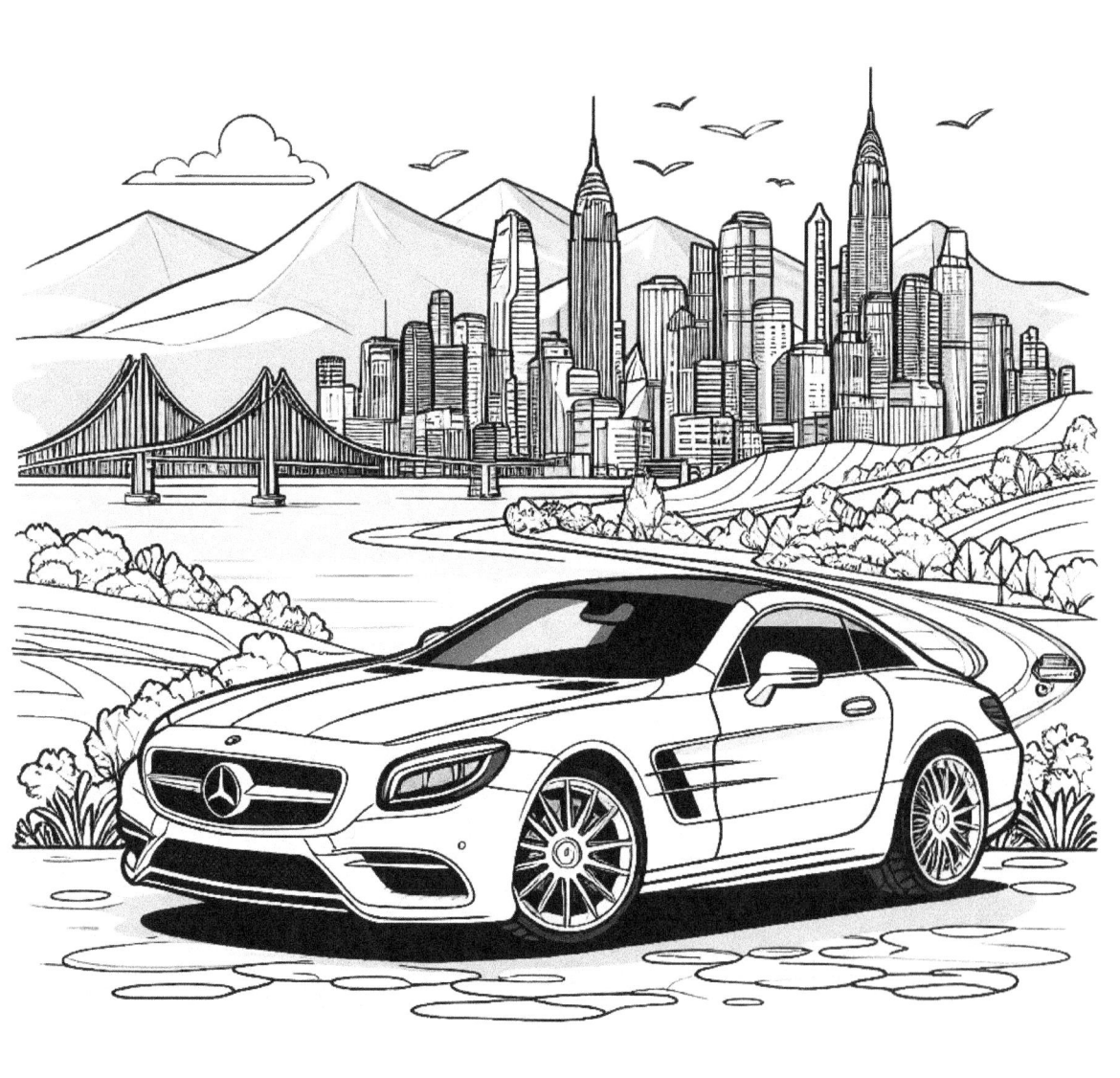

"CREATE YOUR DESIGN HERE"

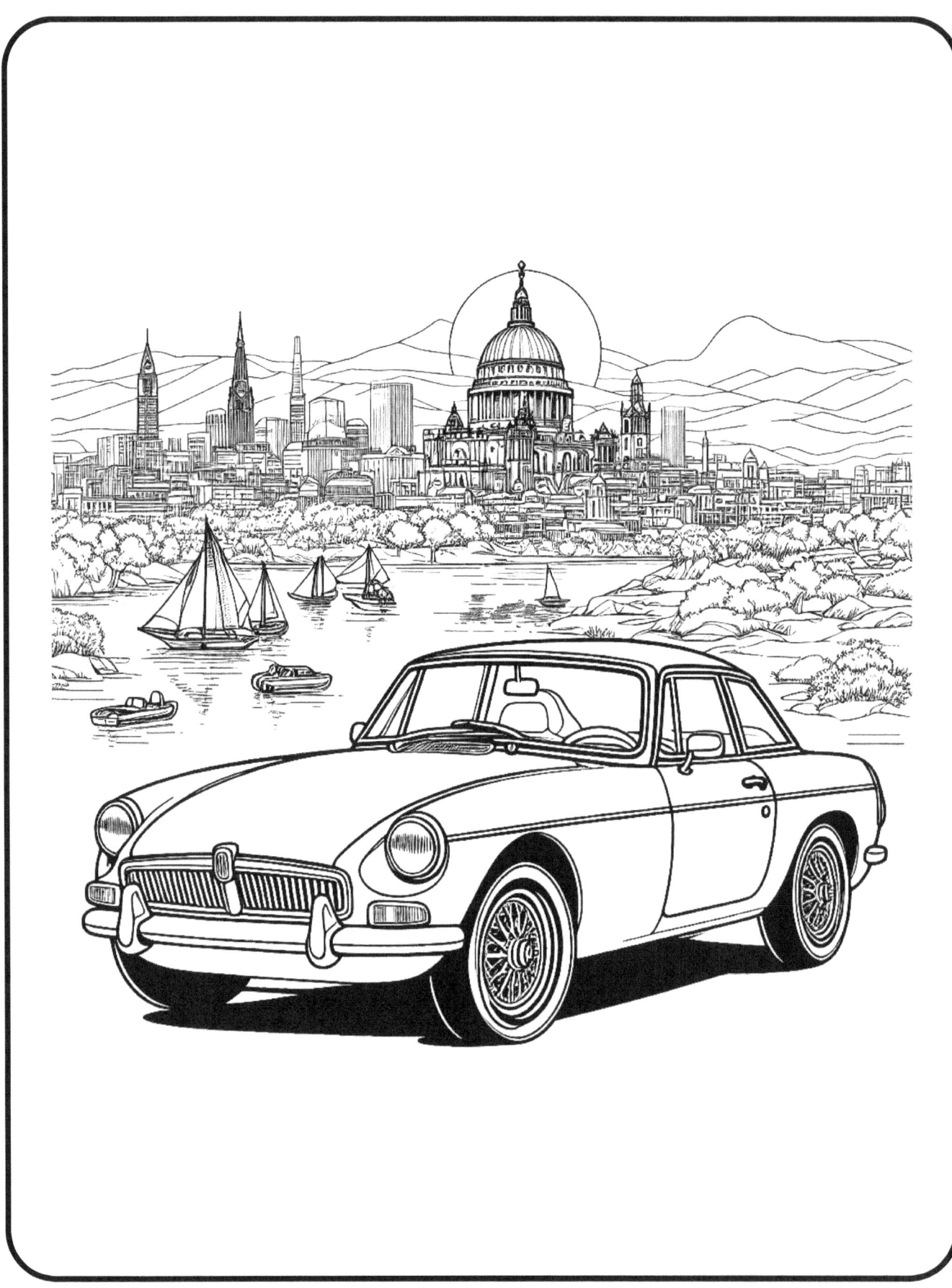

"CREATE YOUR DESIGN HERE"

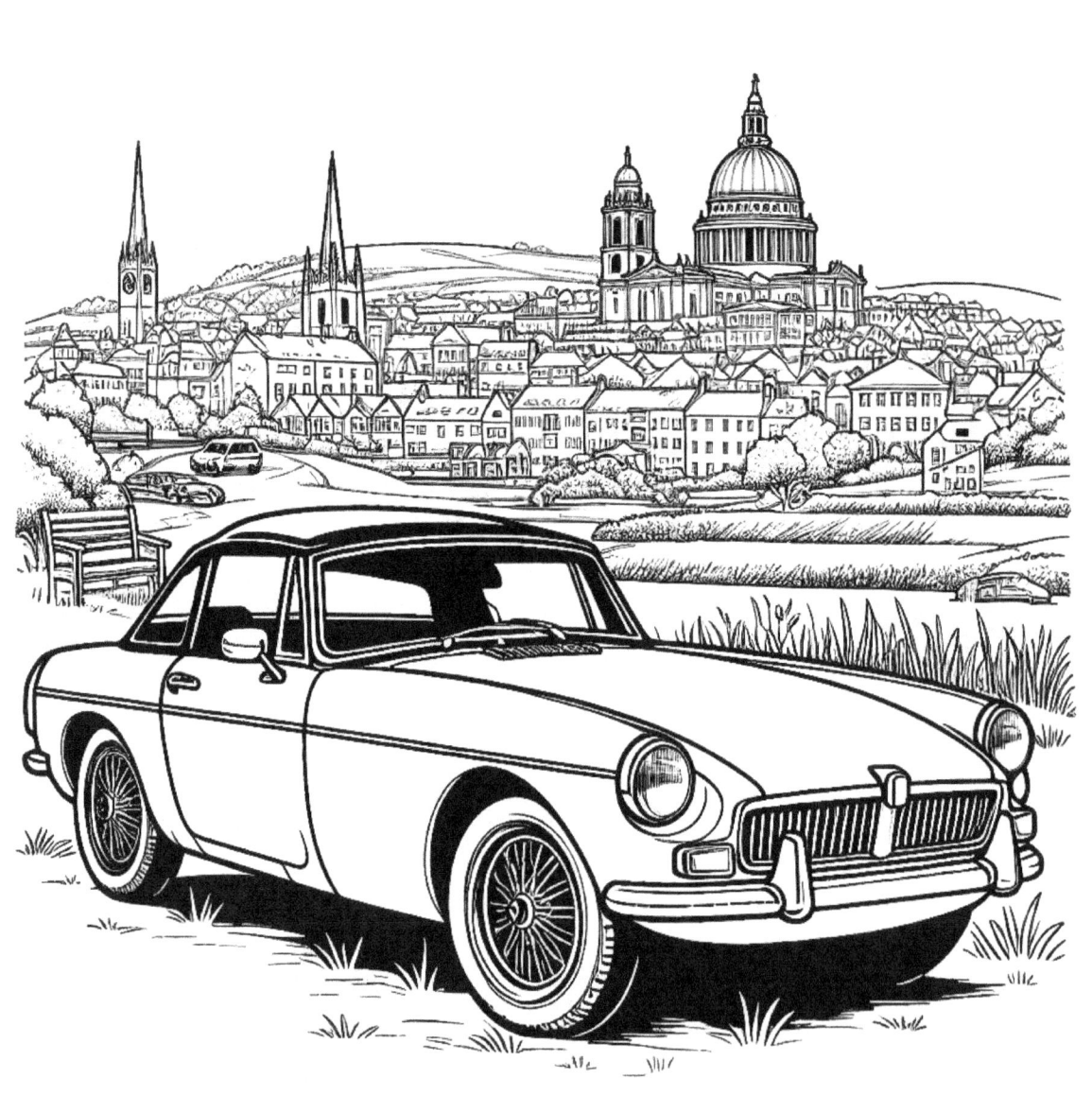

"CREATE YOUR DESIGN HERE"

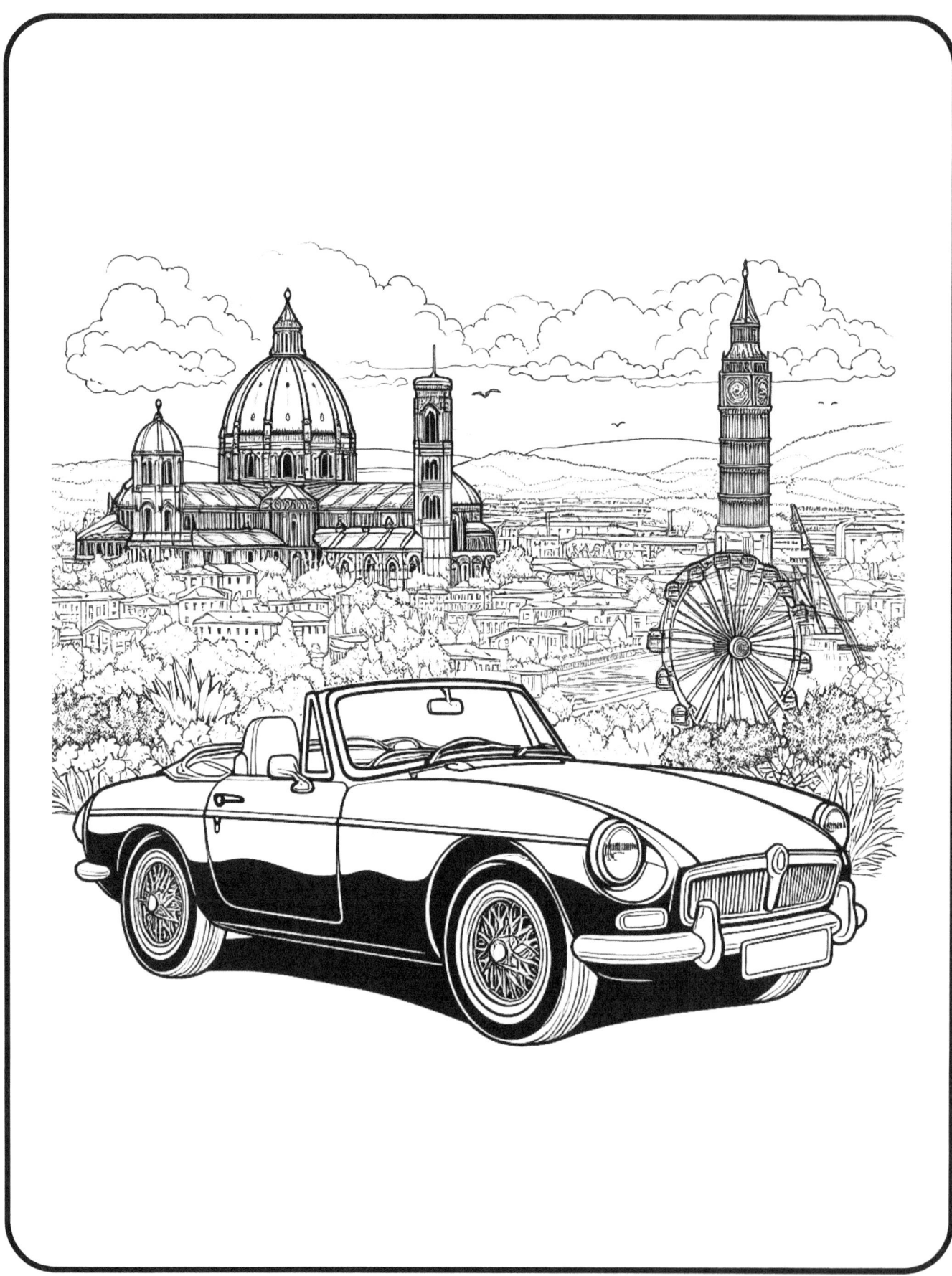

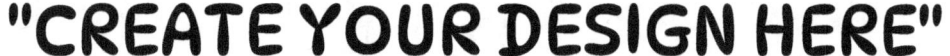

"CREATE YOUR DESIGN HERE"

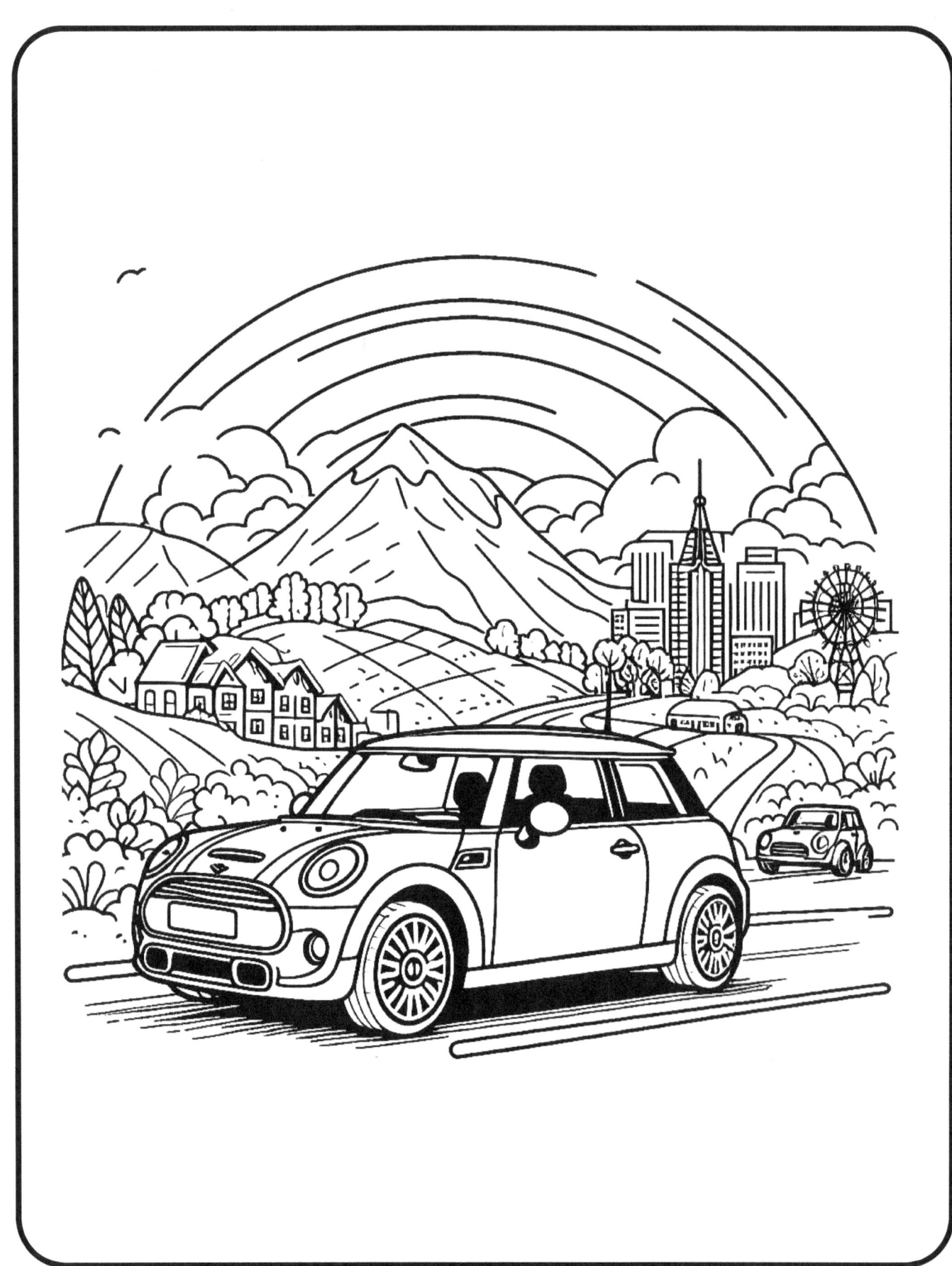

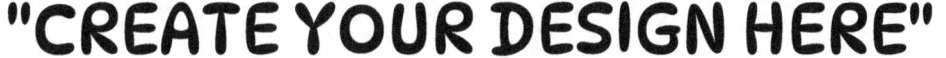

"CREATE YOUR DESIGN HERE"

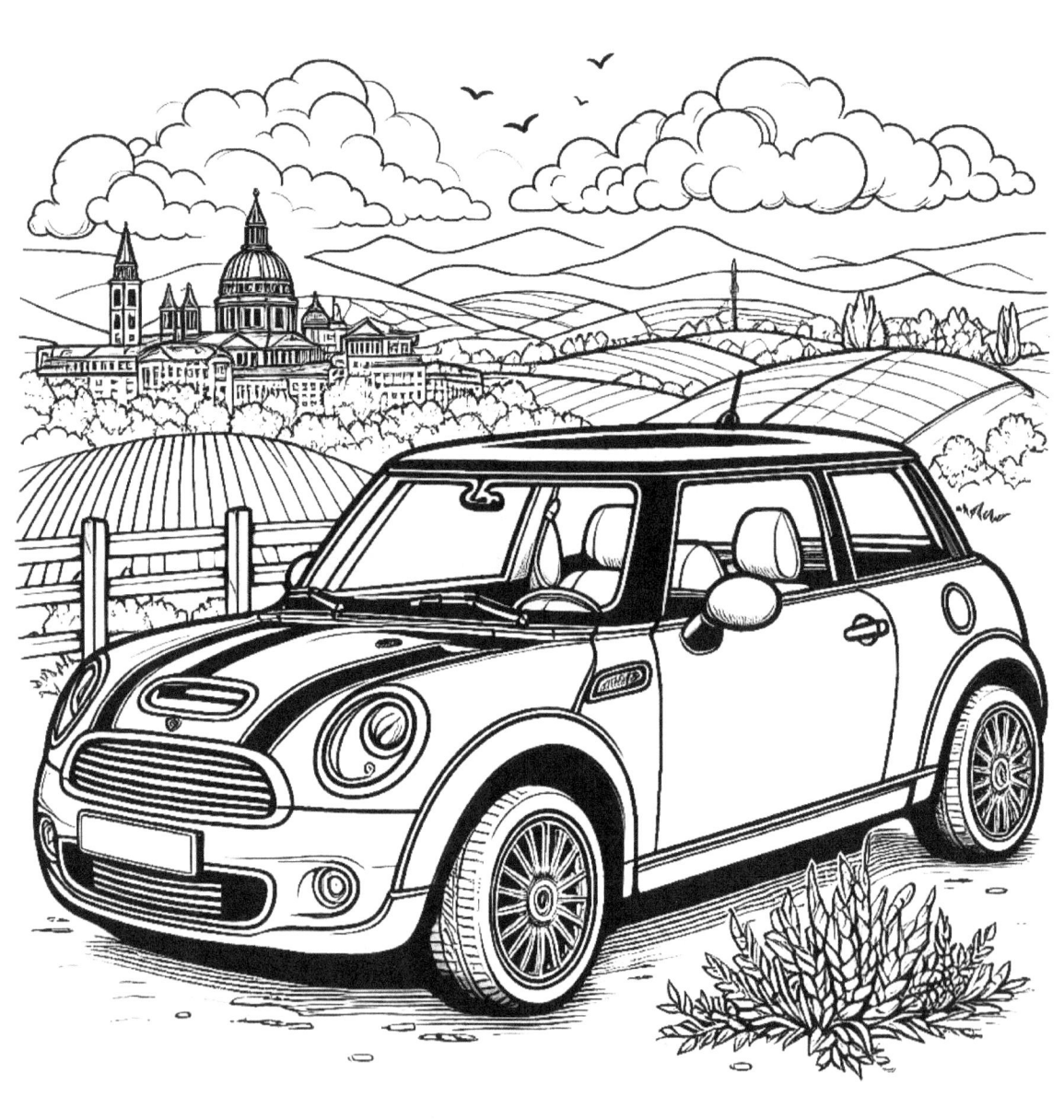

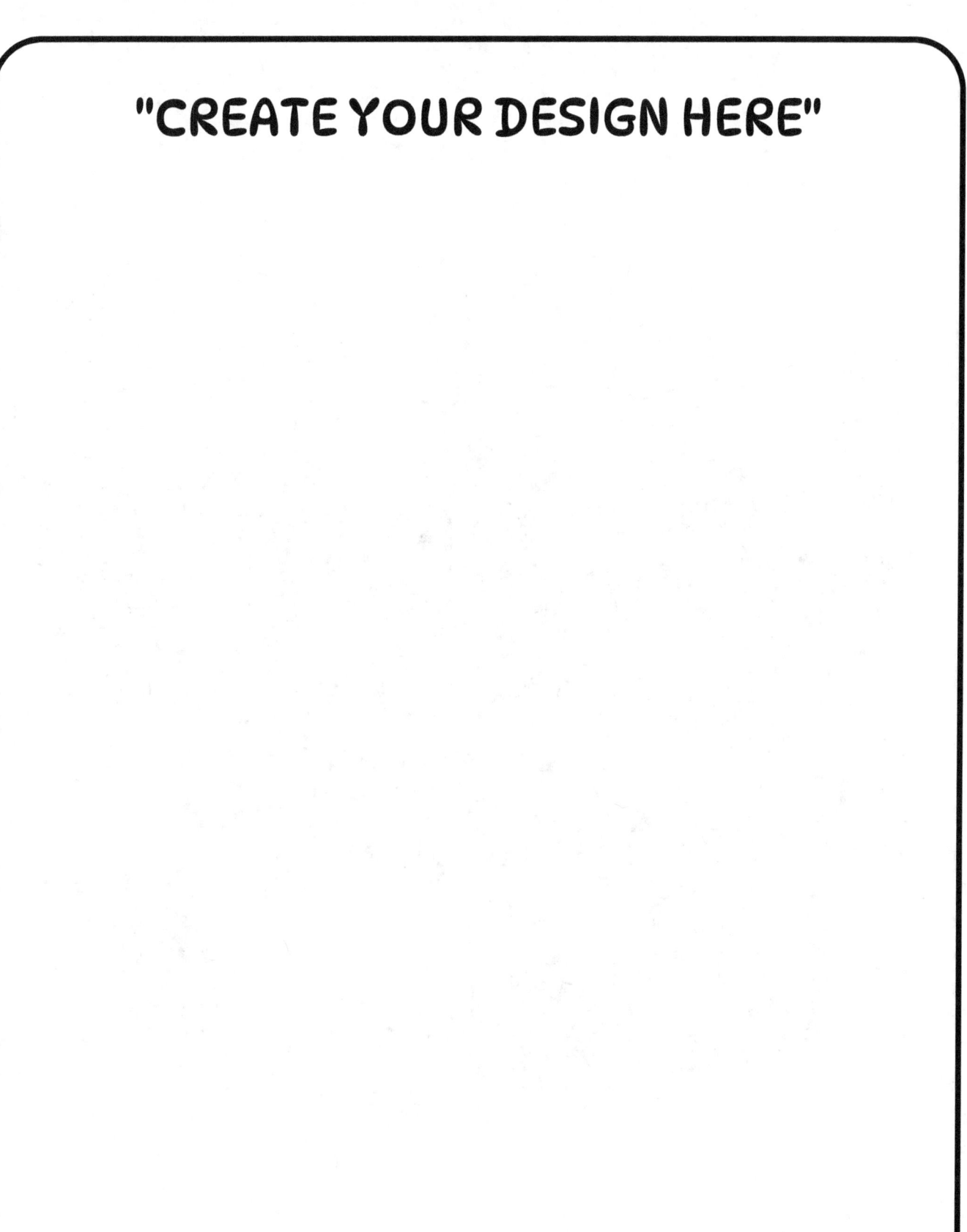
"CREATE YOUR DESIGN HERE"

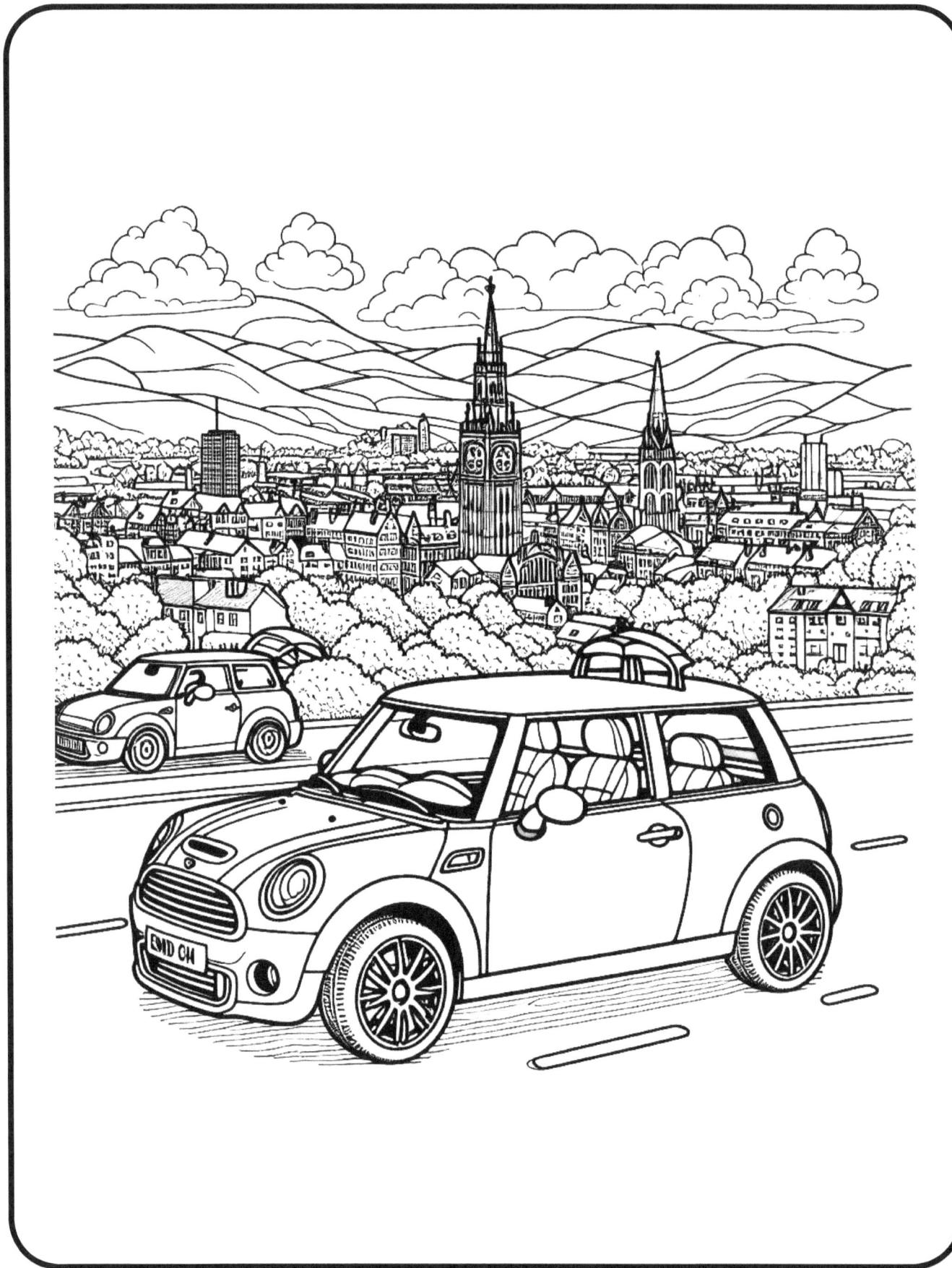

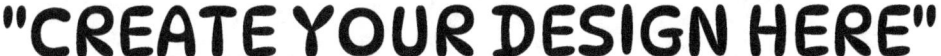

"CREATE YOUR DESIGN HERE"

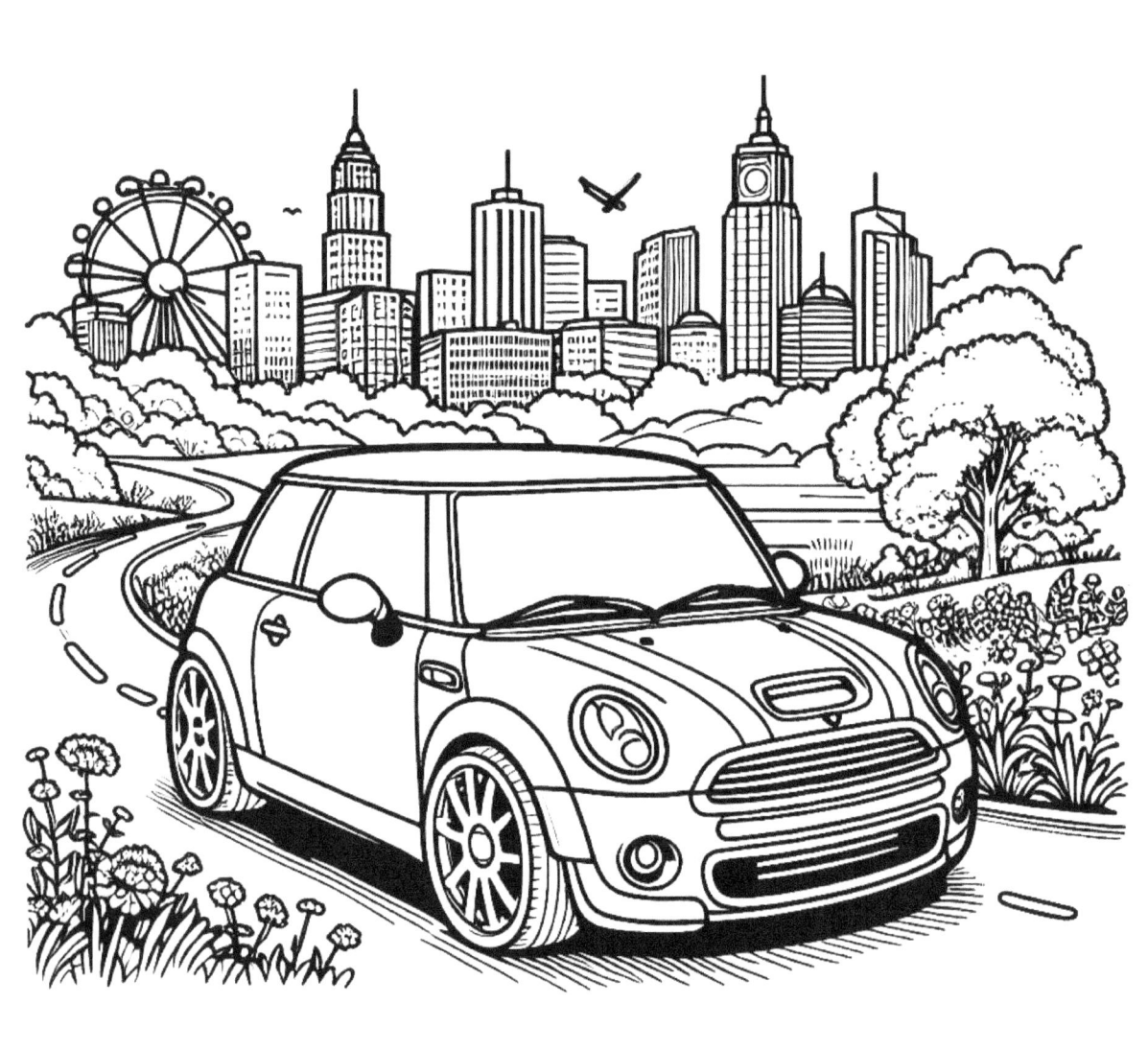

"CREATE YOUR DESIGN HERE"

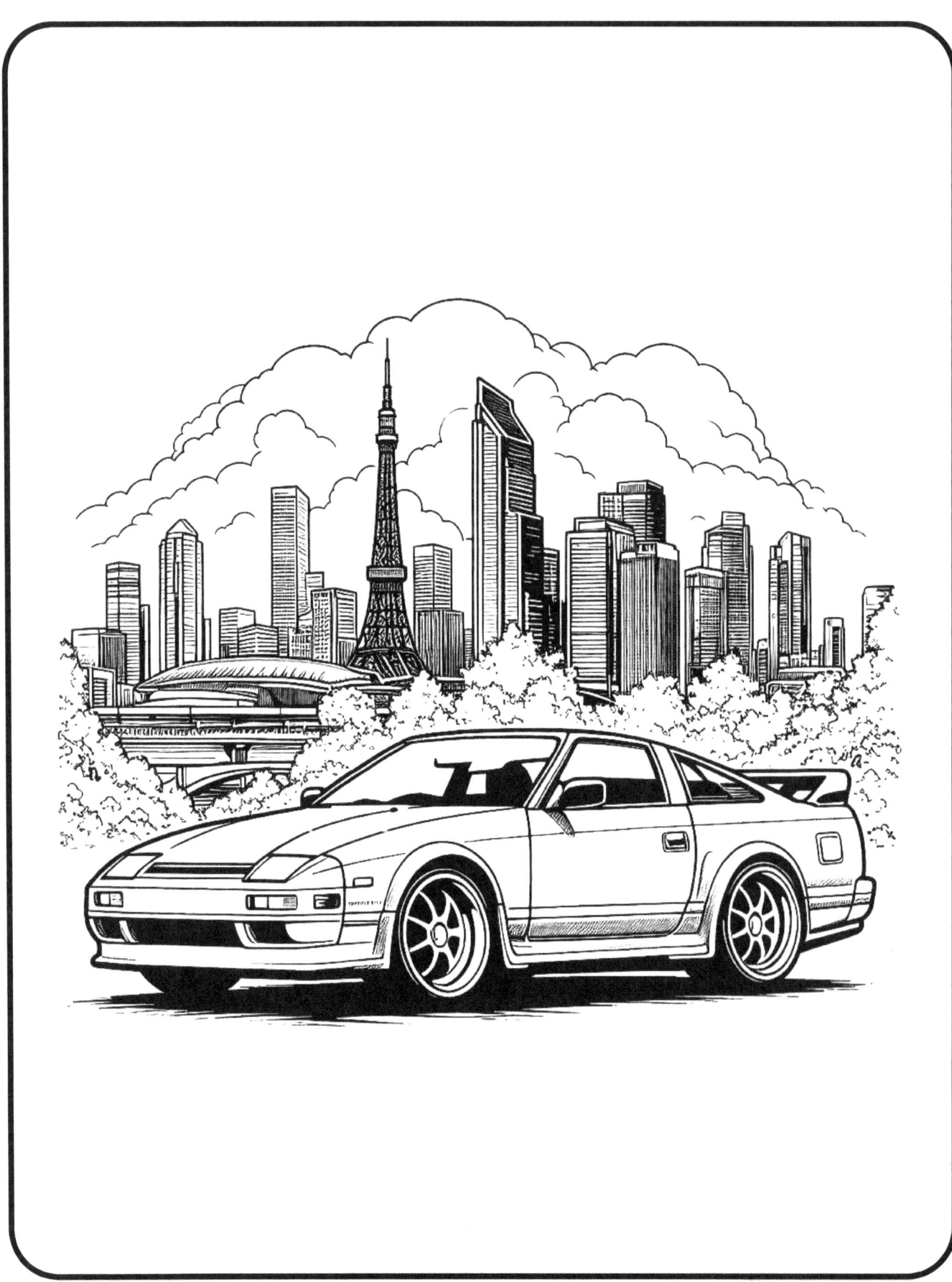

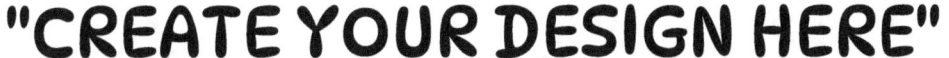

"CREATE YOUR DESIGN HERE"

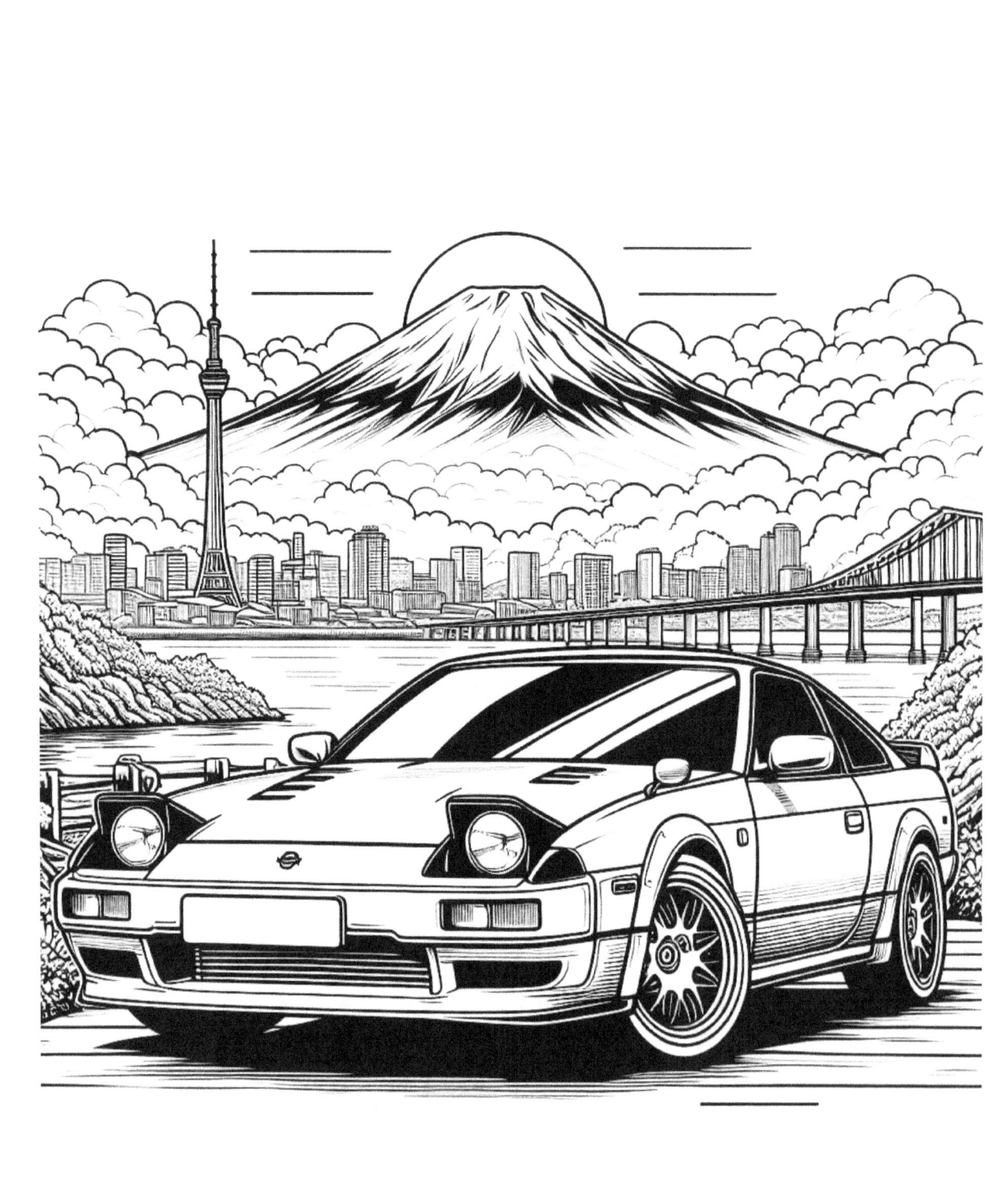

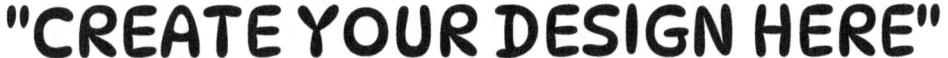

"CREATE YOUR DESIGN HERE"

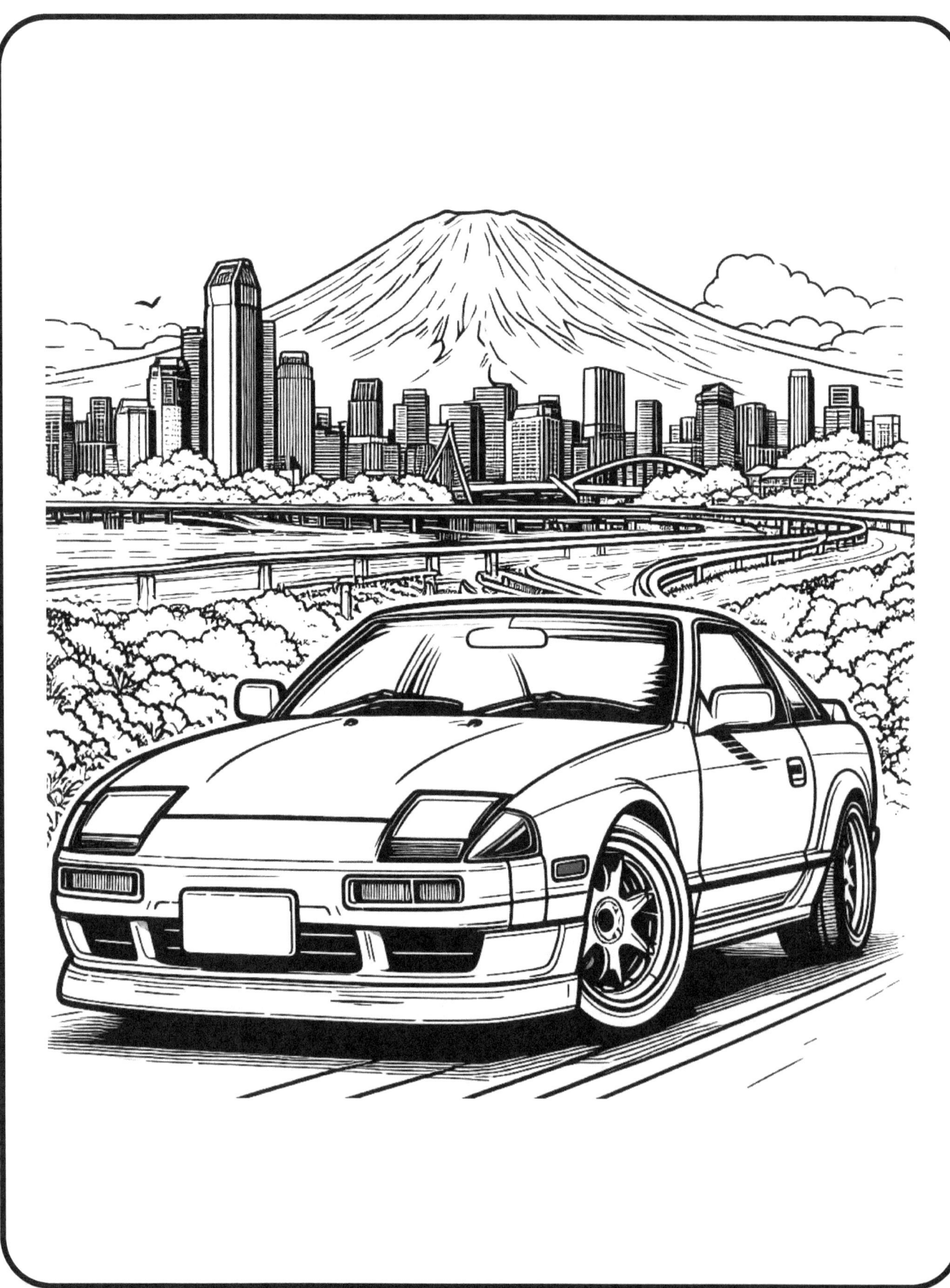

"CREATE YOUR DESIGN HERE"

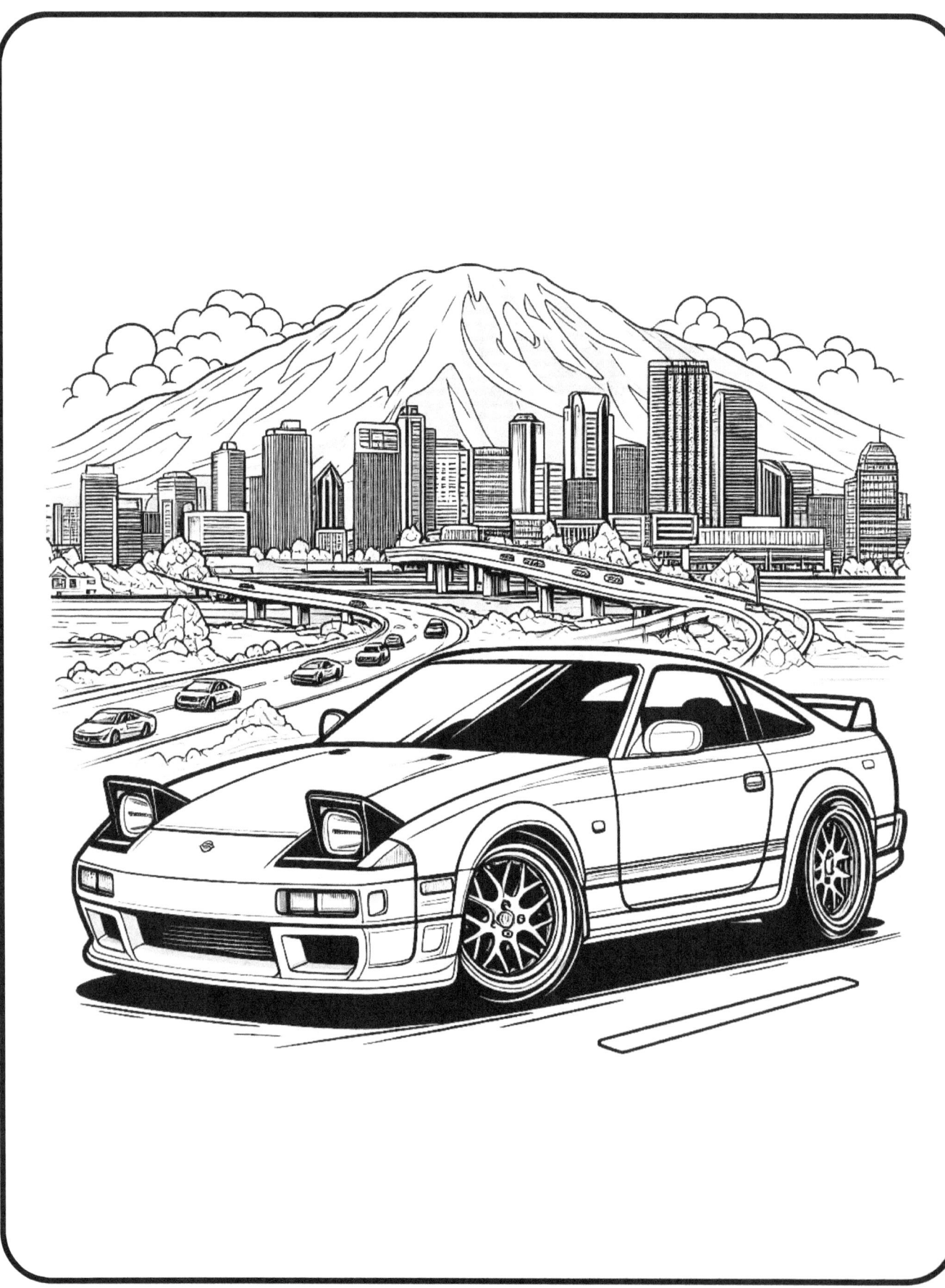

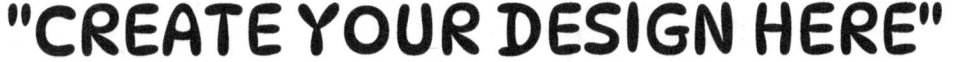

"CREATE YOUR DESIGN HERE"

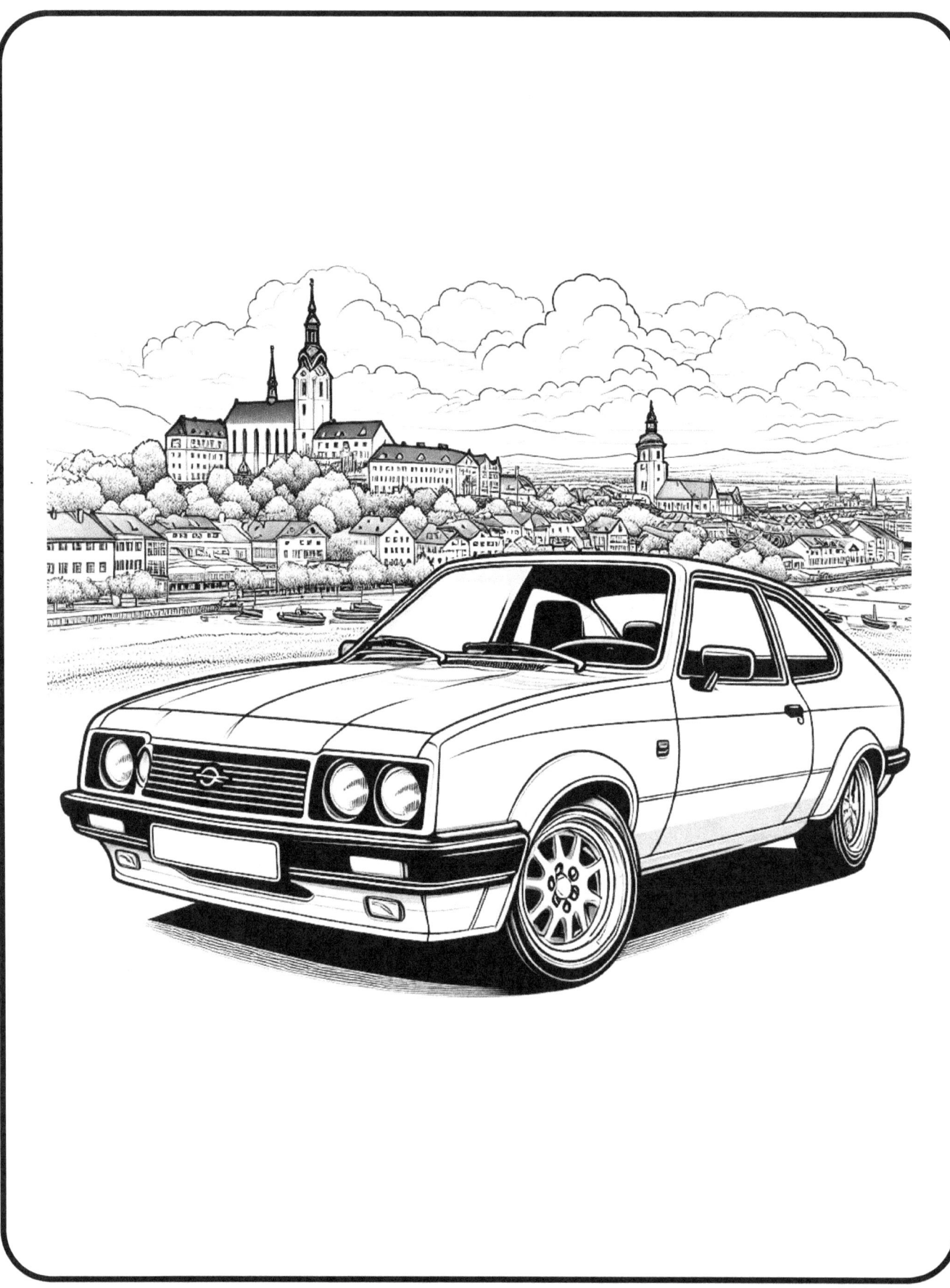

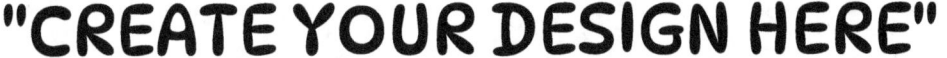

"CREATE YOUR DESIGN HERE"

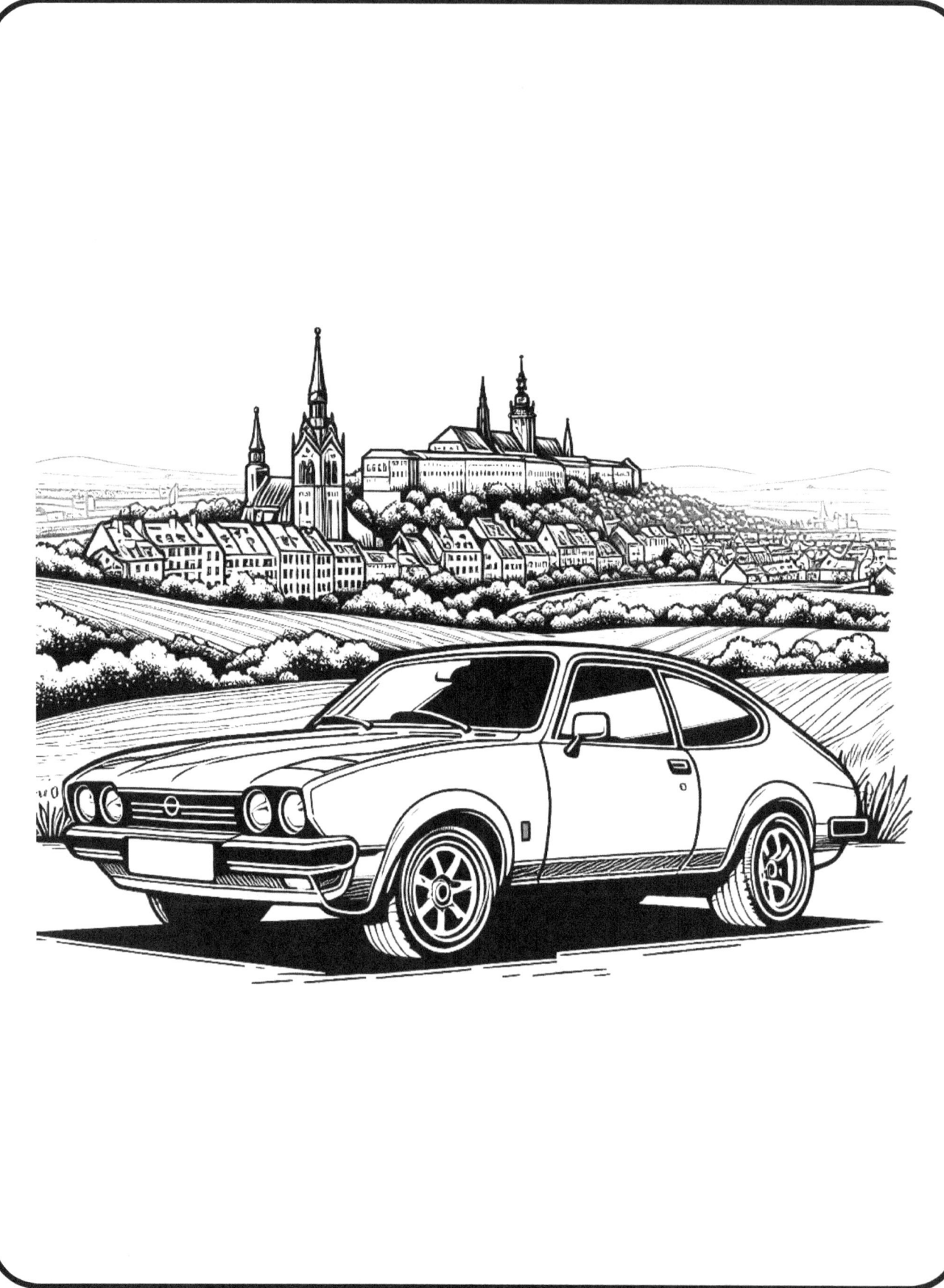

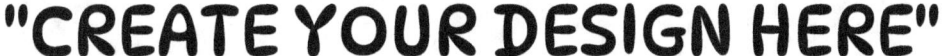

"CREATE YOUR DESIGN HERE"

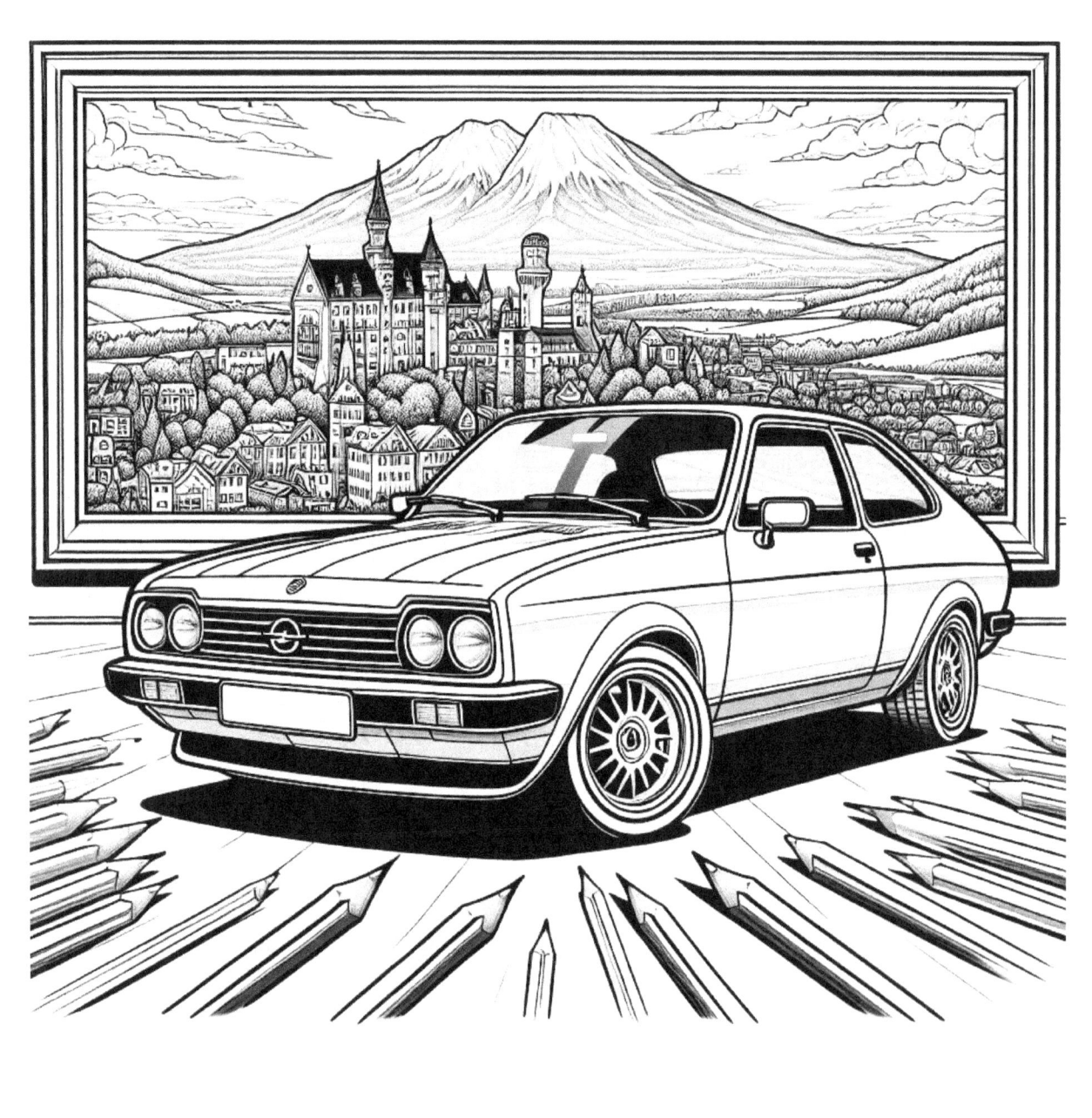

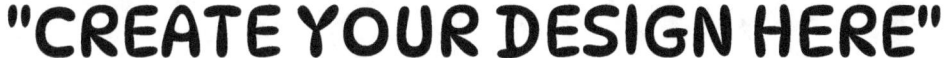
"CREATE YOUR DESIGN HERE"

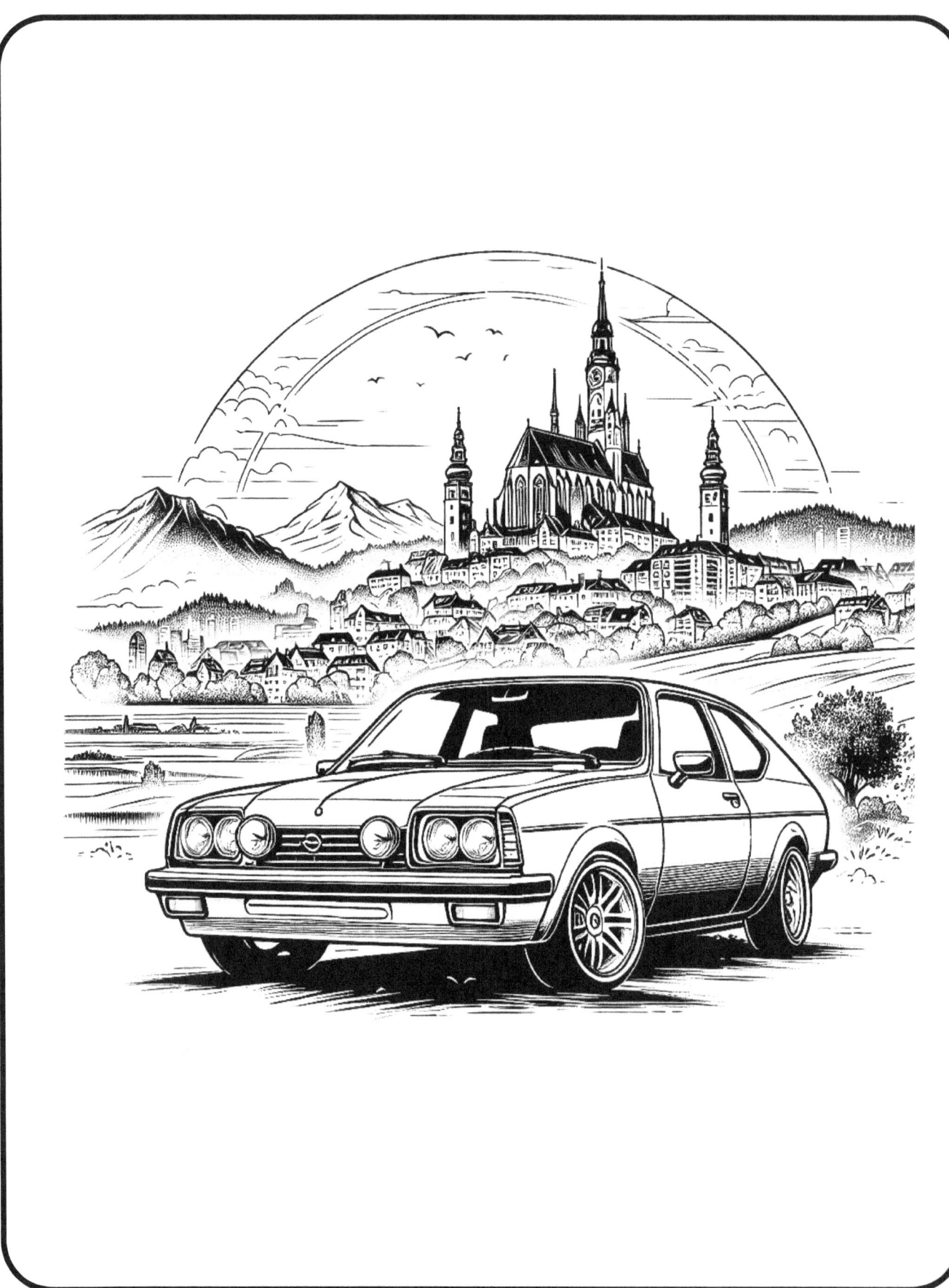

"CREATE YOUR DESIGN HERE"

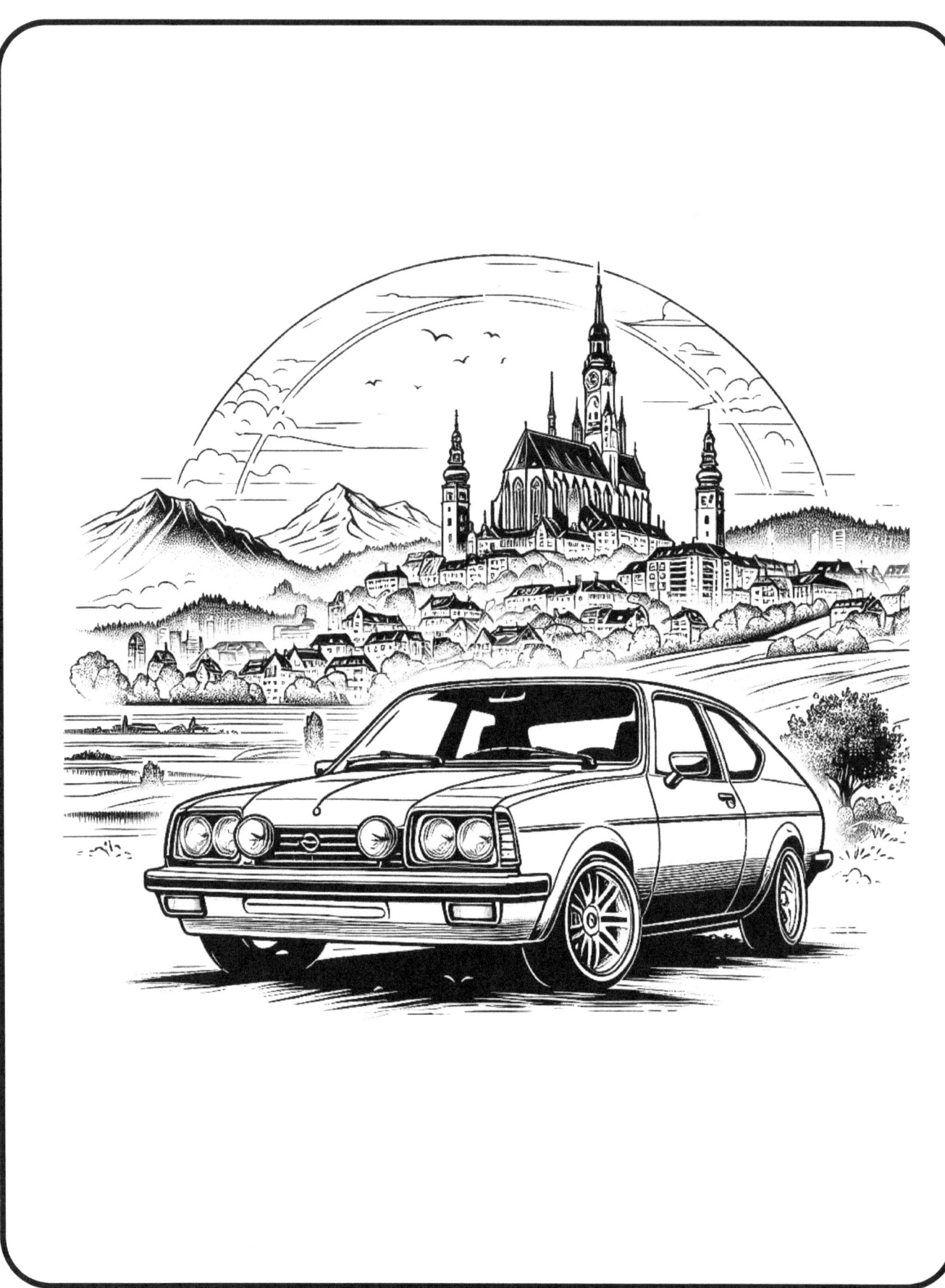

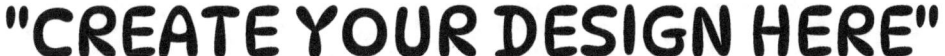

"CREATE YOUR DESIGN HERE"

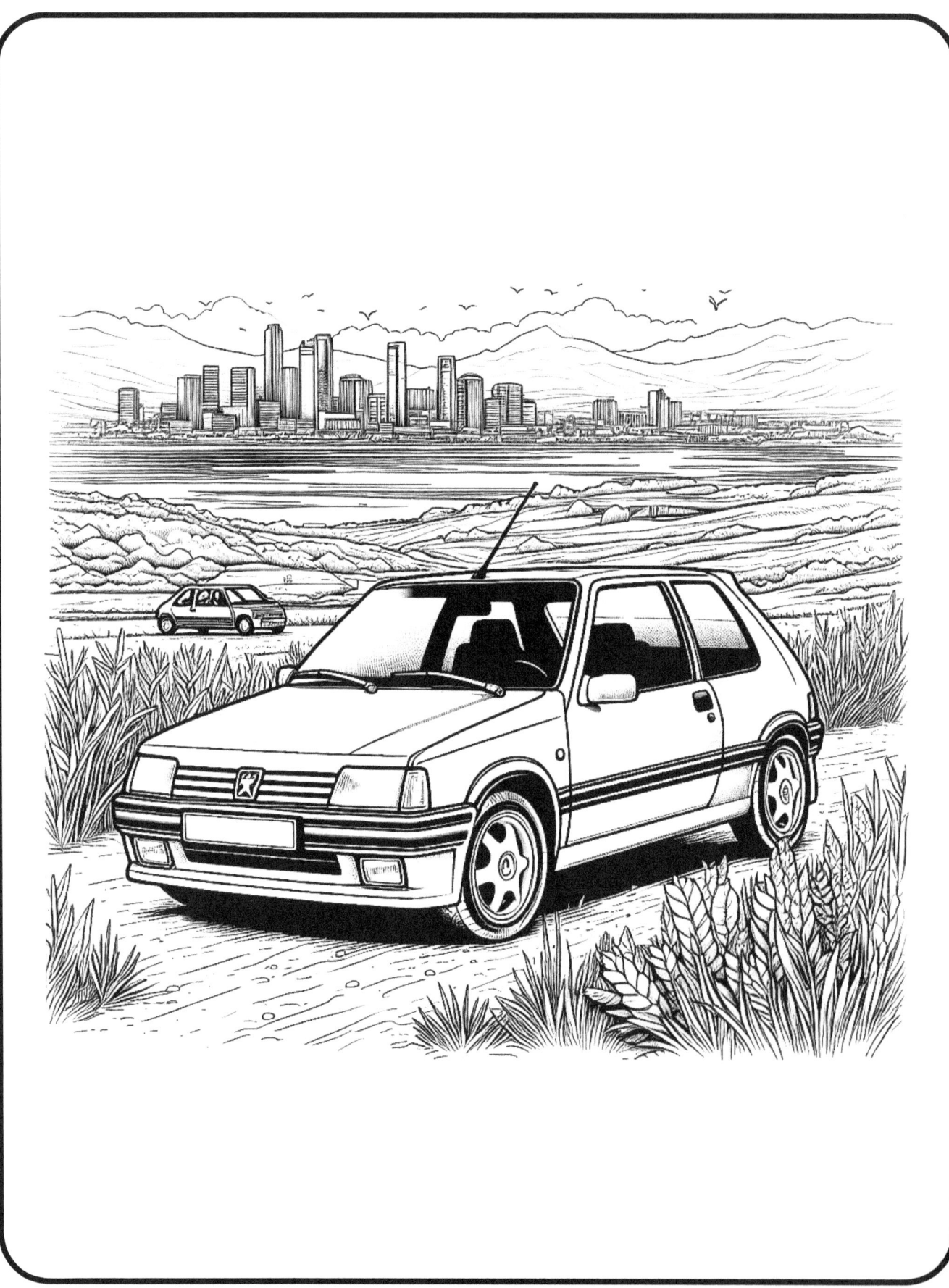

"CREATE YOUR DESIGN HERE"

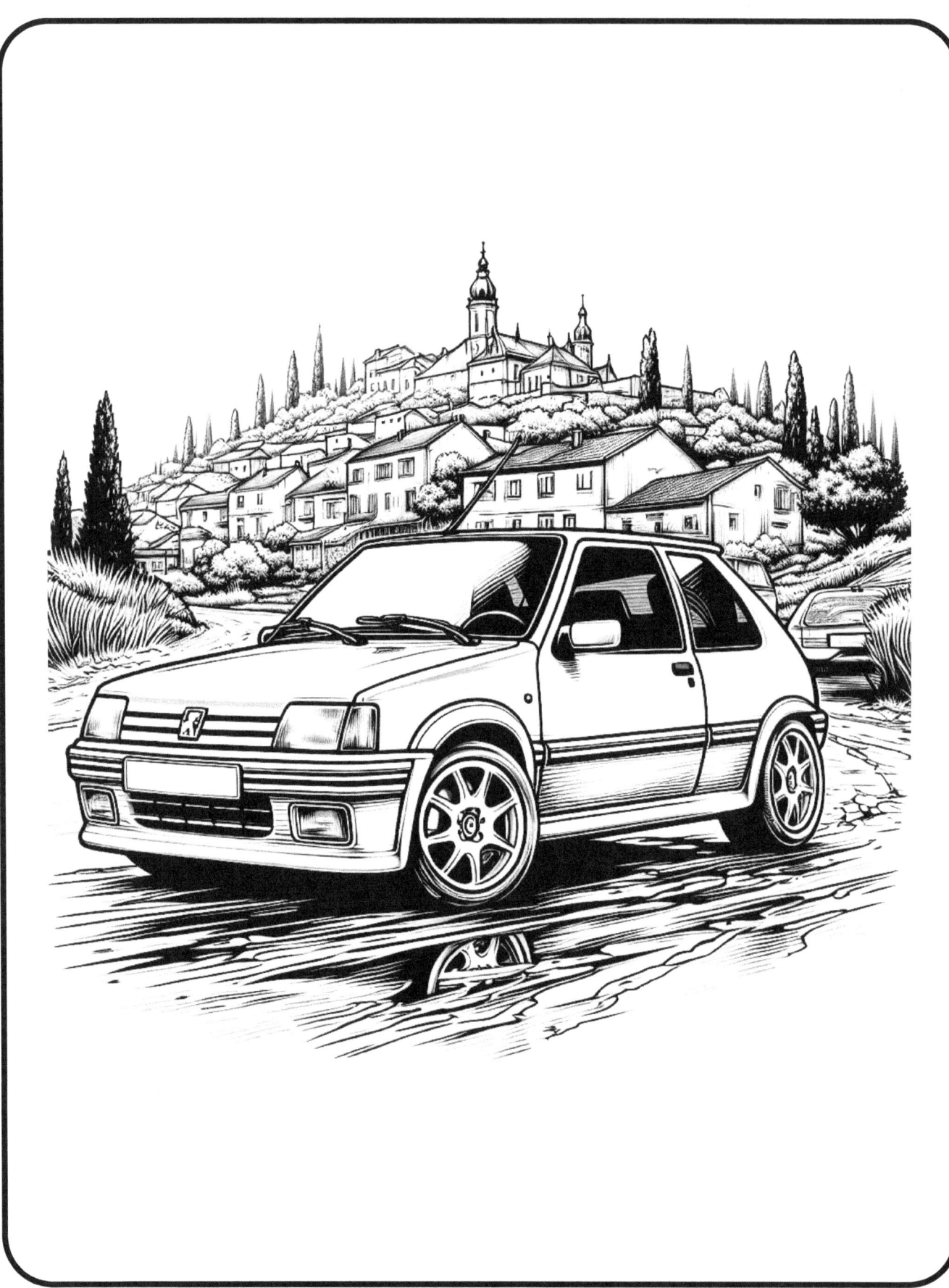

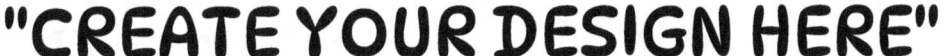

"CREATE YOUR DESIGN HERE"

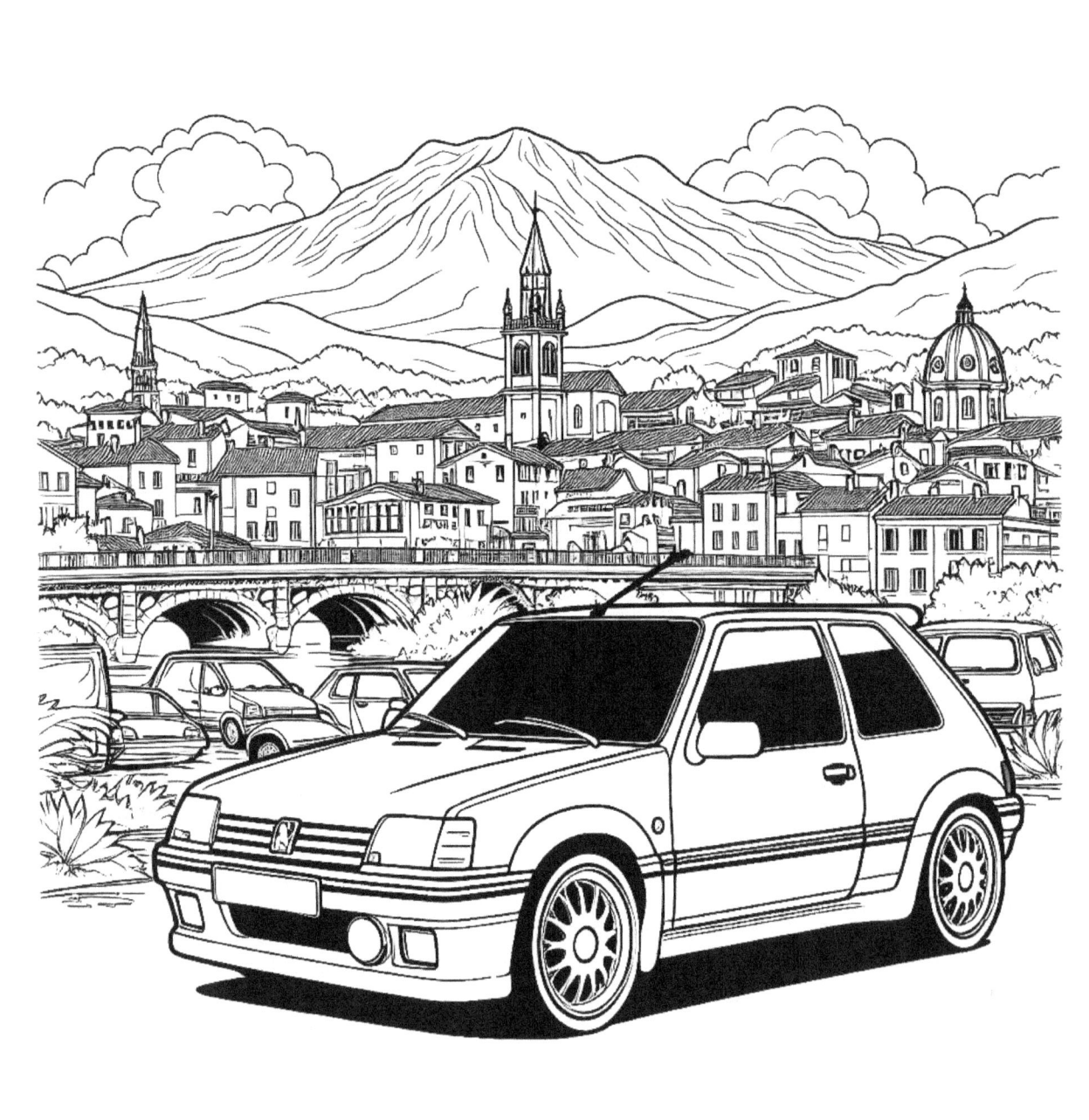

"CREATE YOUR DESIGN HERE"

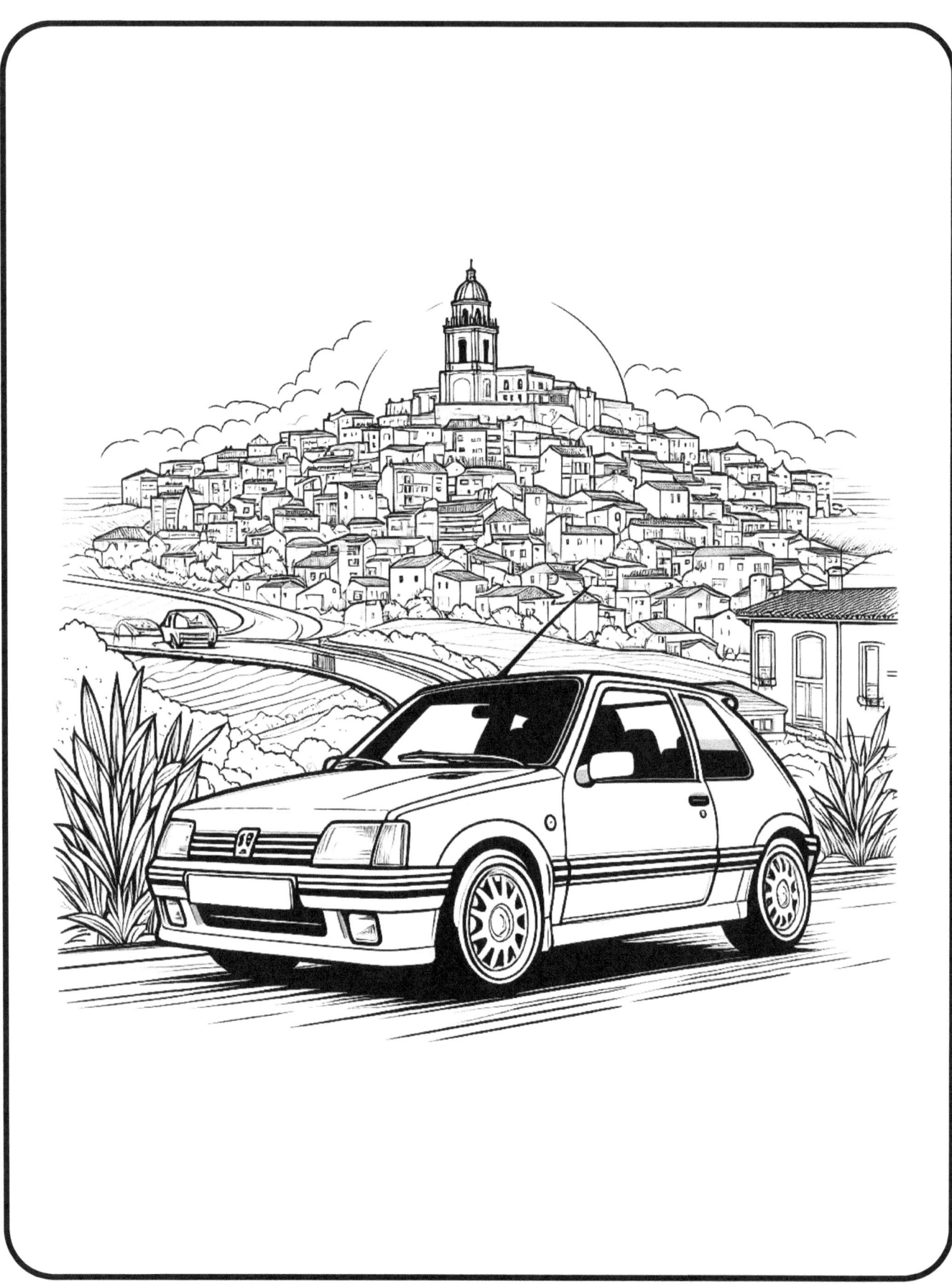

"CREATE YOUR DESIGN HERE"

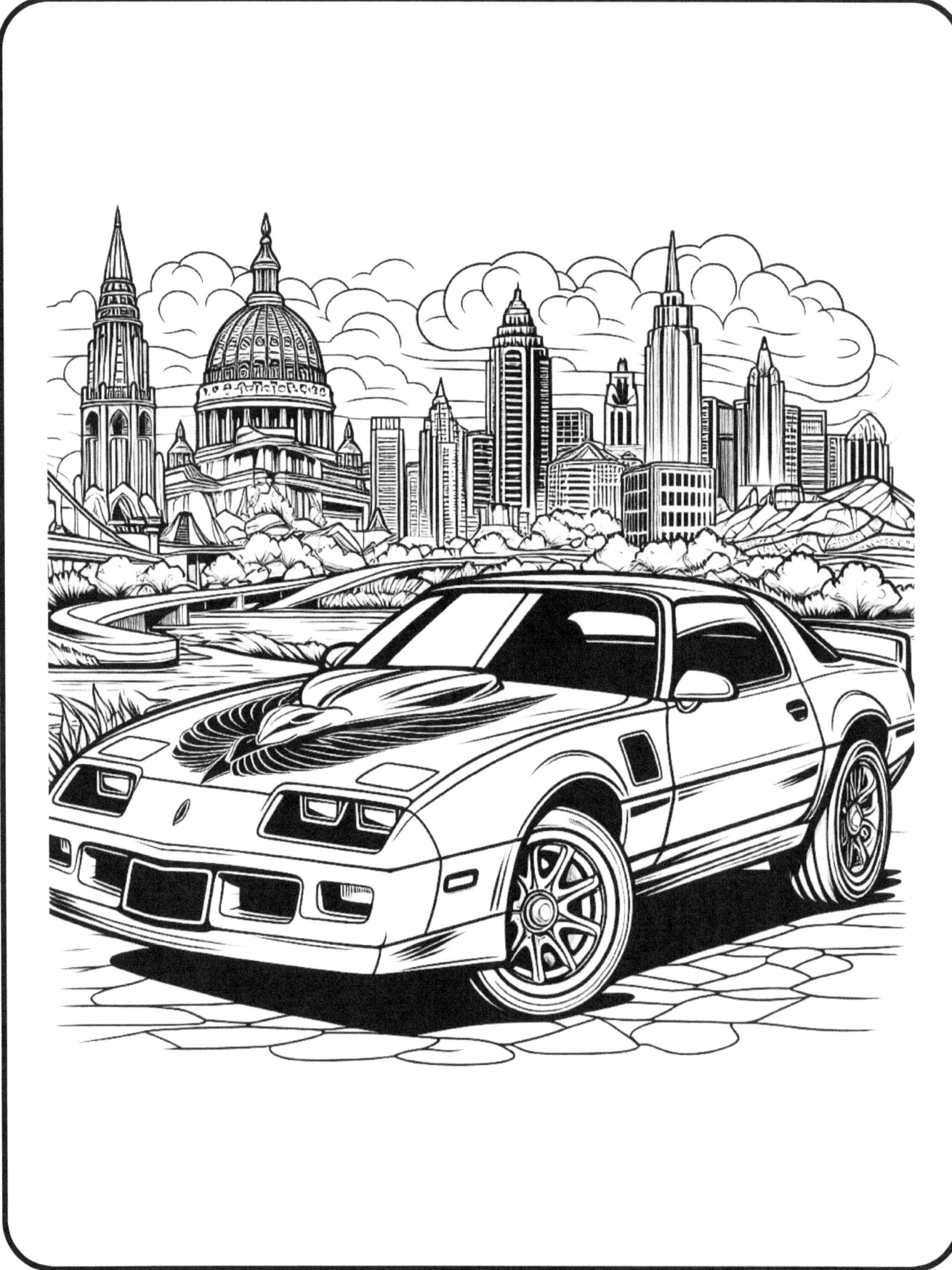

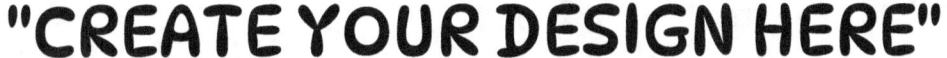

"CREATE YOUR DESIGN HERE"

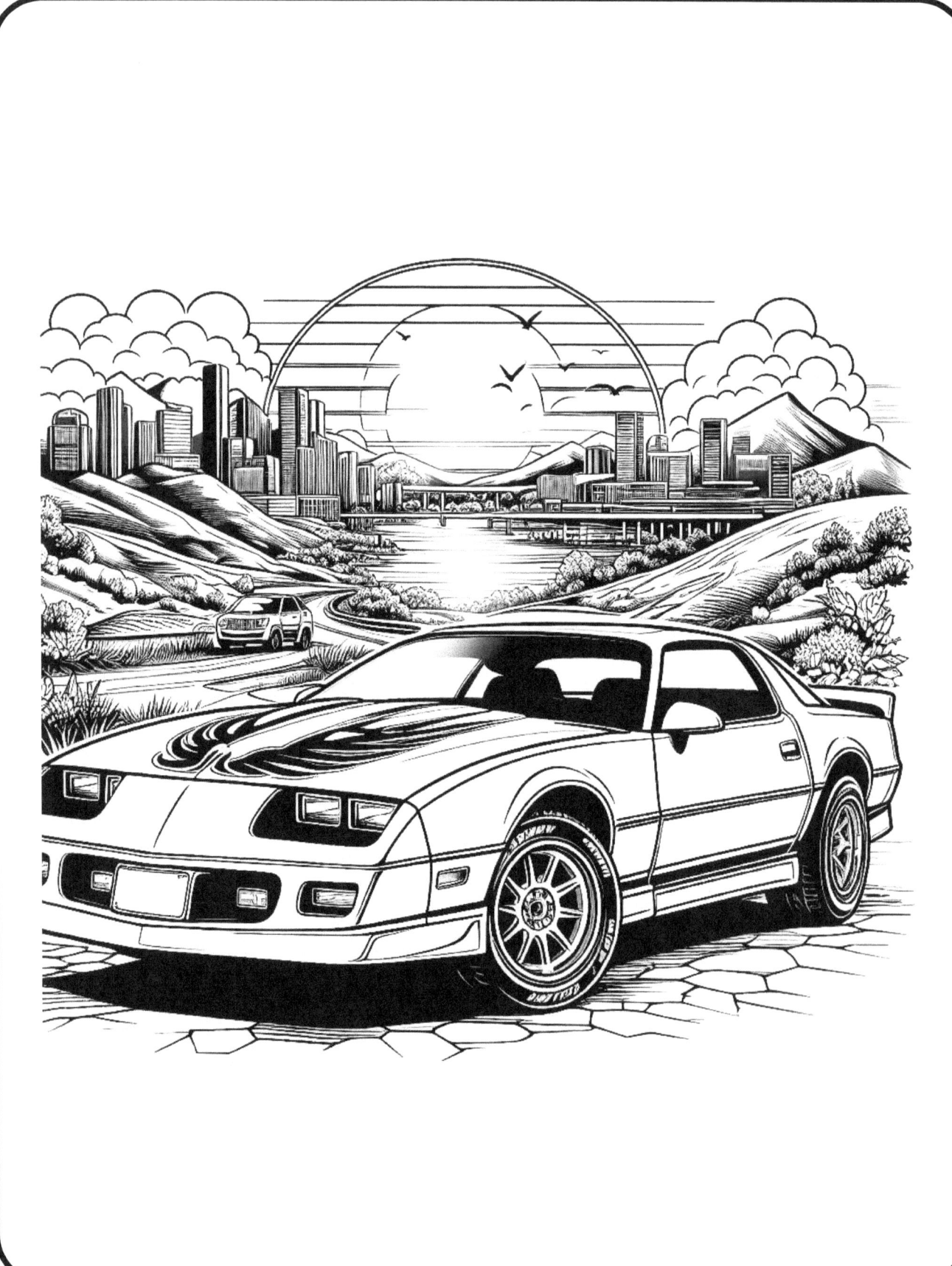

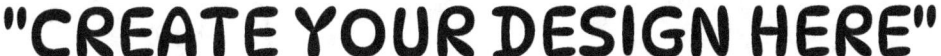

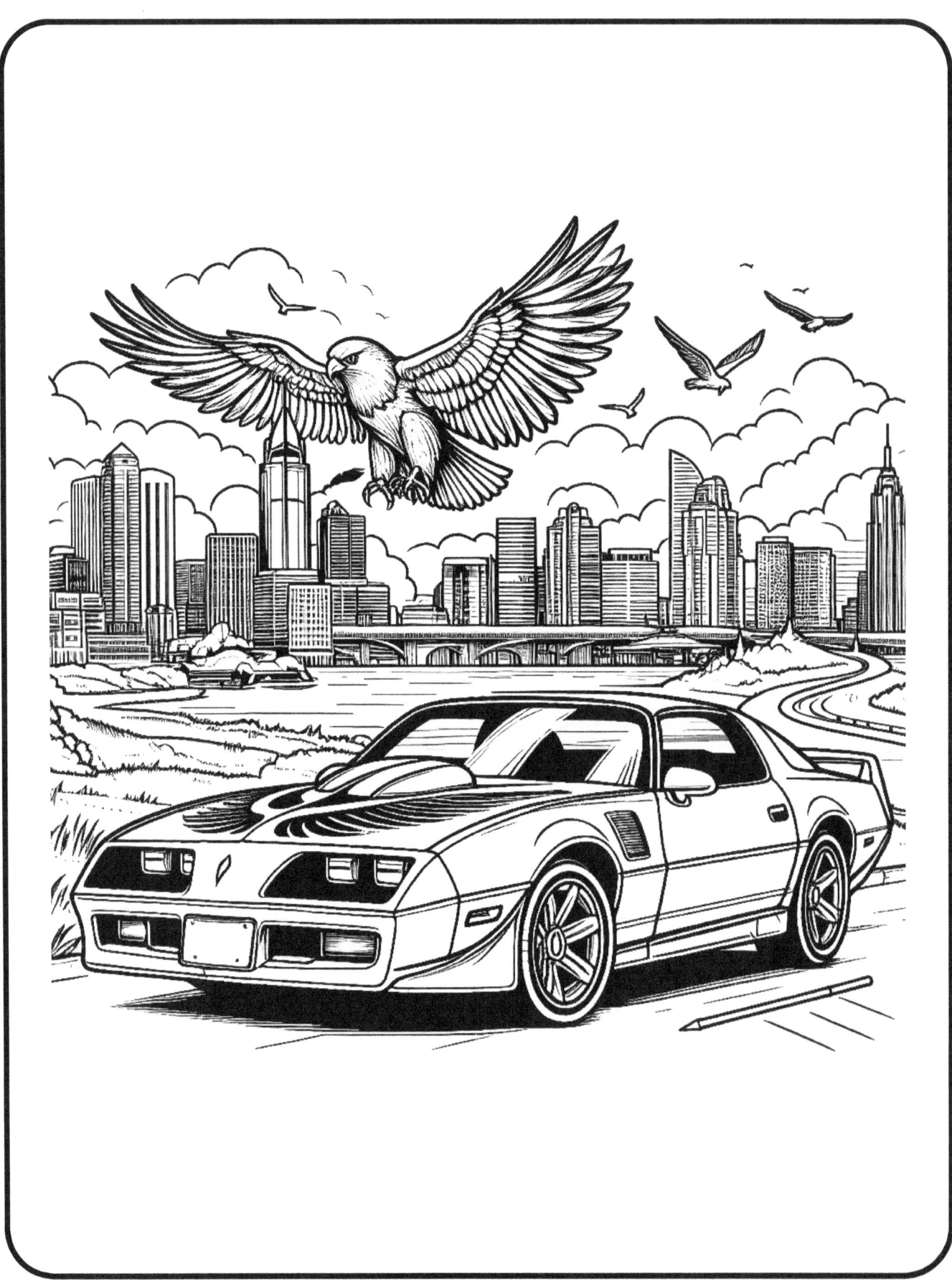

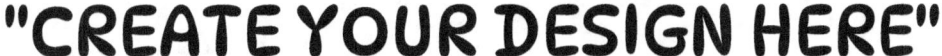

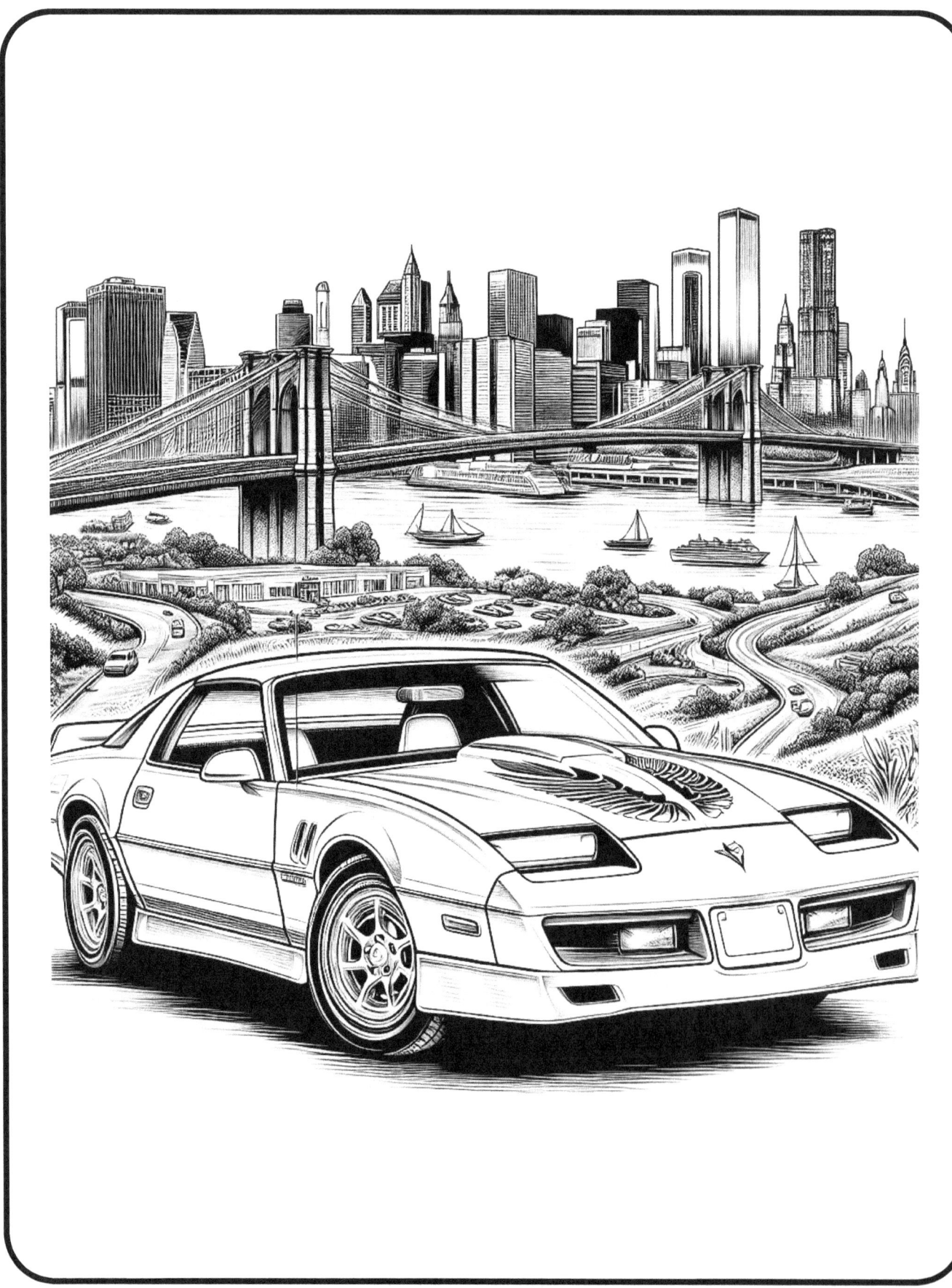

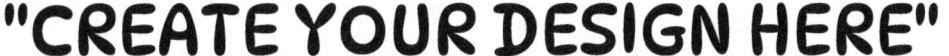

"CREATE YOUR DESIGN HERE"

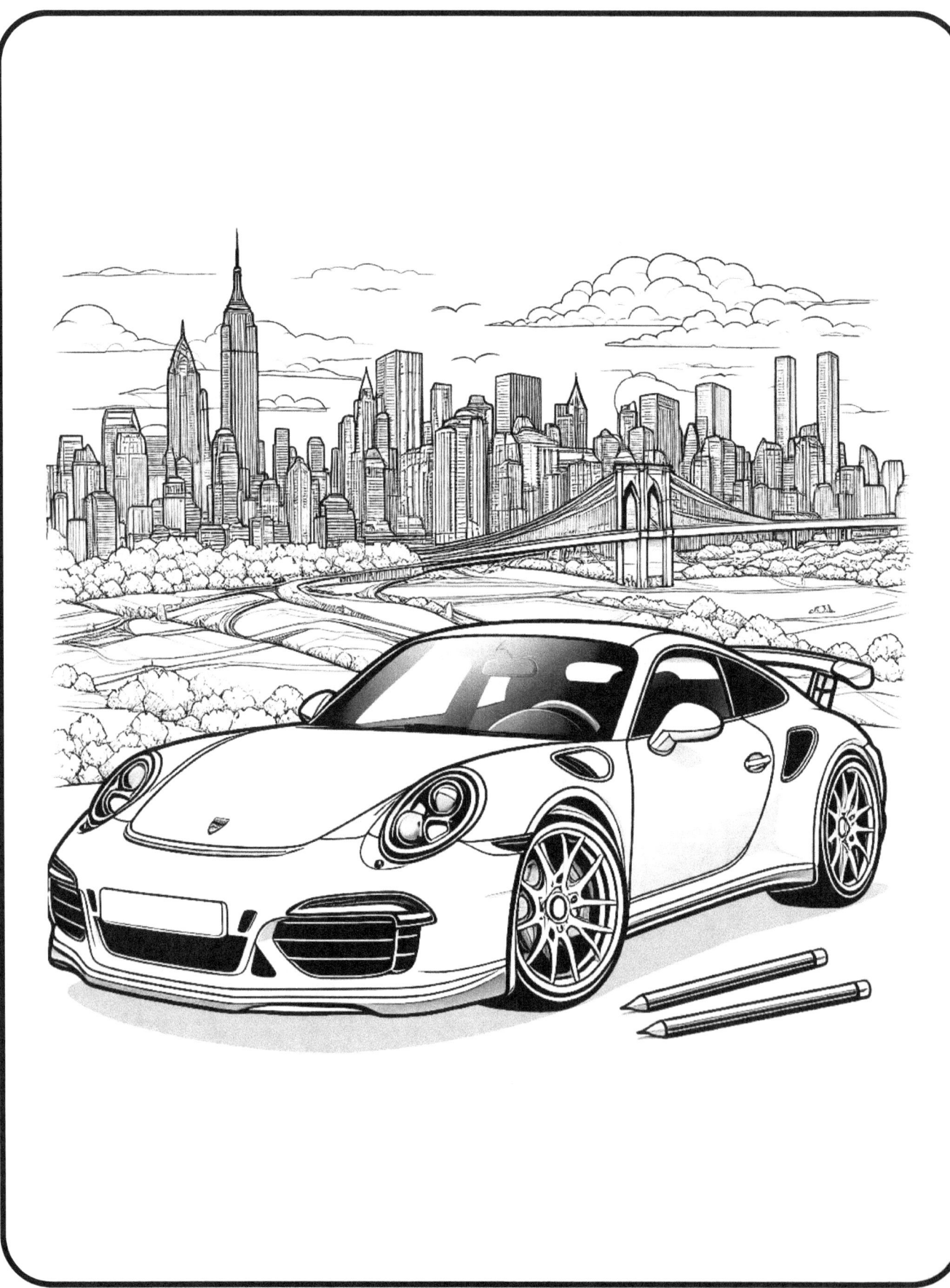

"CREATE YOUR DESIGN HERE"

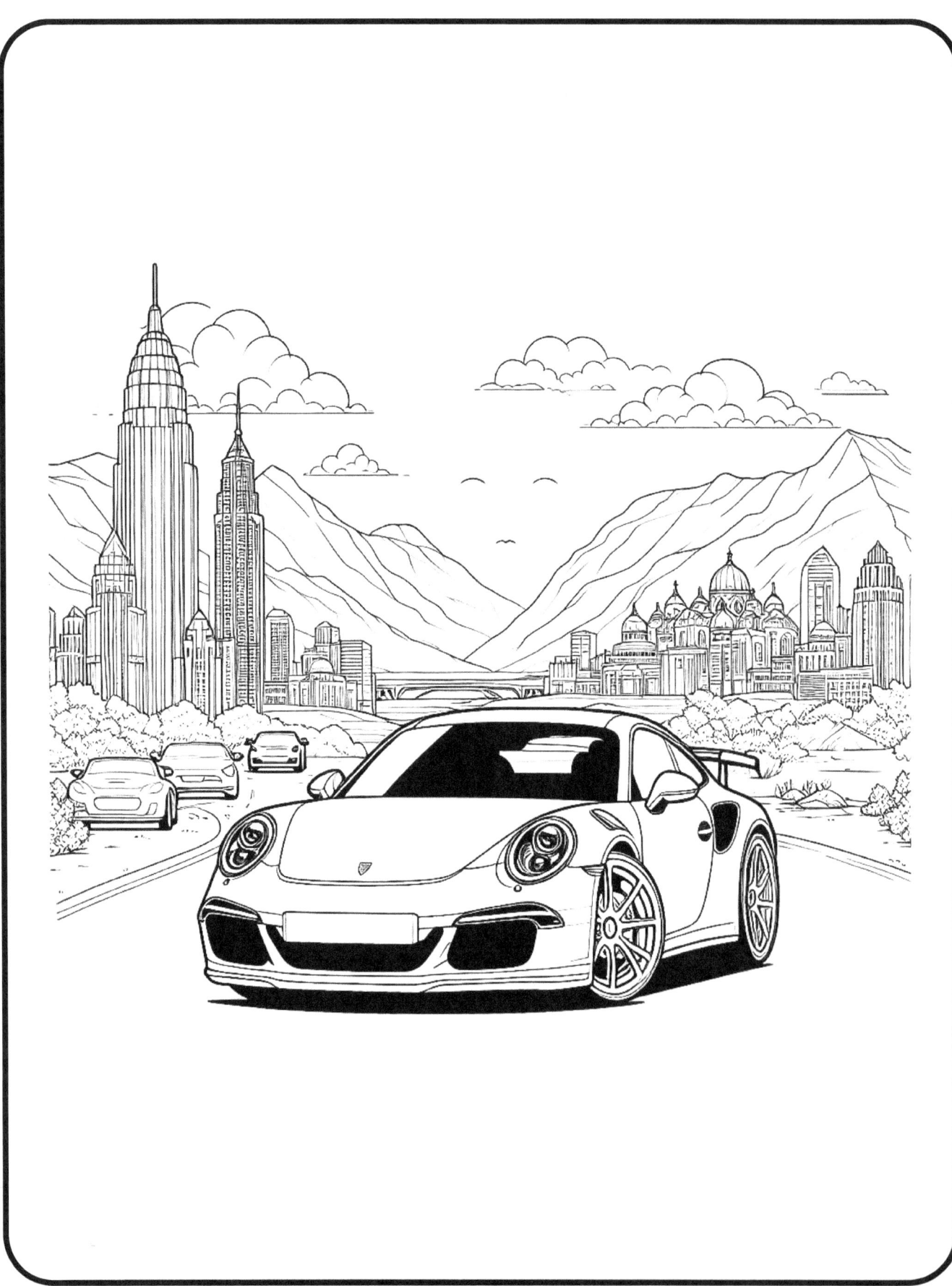

"CREATE YOUR DESIGN HERE"

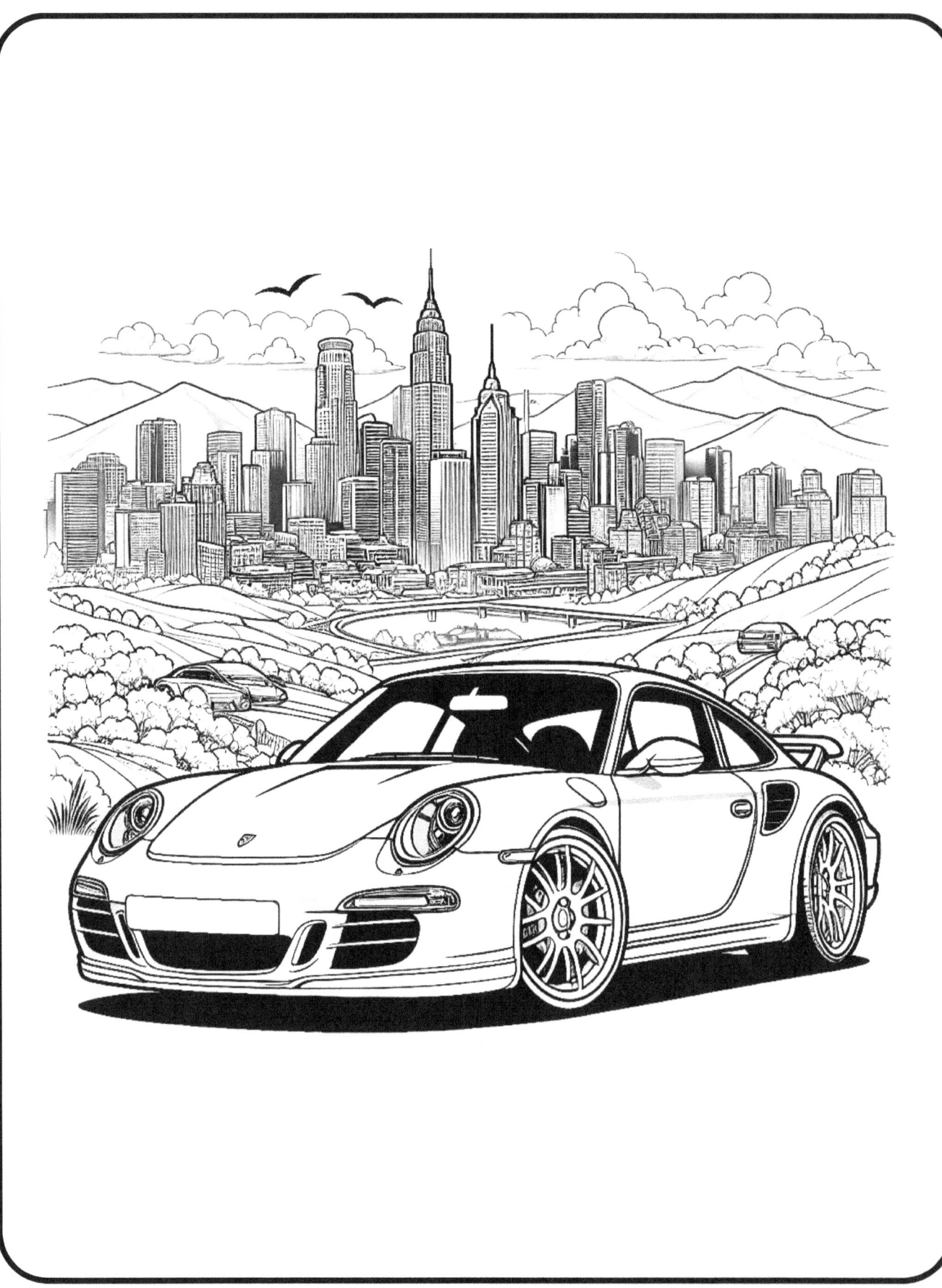

"CREATE YOUR DESIGN HERE"

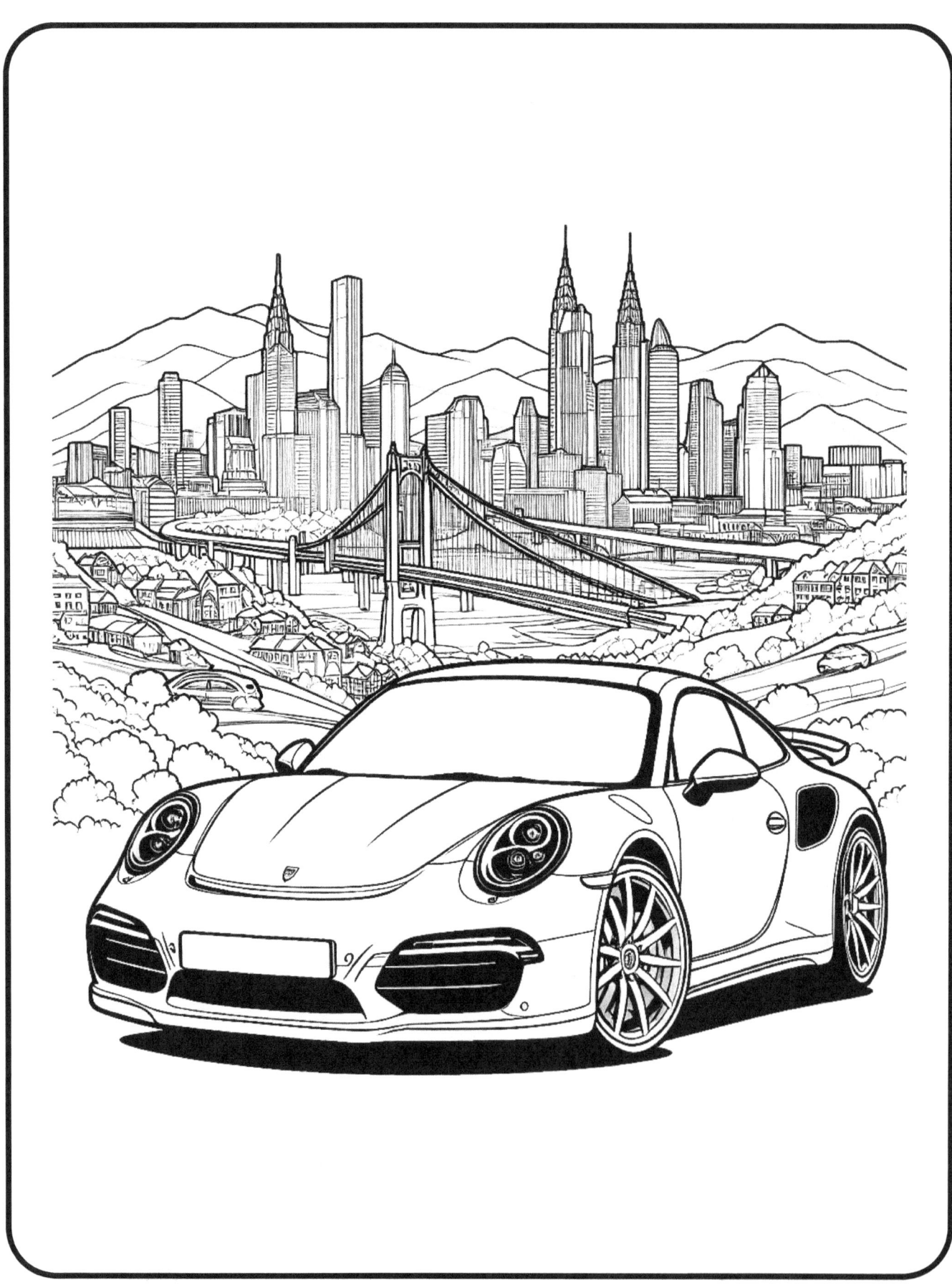

"CREATE YOUR DESIGN HERE"

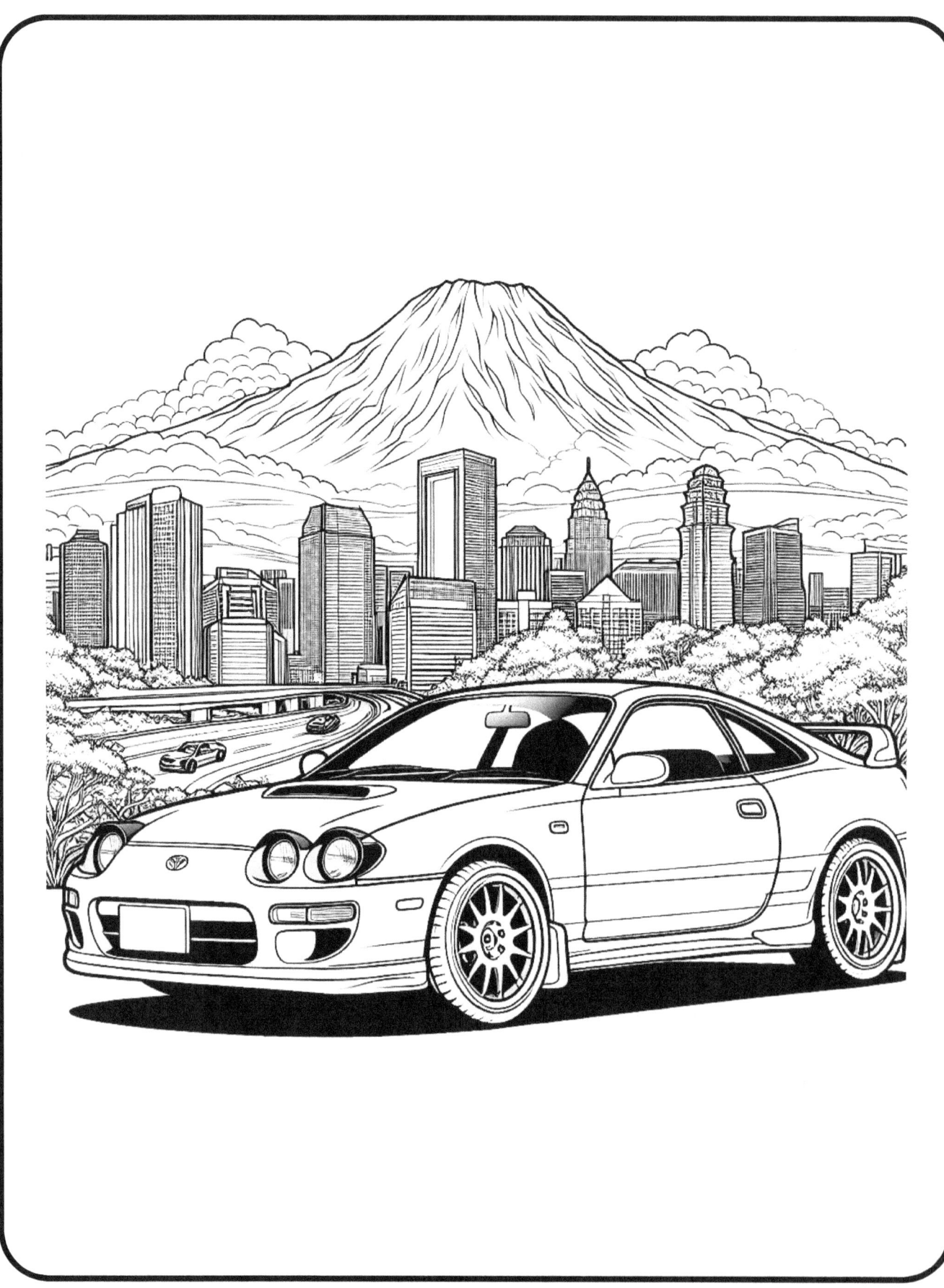

"CREATE YOUR DESIGN HERE"

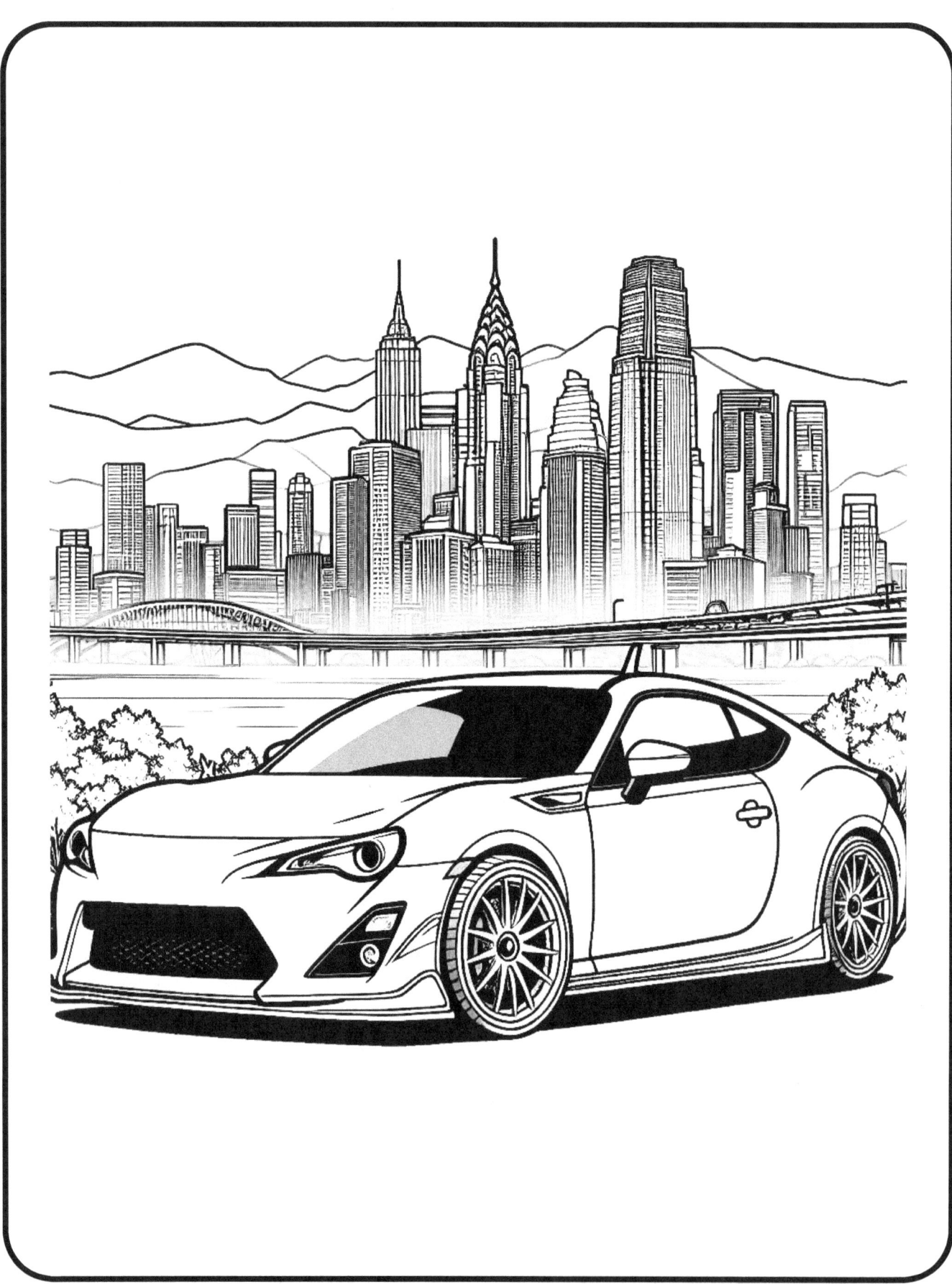

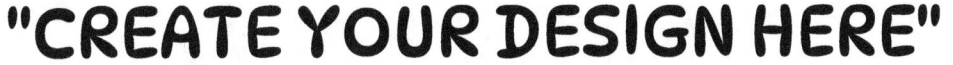
"CREATE YOUR DESIGN HERE"

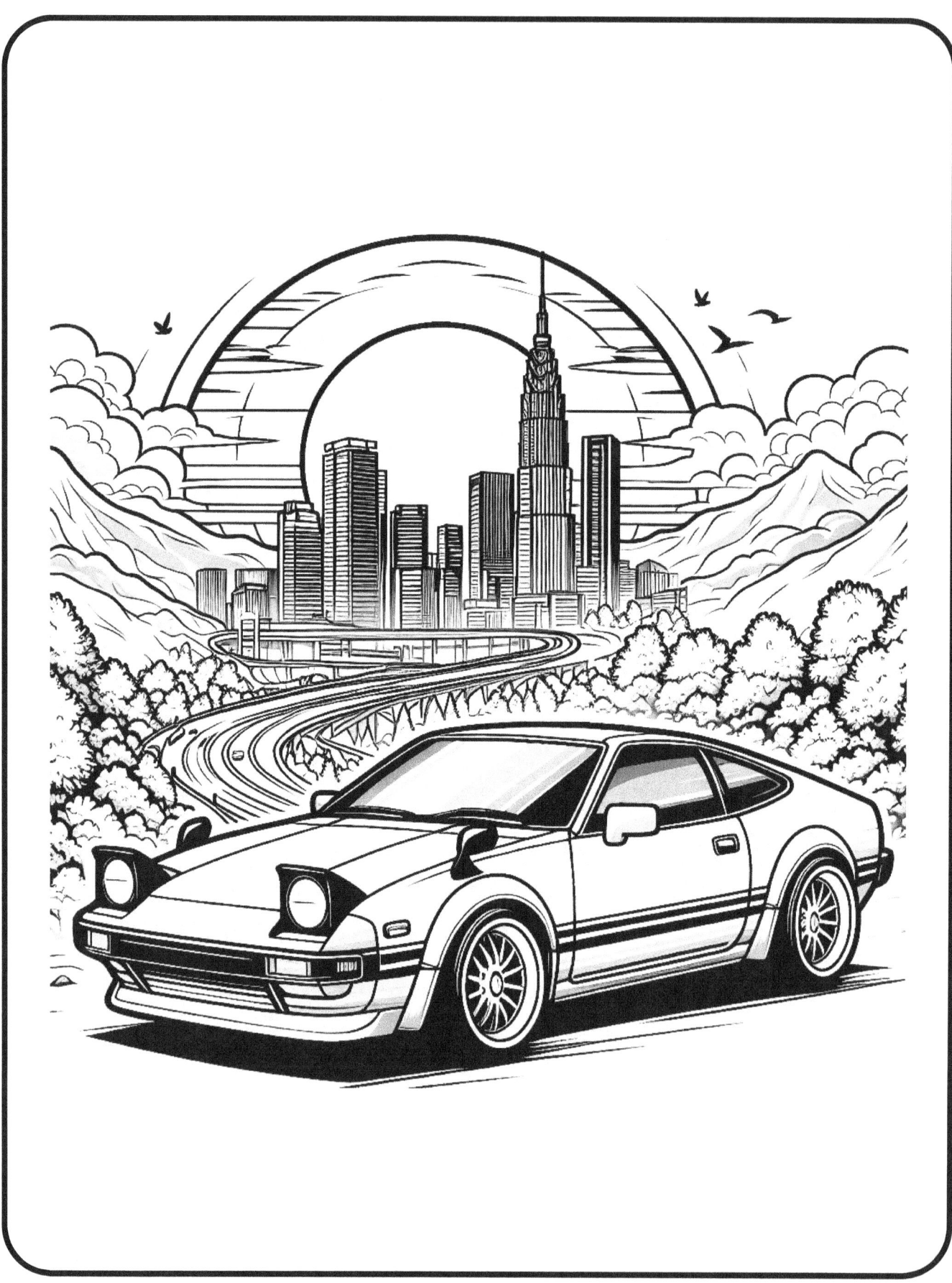

"CREATE YOUR DESIGN HERE"

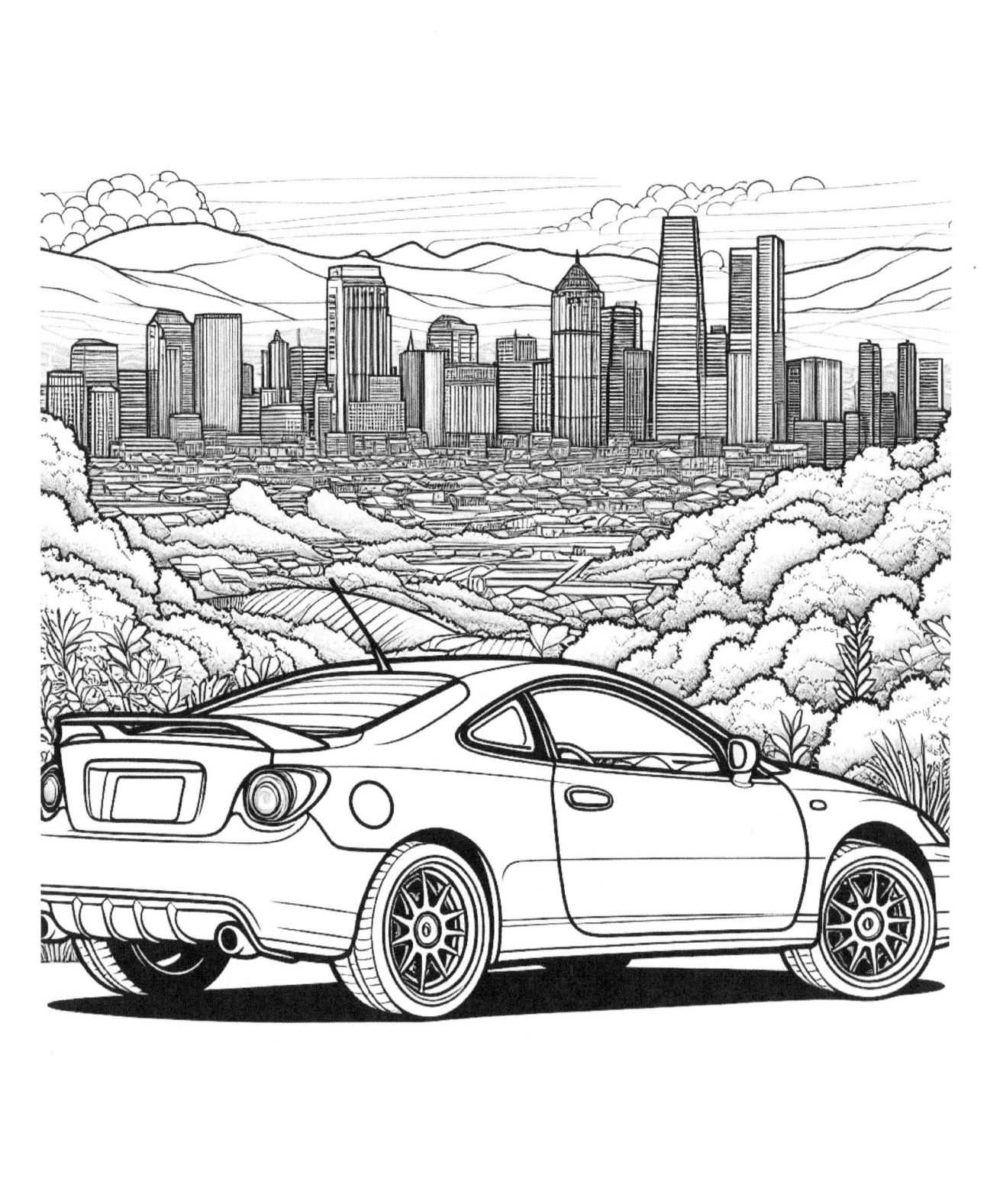

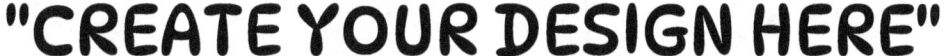

"CREATE YOUR DESIGN HERE"

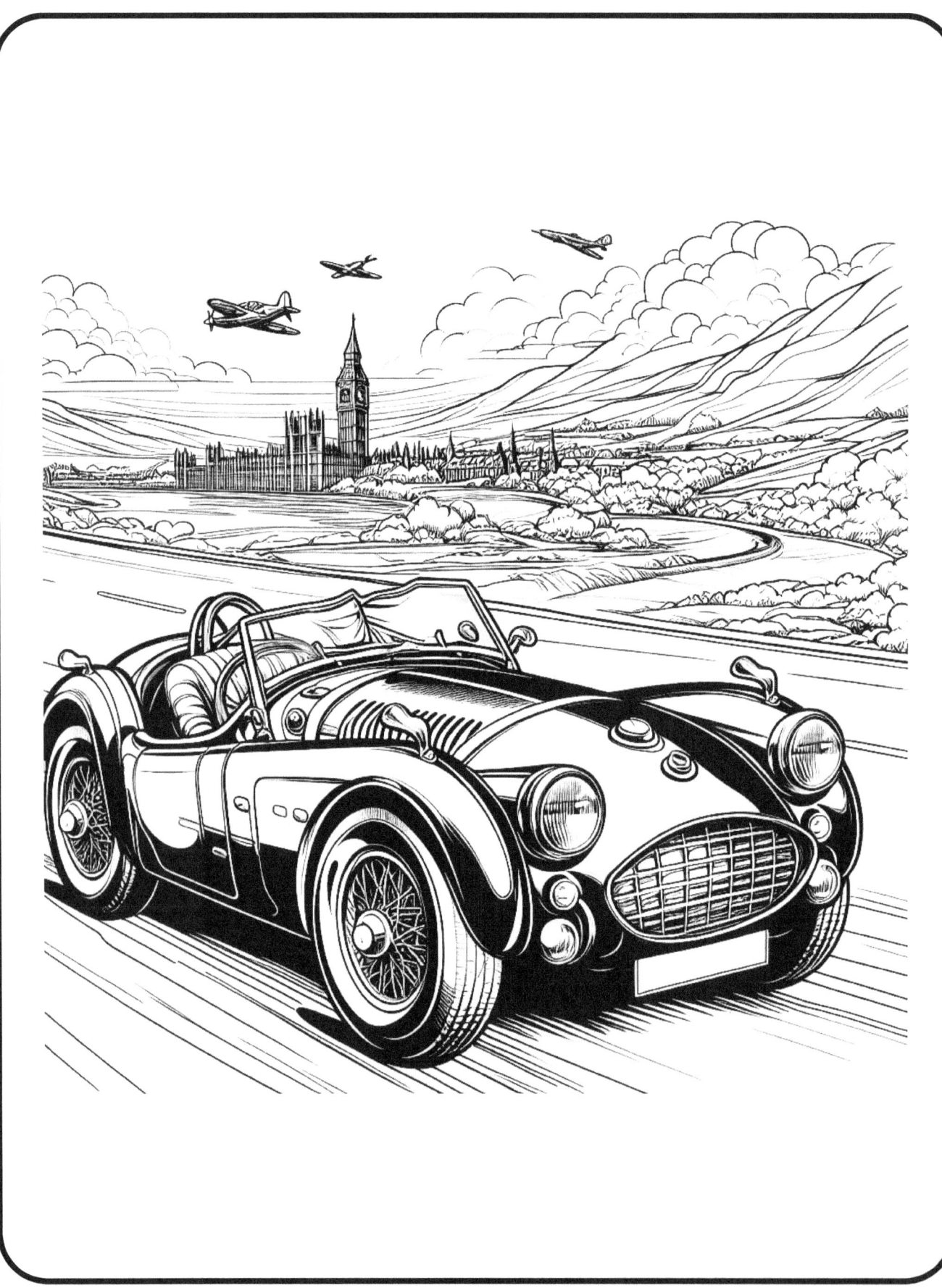

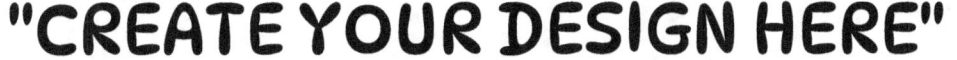
"CREATE YOUR DESIGN HERE"

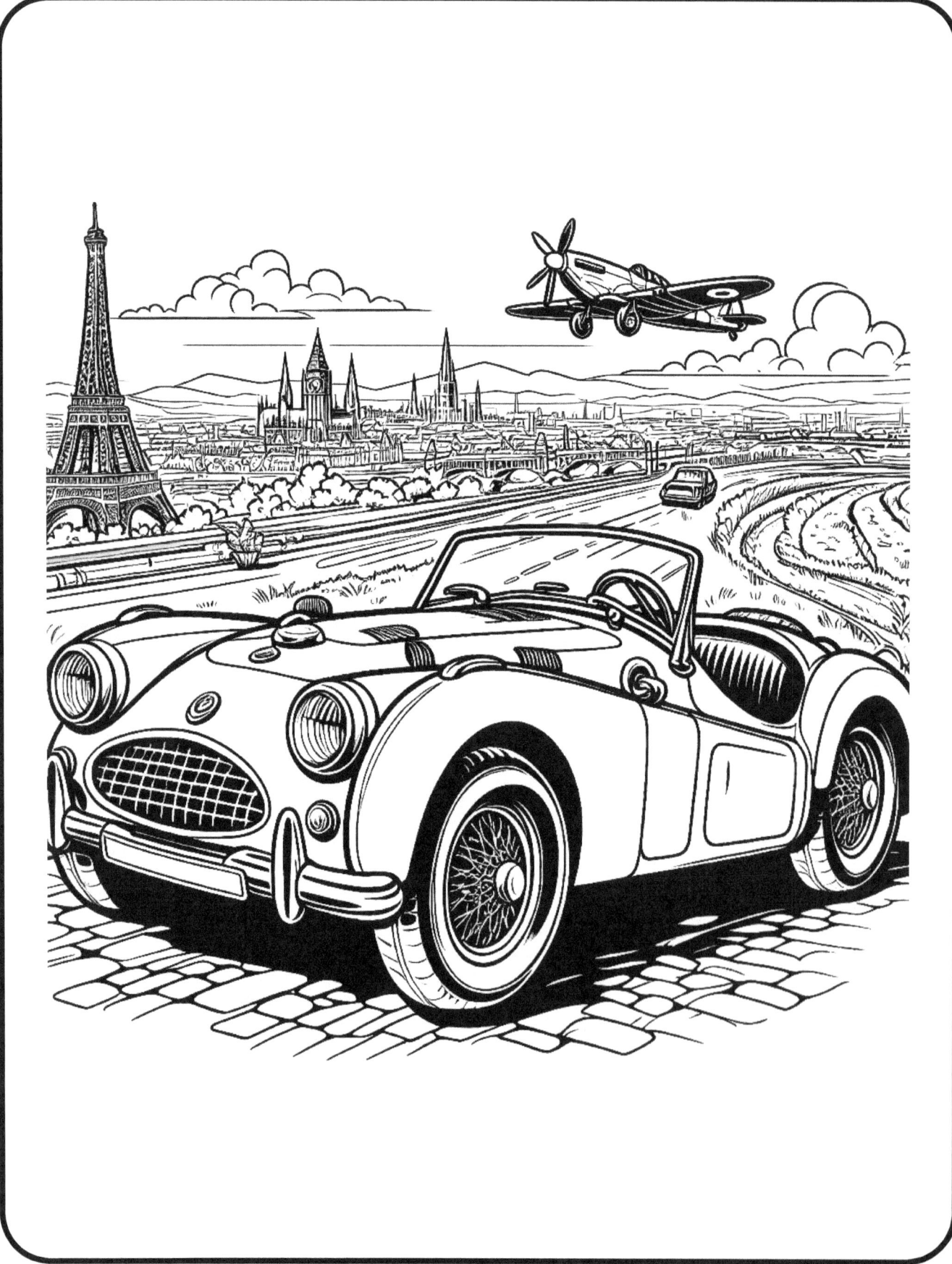

"CREATE YOUR DESIGN HERE"

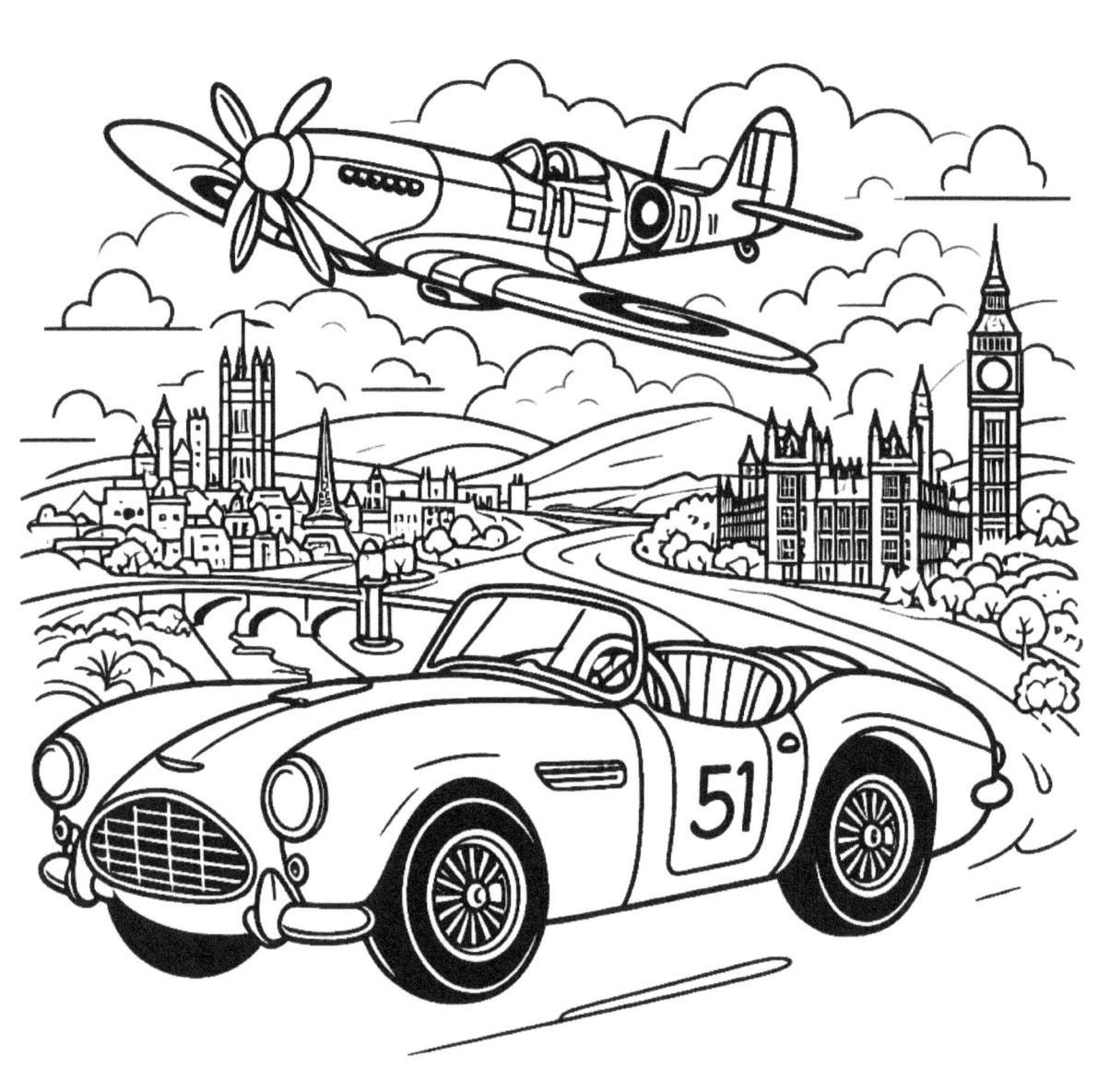

"CREATE YOUR DESIGN HERE"

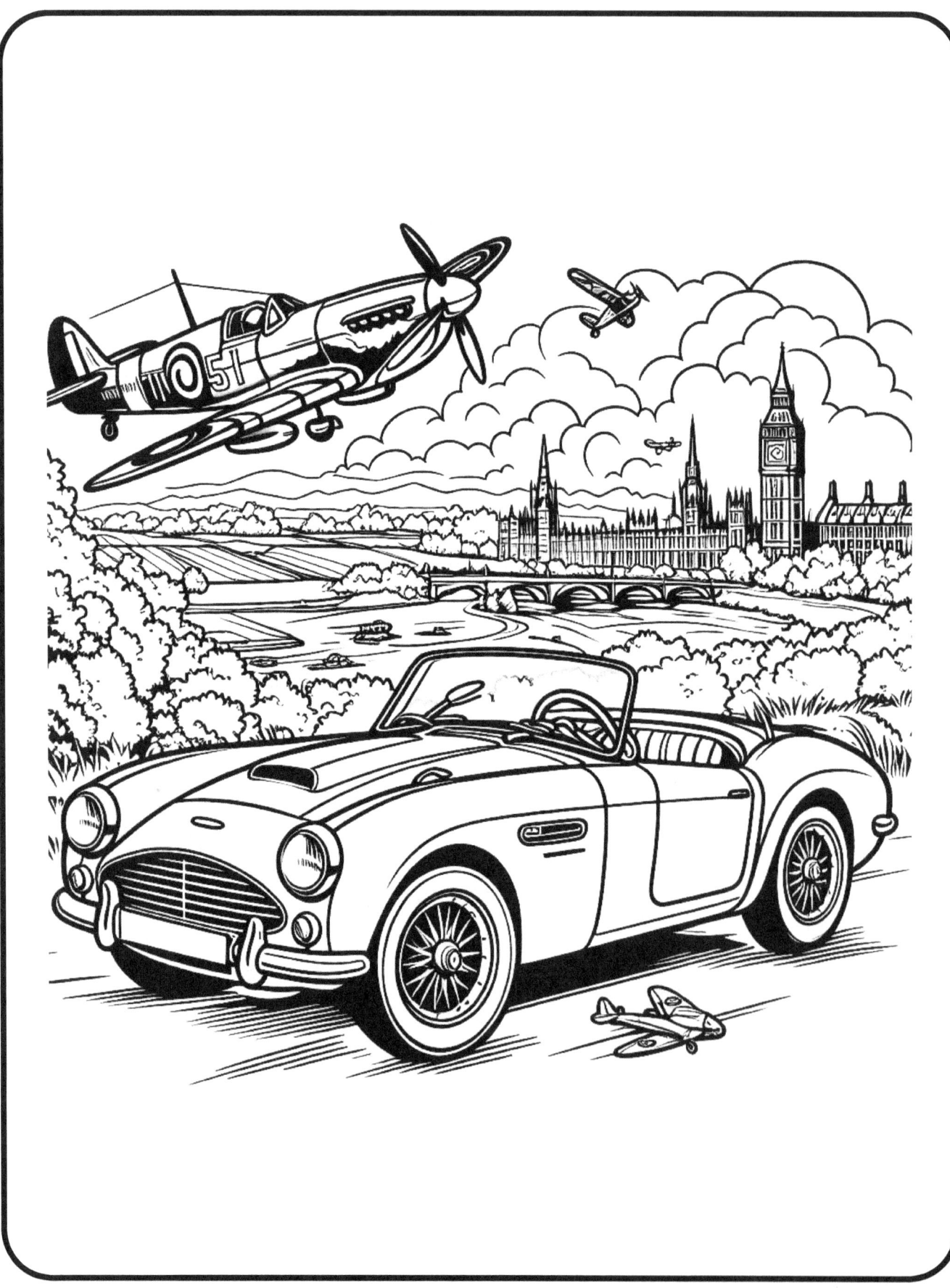

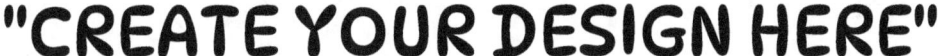

"CREATE YOUR DESIGN HERE"

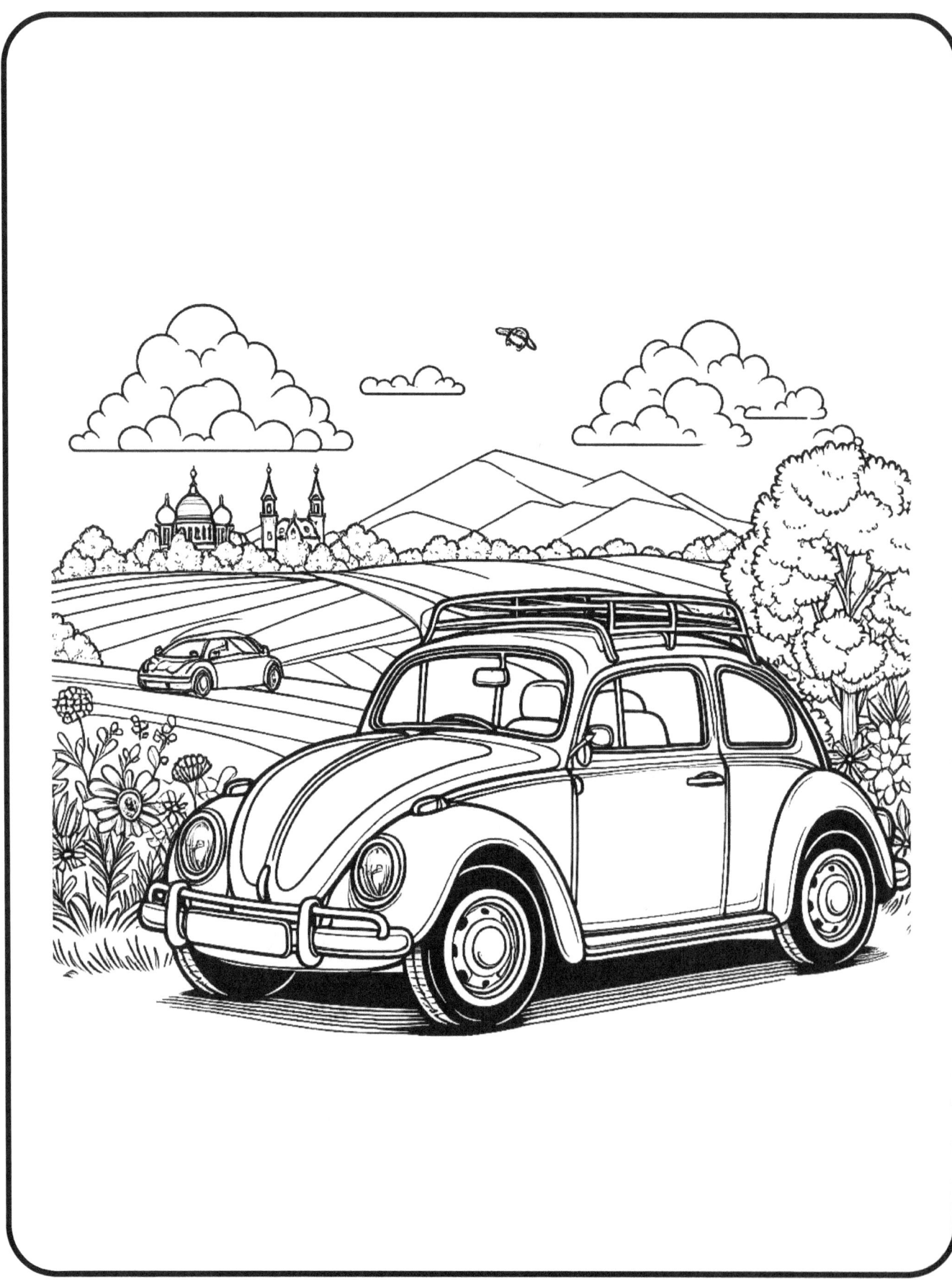

"CREATE YOUR DESIGN HERE"

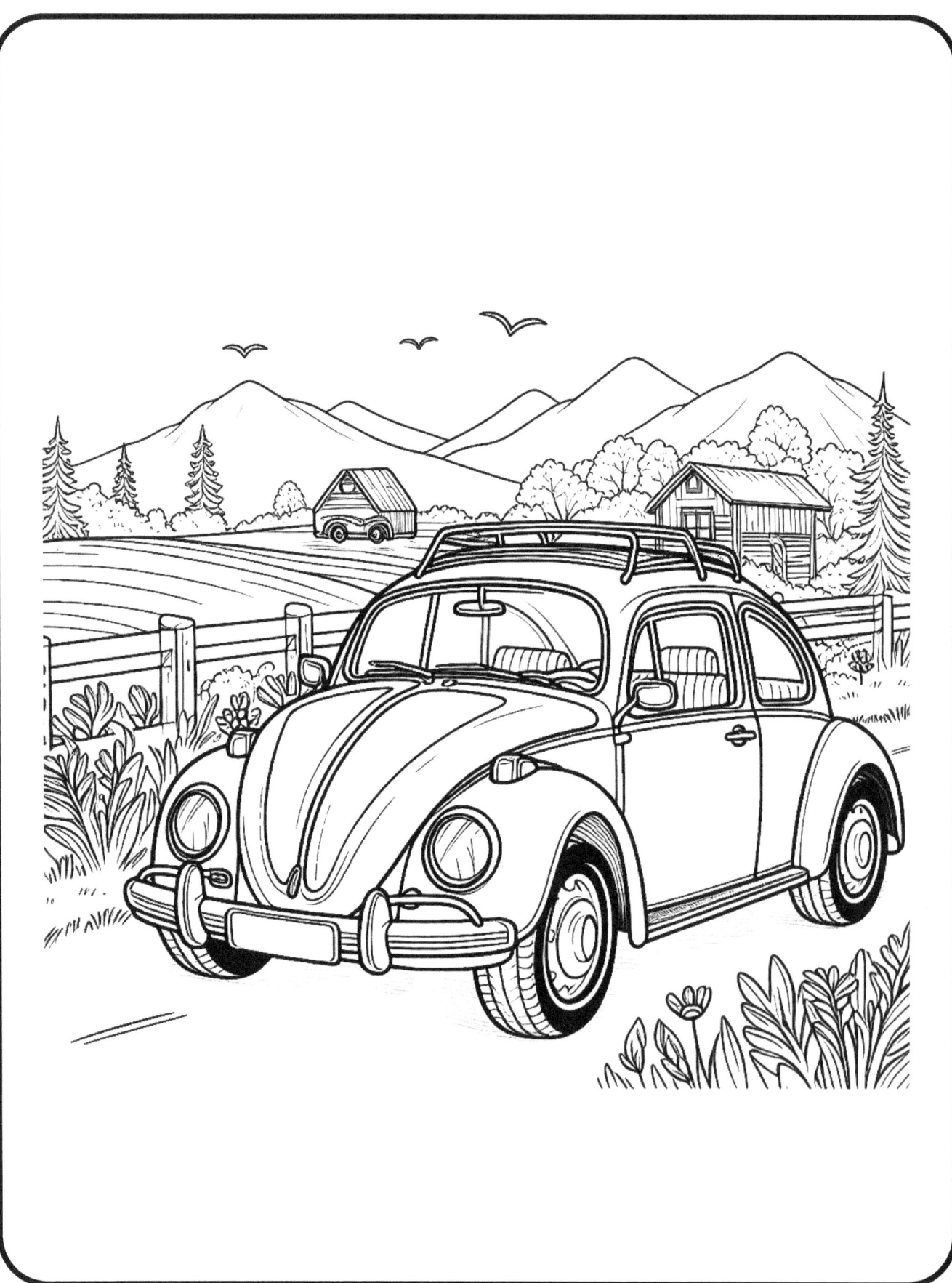

"CREATE YOUR DESIGN HERE"

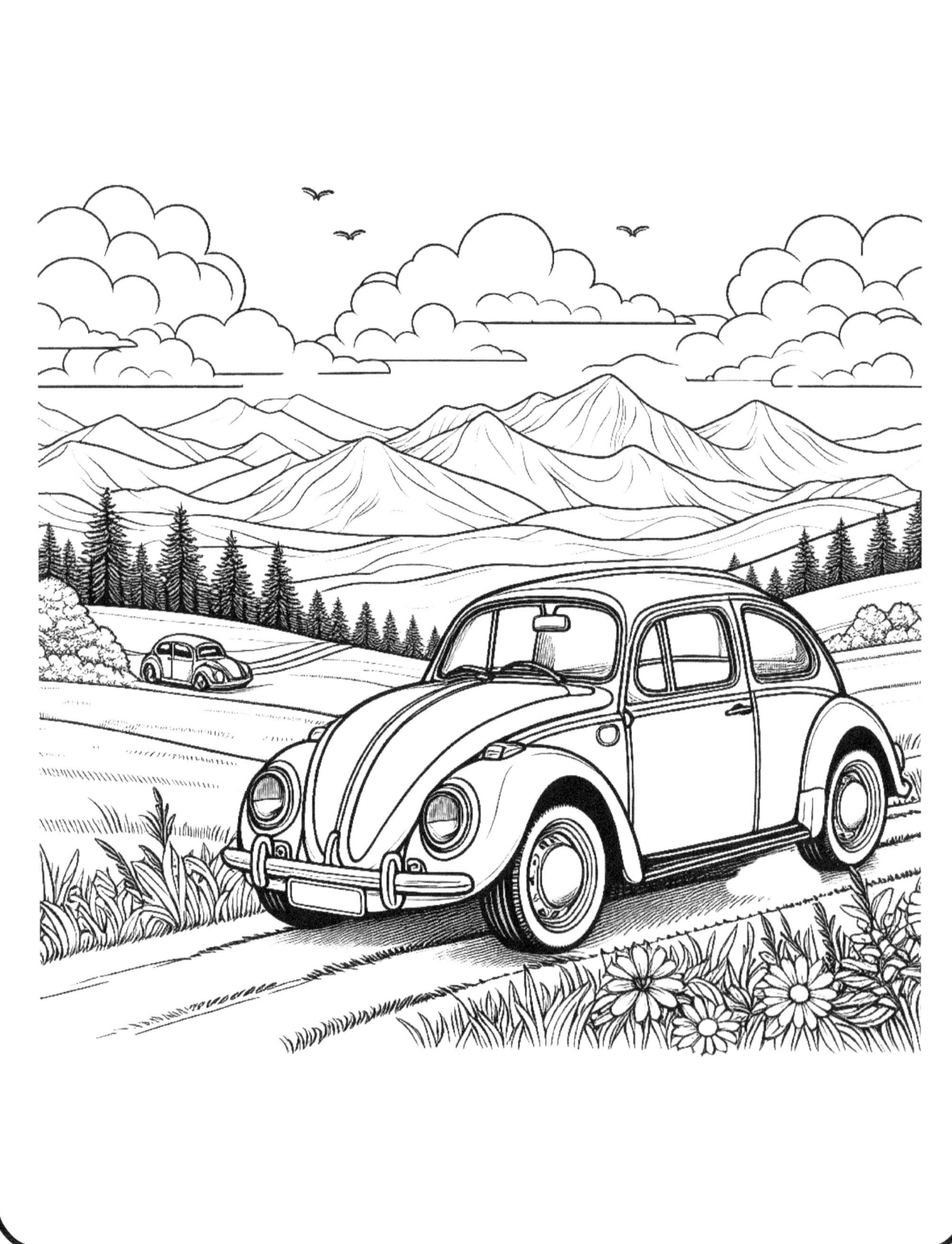

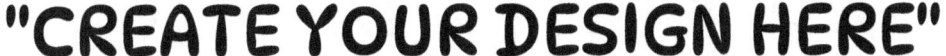

"CREATE YOUR DESIGN HERE"

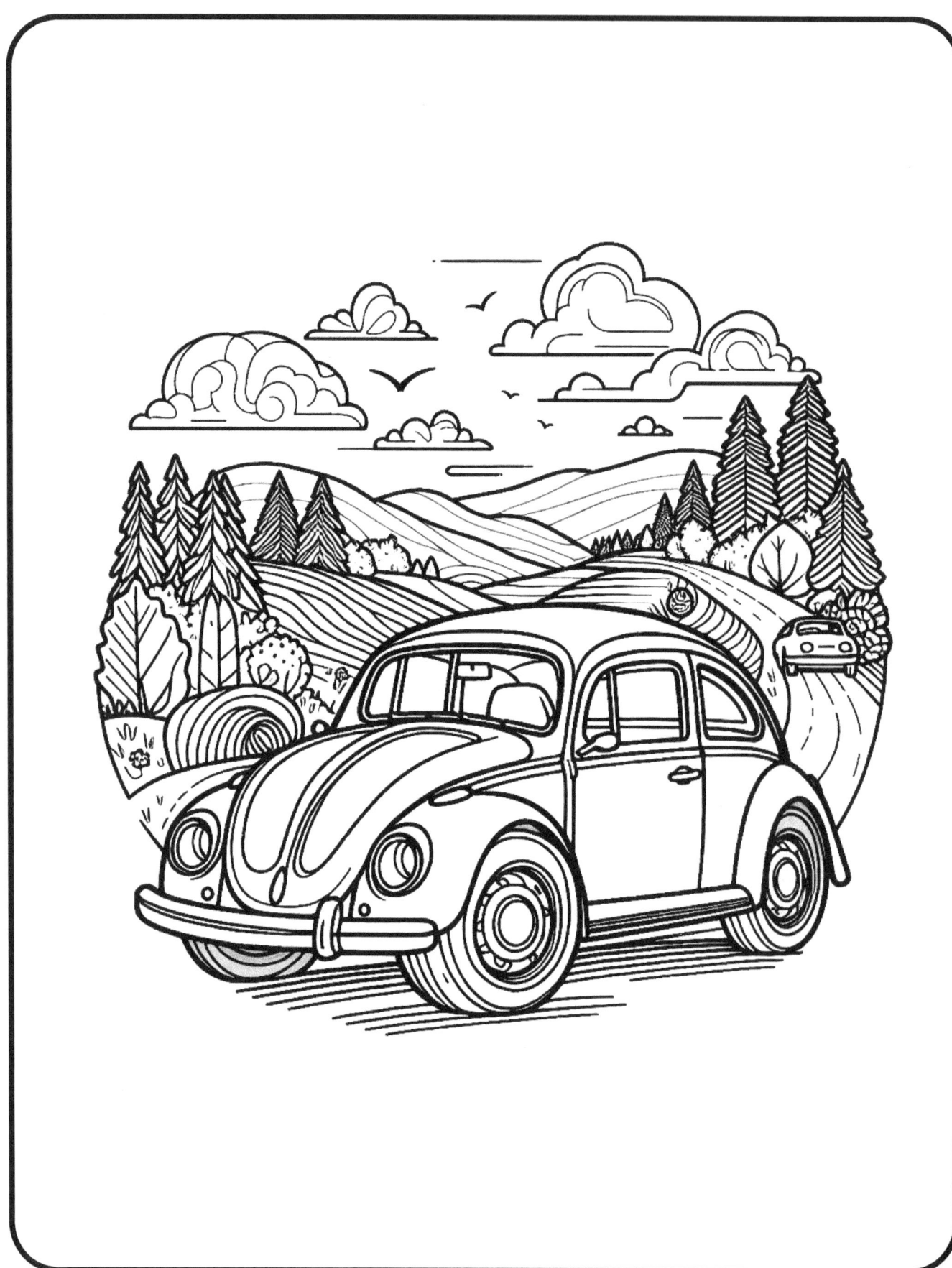

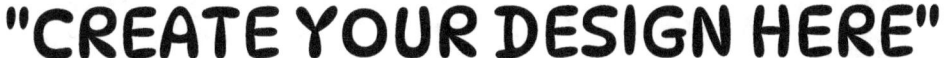
"CREATE YOUR DESIGN HERE"

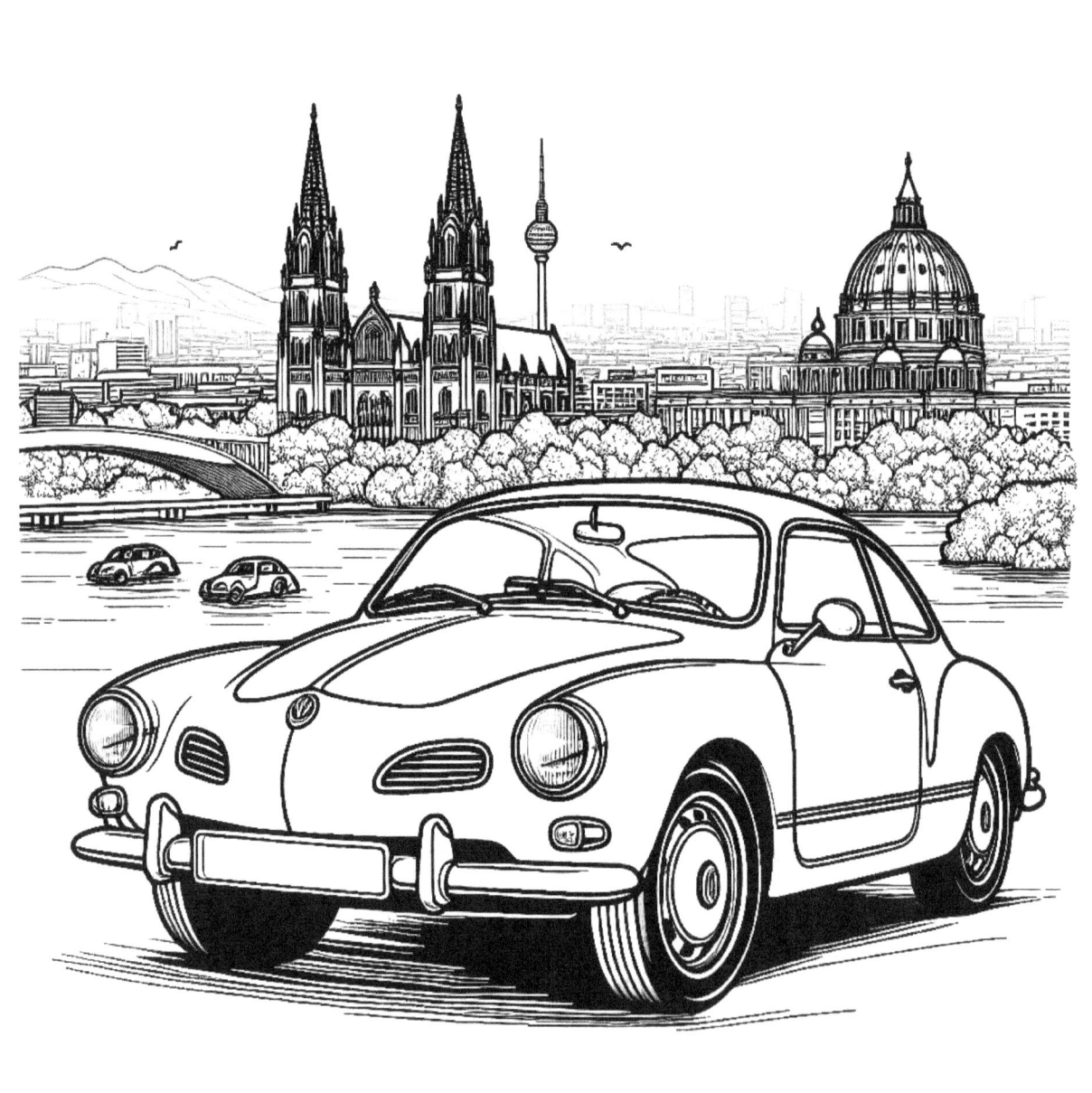

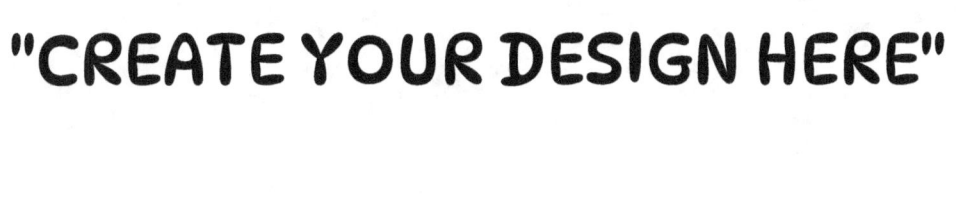

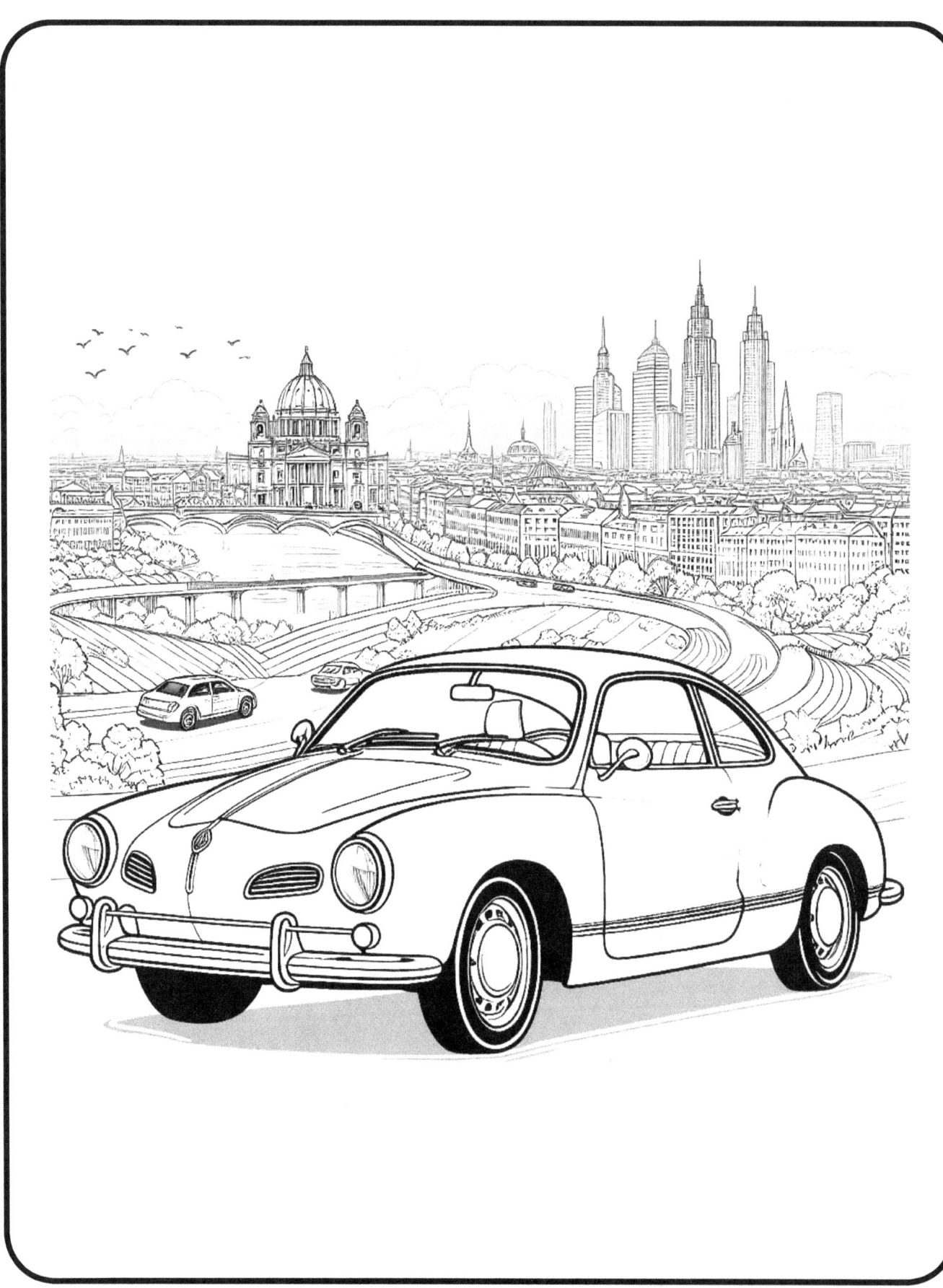

"CREATE YOUR DESIGN HERE"

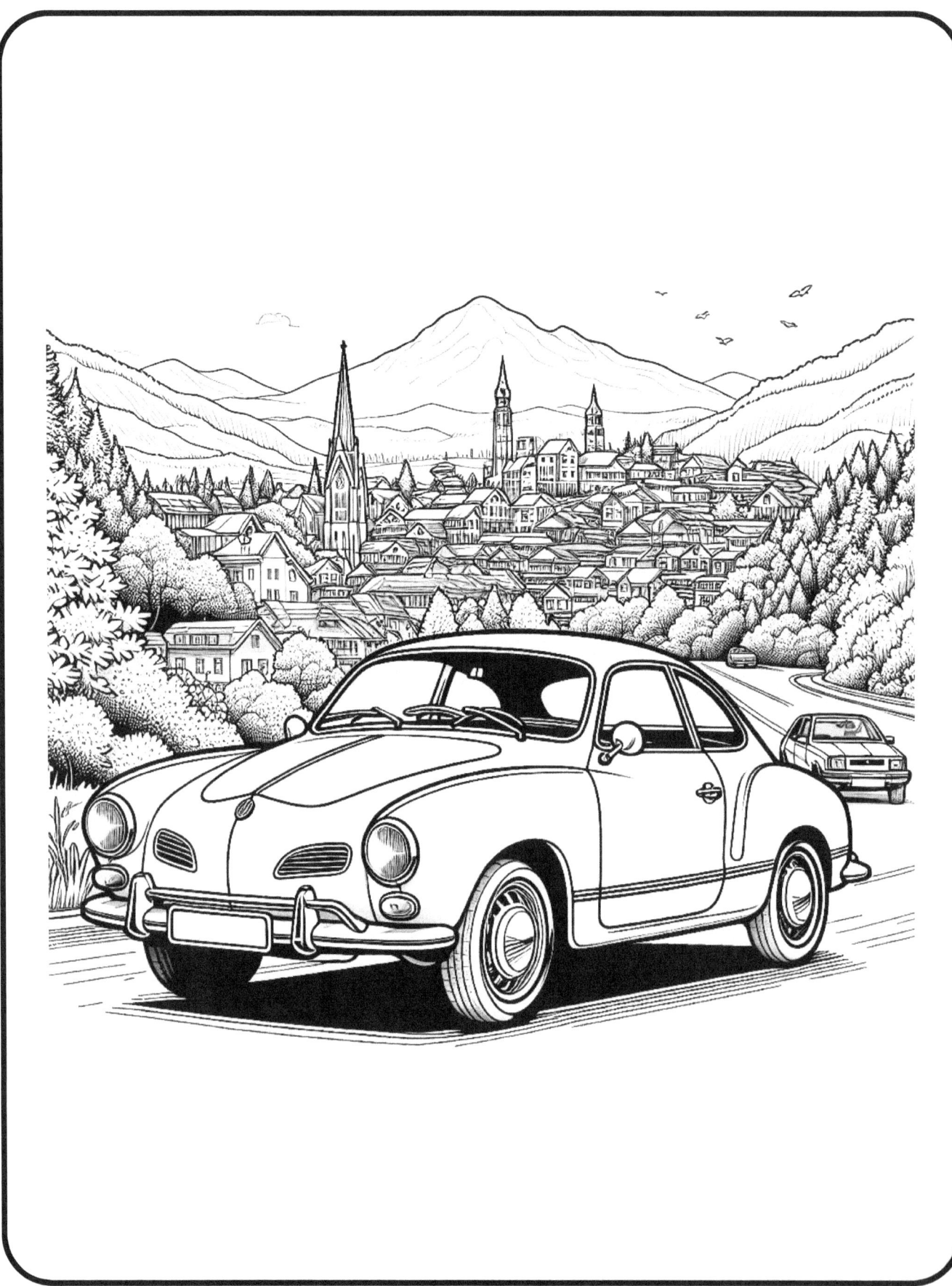

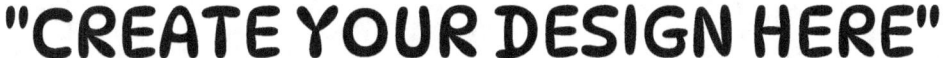

"CREATE YOUR DESIGN HERE"

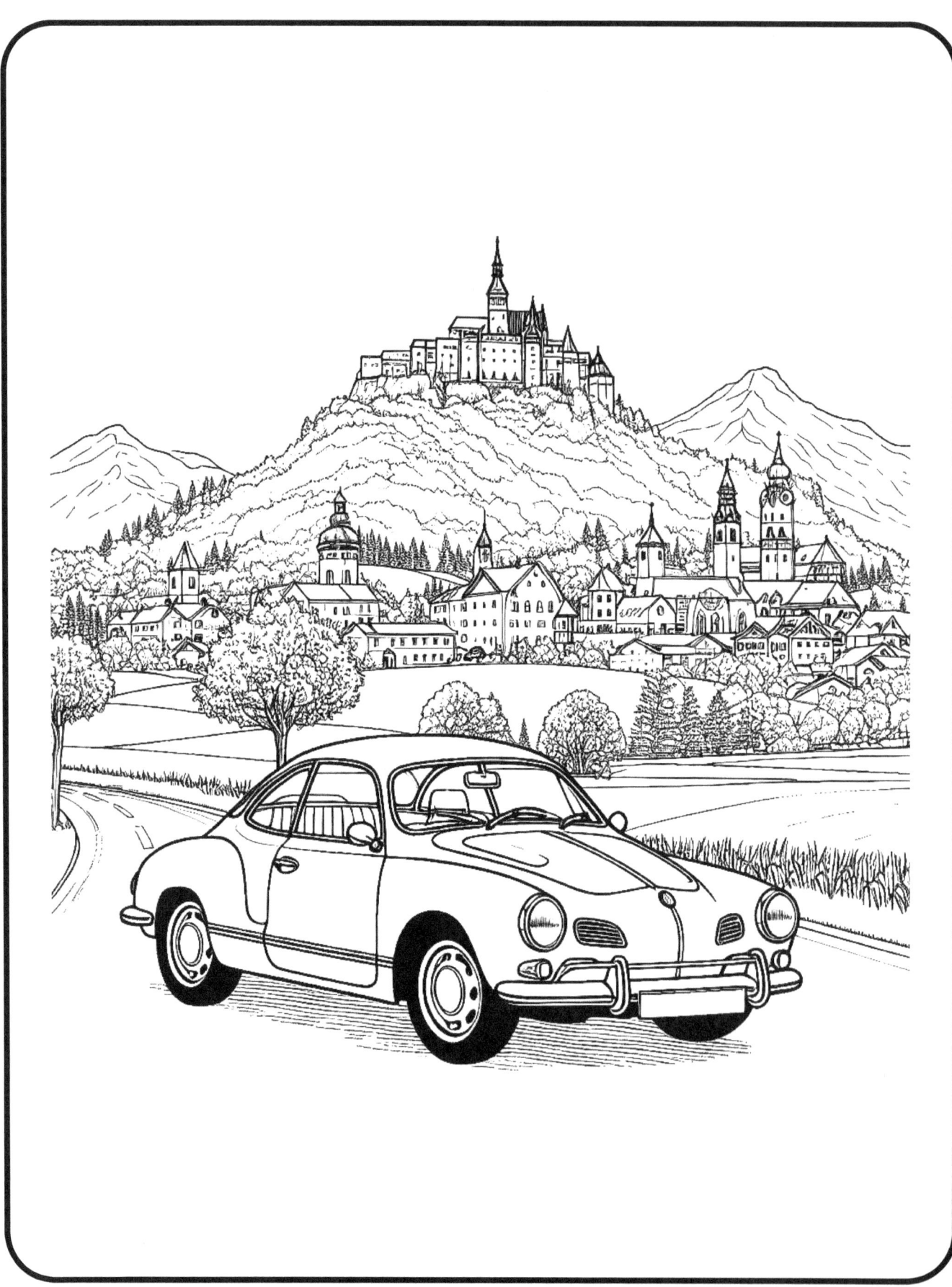

"CREATE YOUR DESIGN HERE"

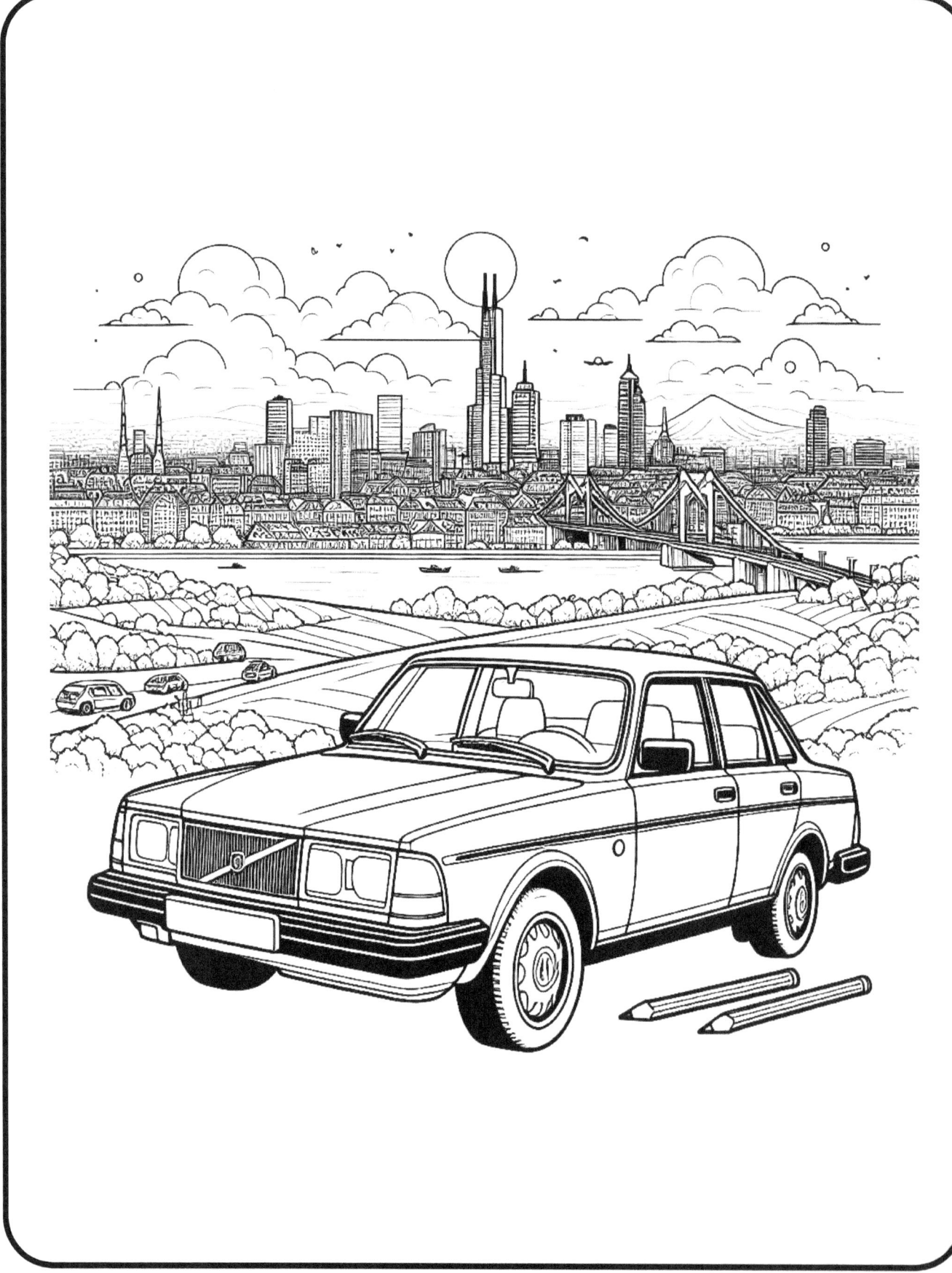

"CREATE YOUR DESIGN HERE"

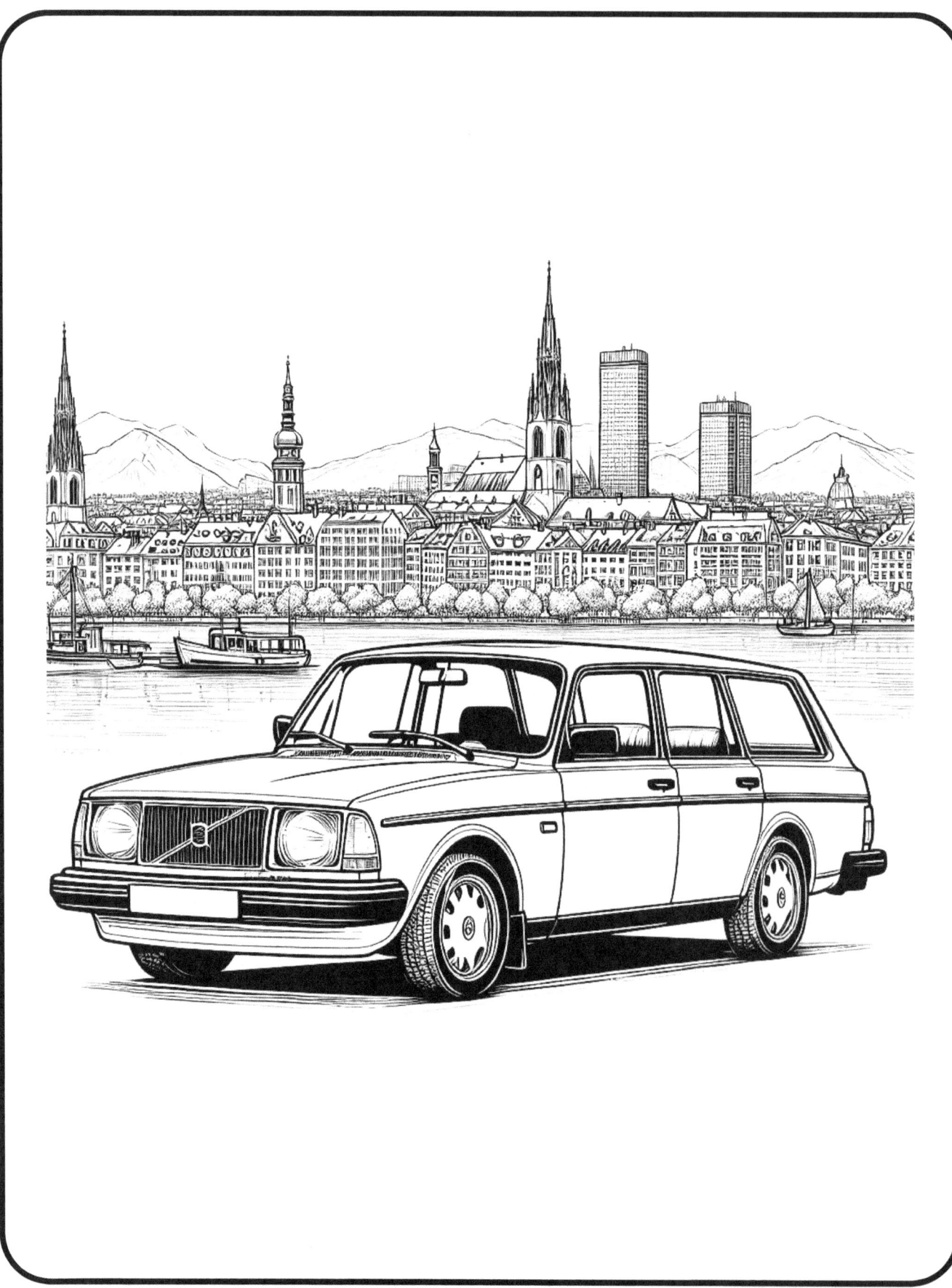

"CREATE YOUR DESIGN HERE"

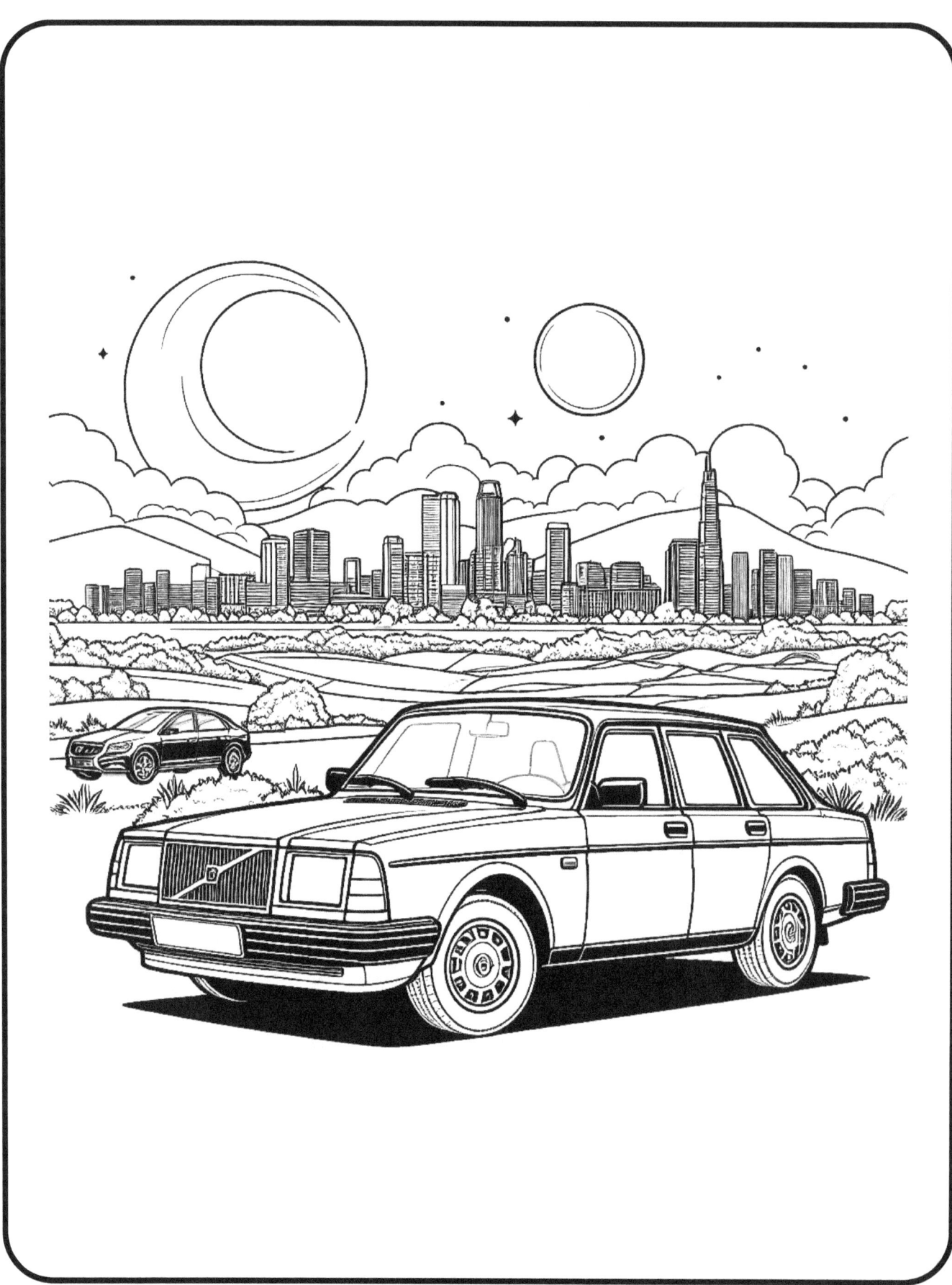

"CREATE YOUR DESIGN HERE"

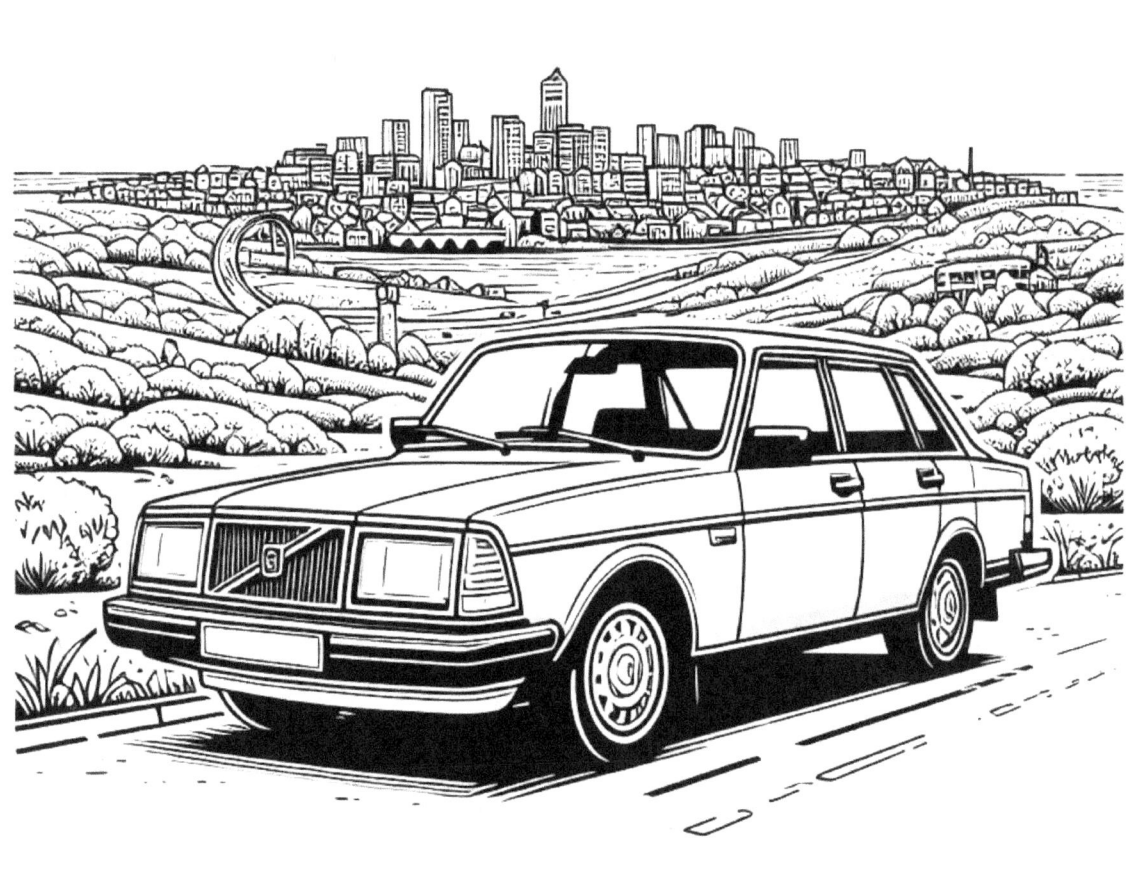

"CREATE YOUR DESIGN HERE"

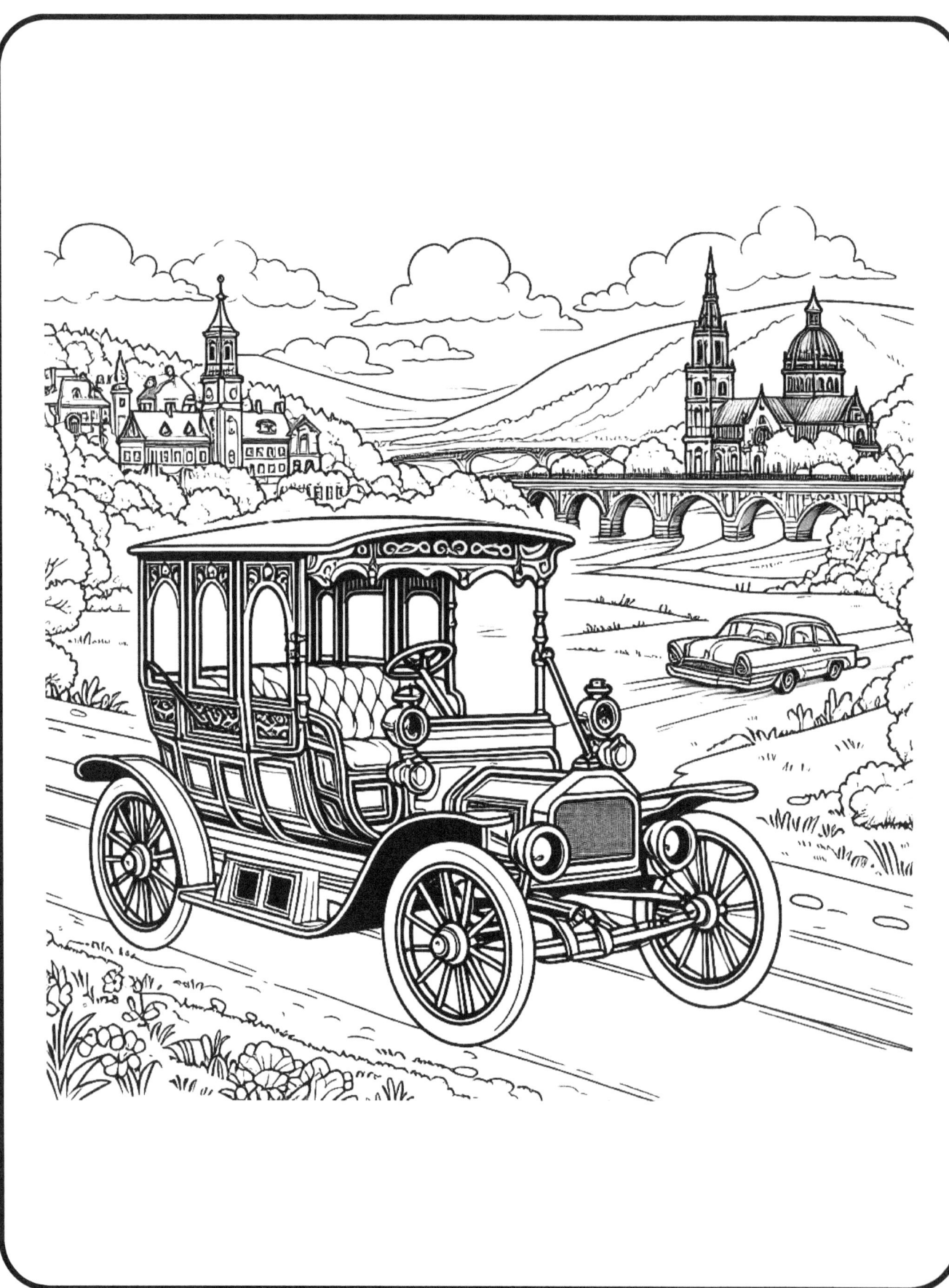

"CREATE YOUR DESIGN HERE"

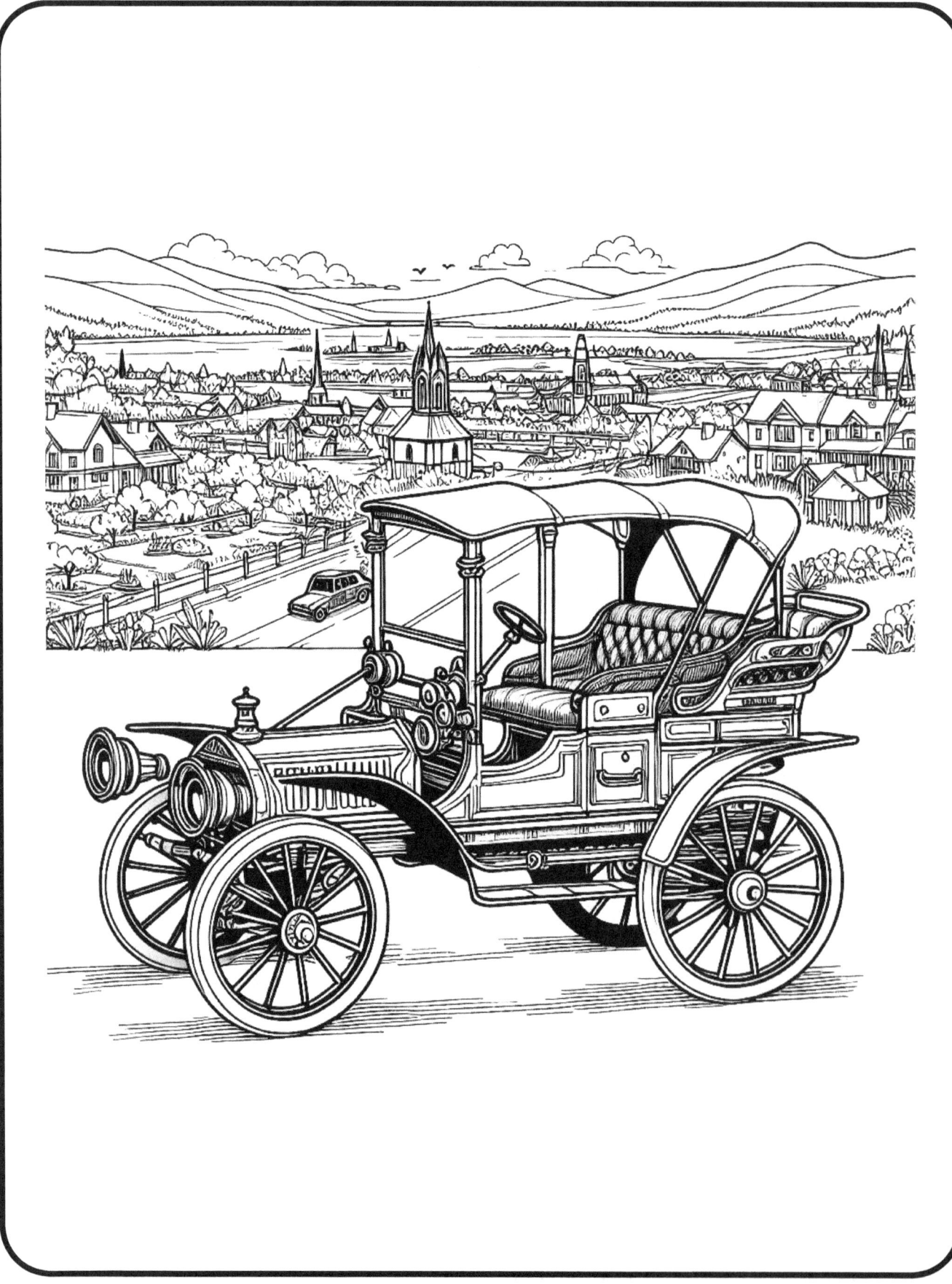

"CREATE YOUR DESIGN HERE"

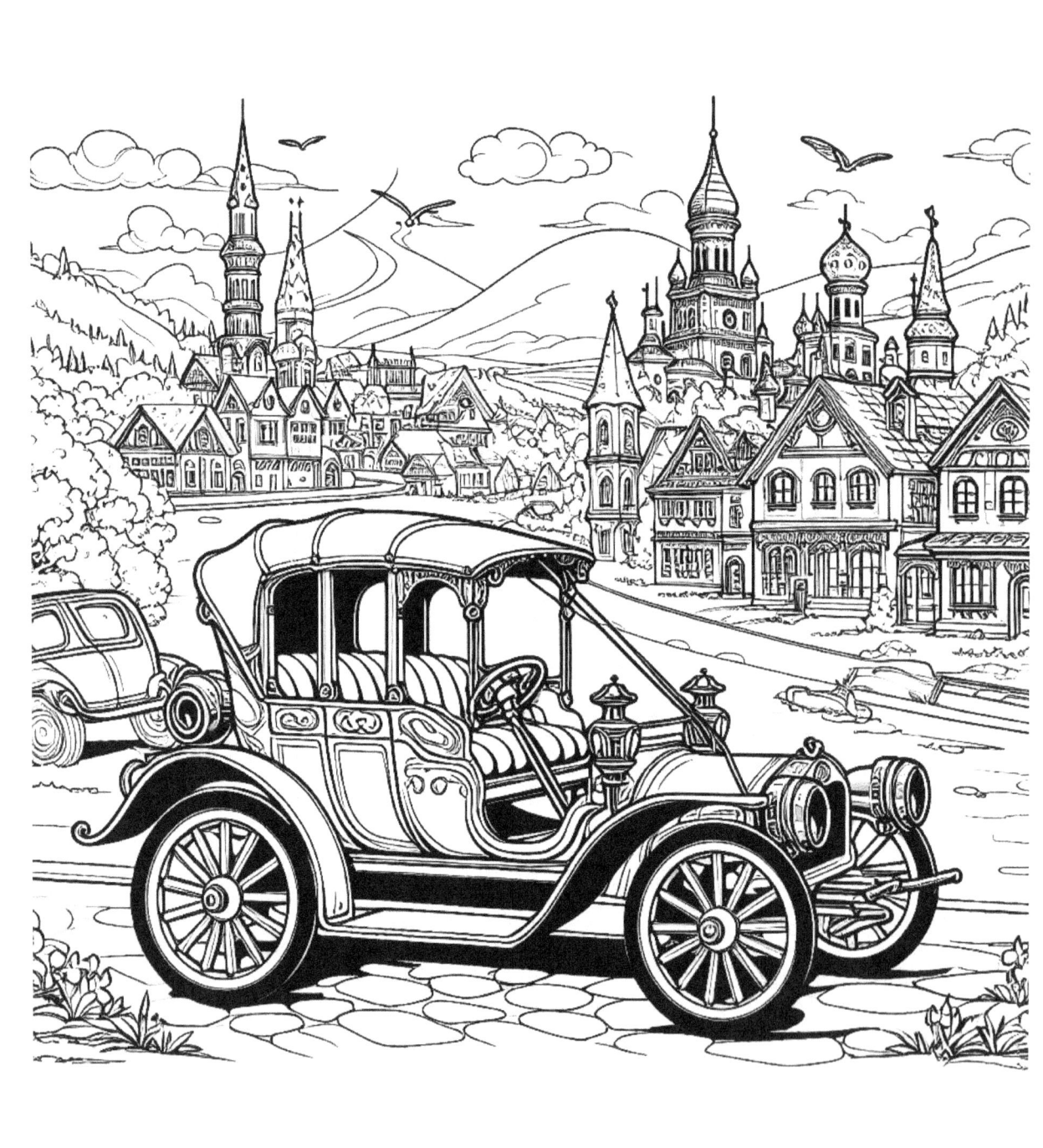

"CREATE YOUR DESIGN HERE"

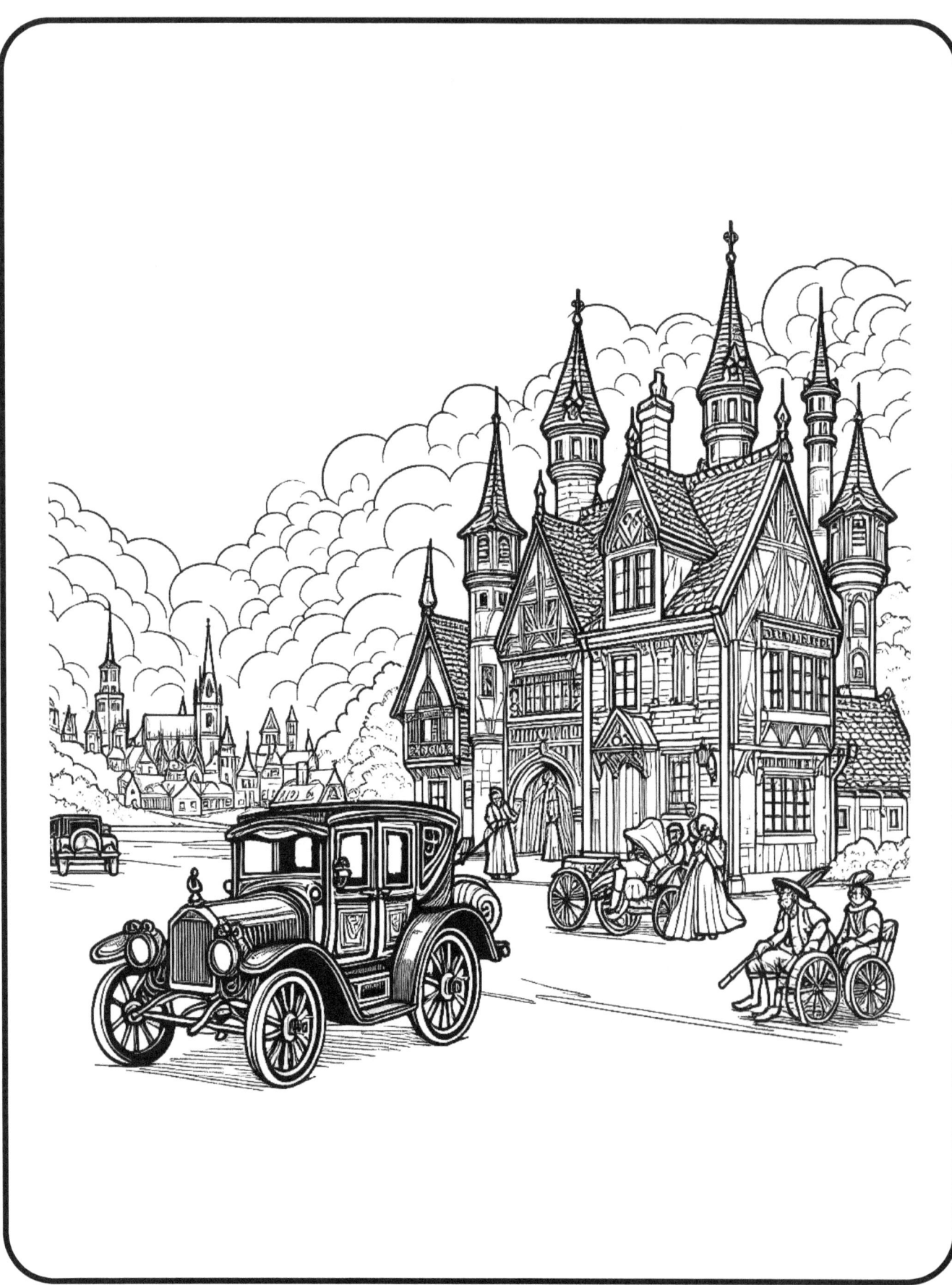

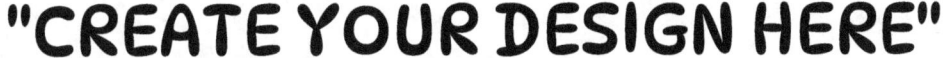
"CREATE YOUR DESIGN HERE"

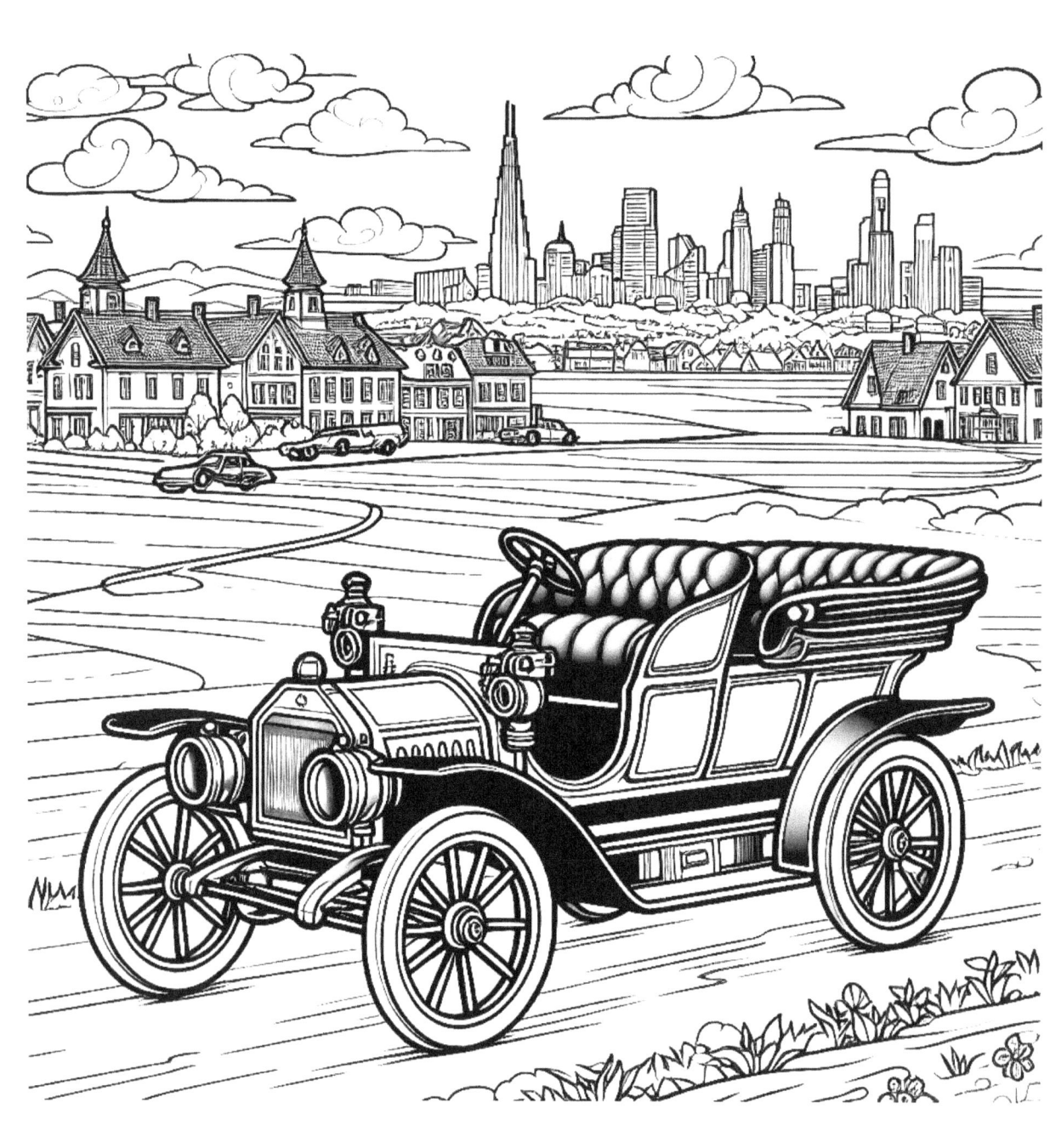

"CREATE YOUR DESIGN HERE"

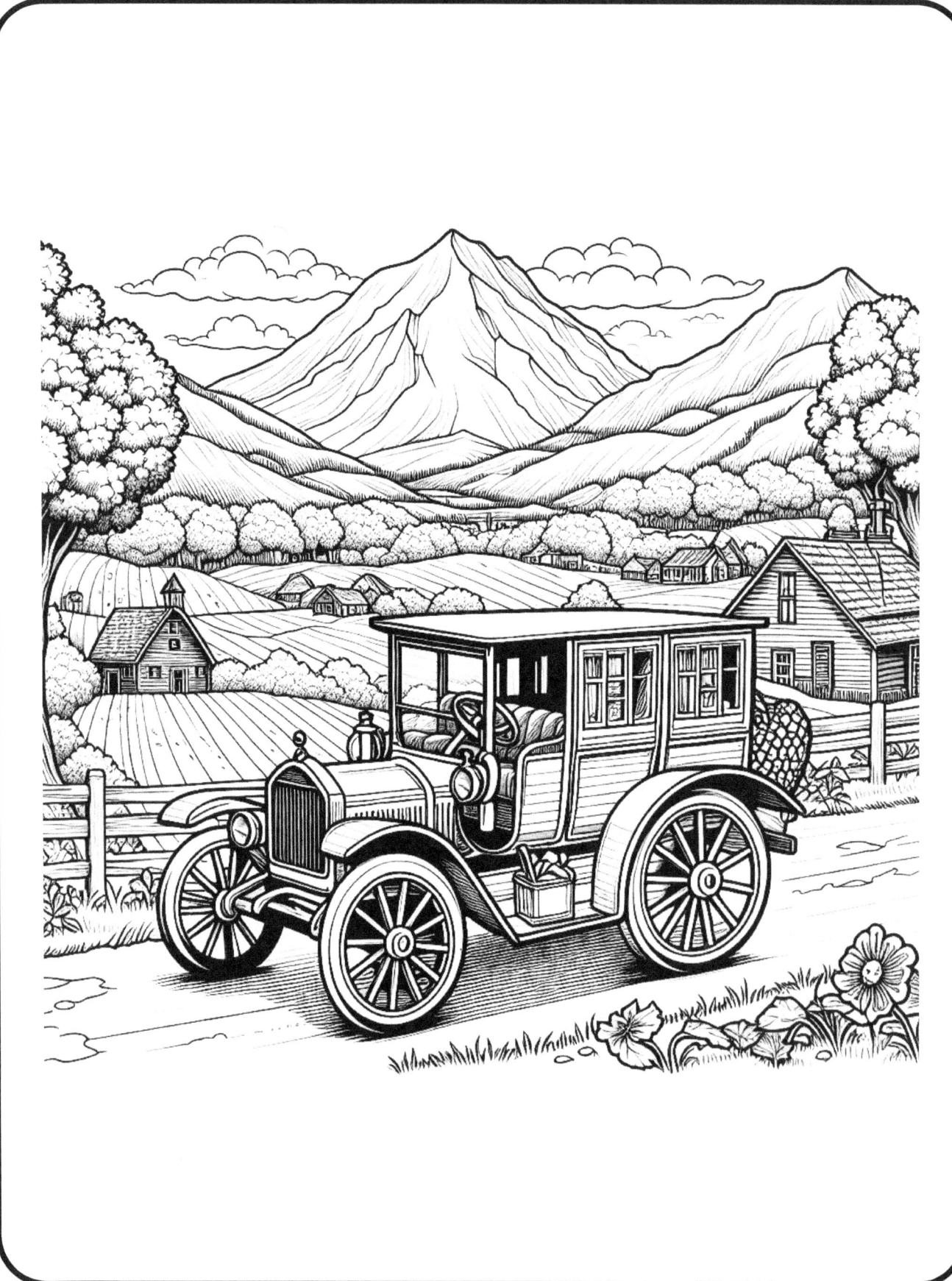

"CREATE YOUR DESIGN HERE"

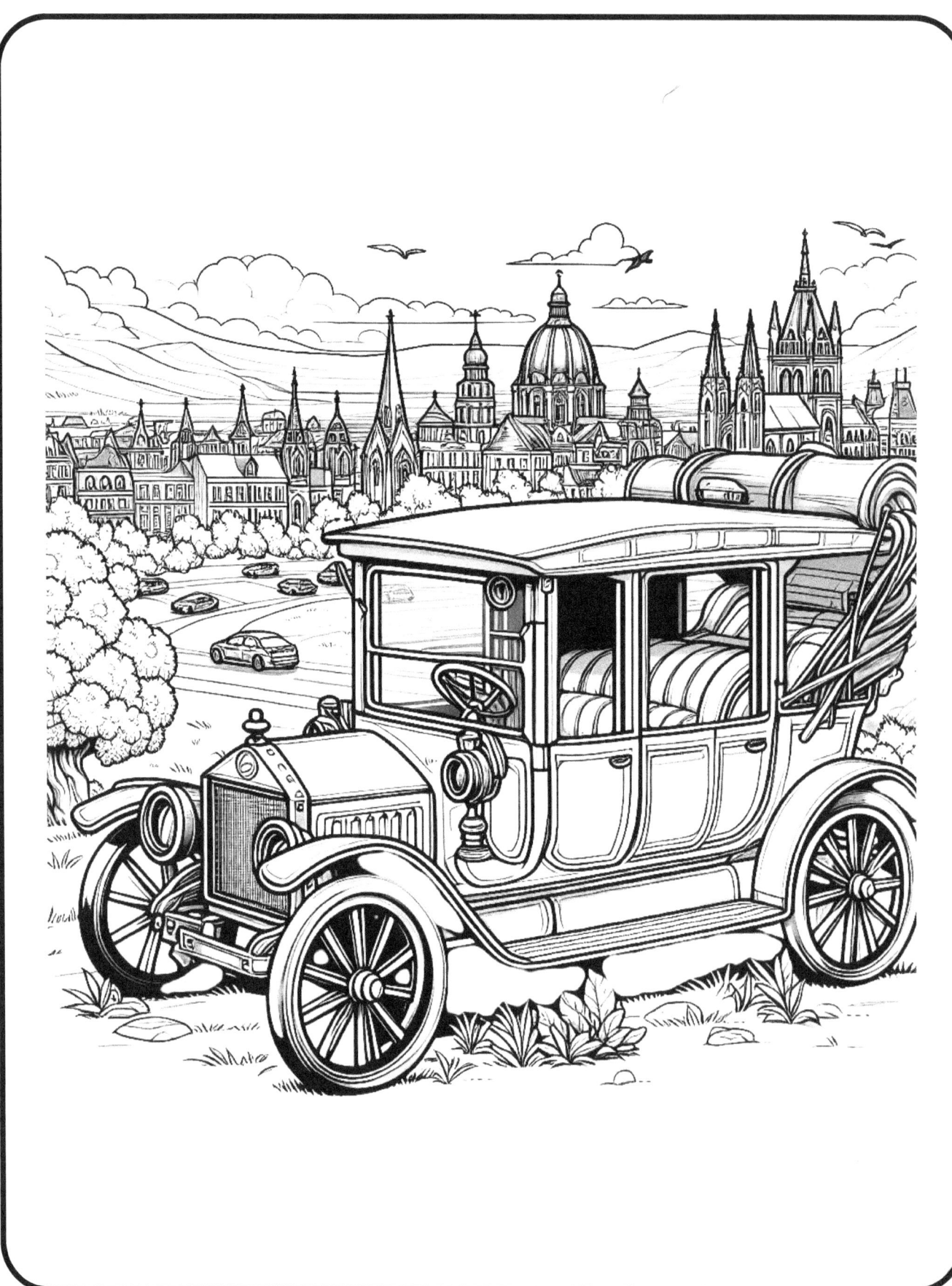

"CREATE YOUR DESIGN HERE"

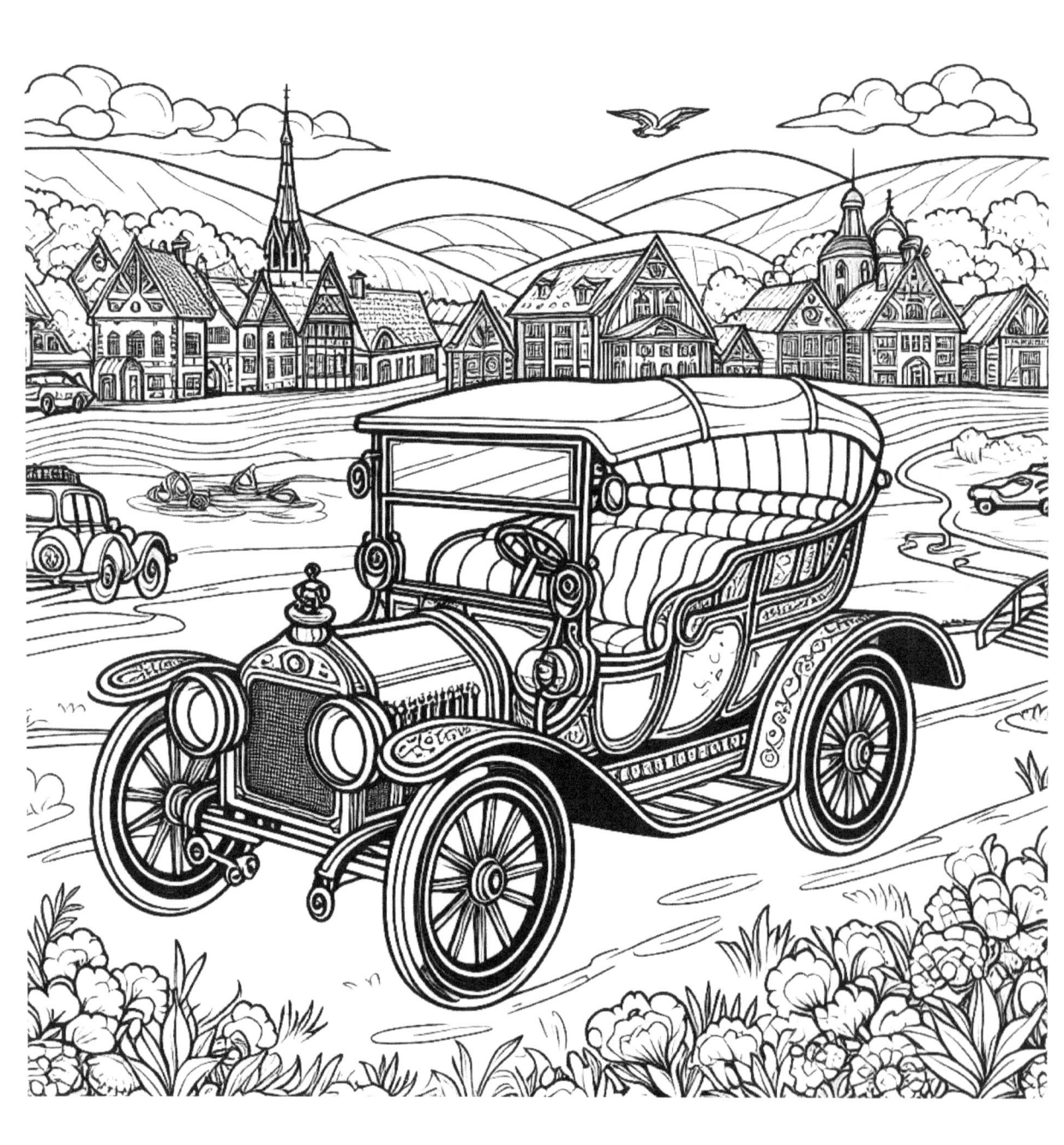

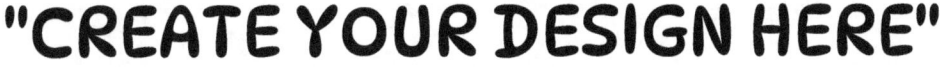

"CREATE YOUR DESIGN HERE"

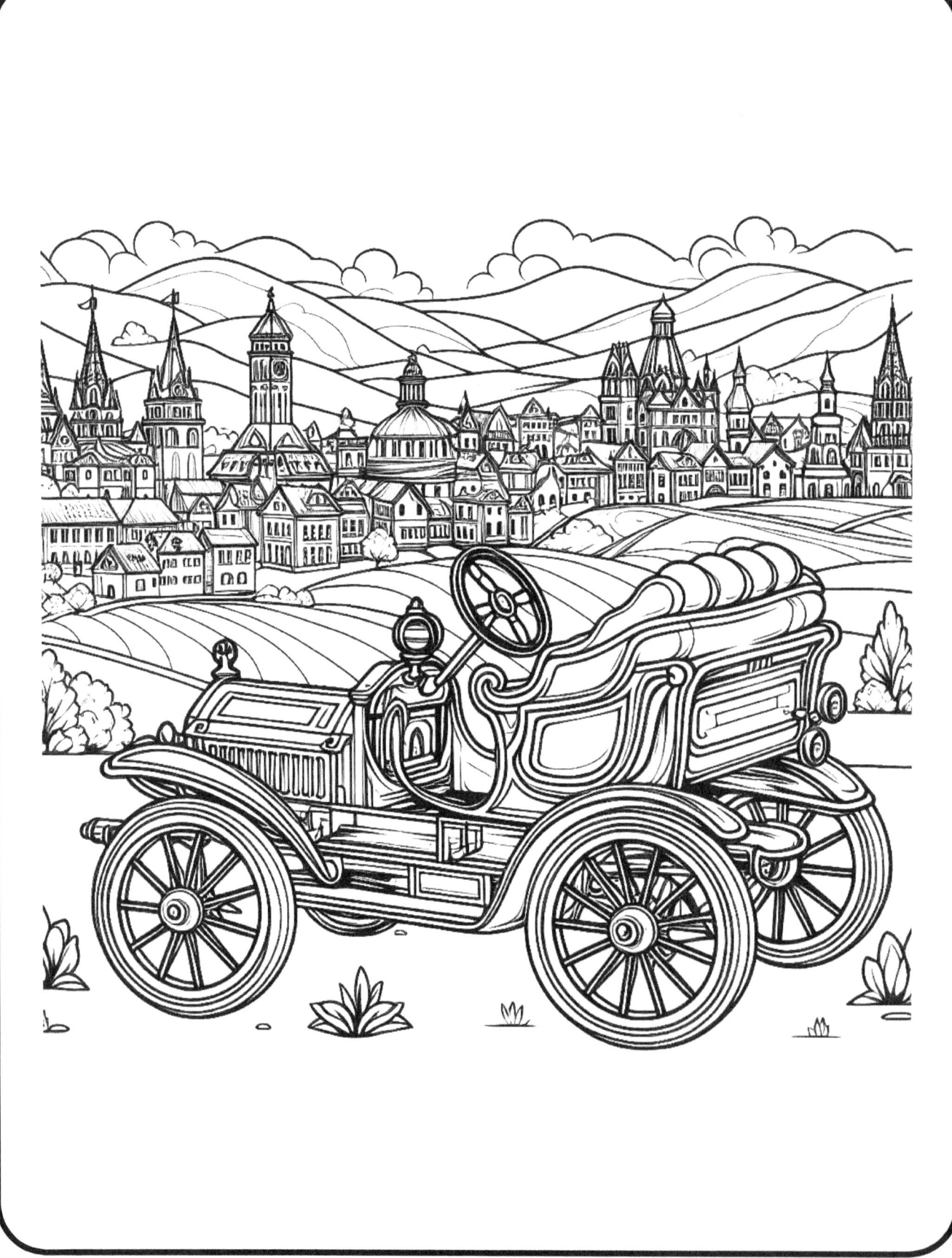

"CREATE YOUR DESIGN HERE"

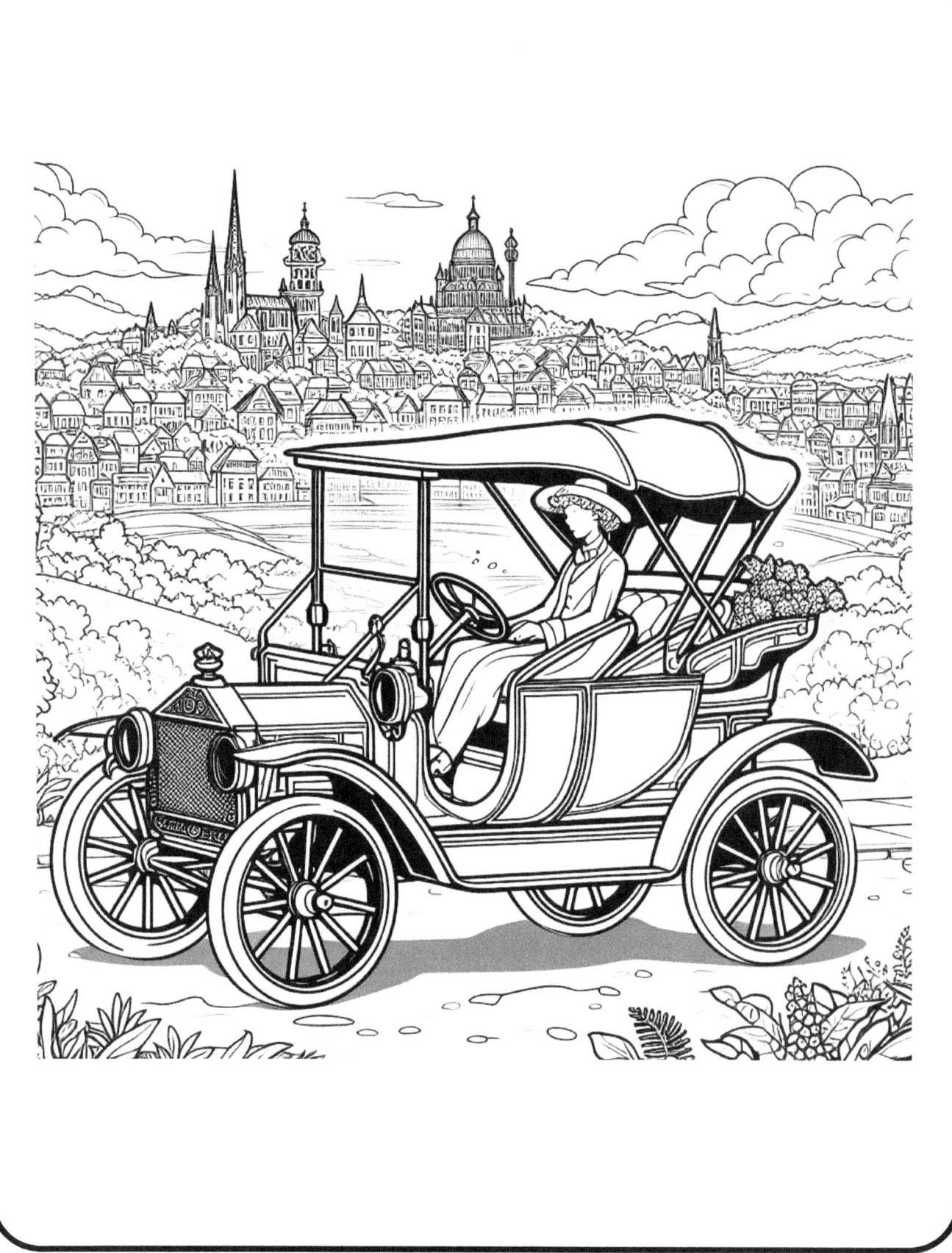

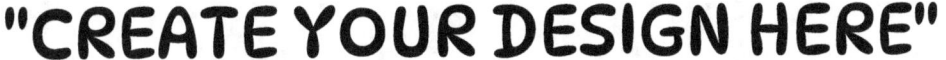

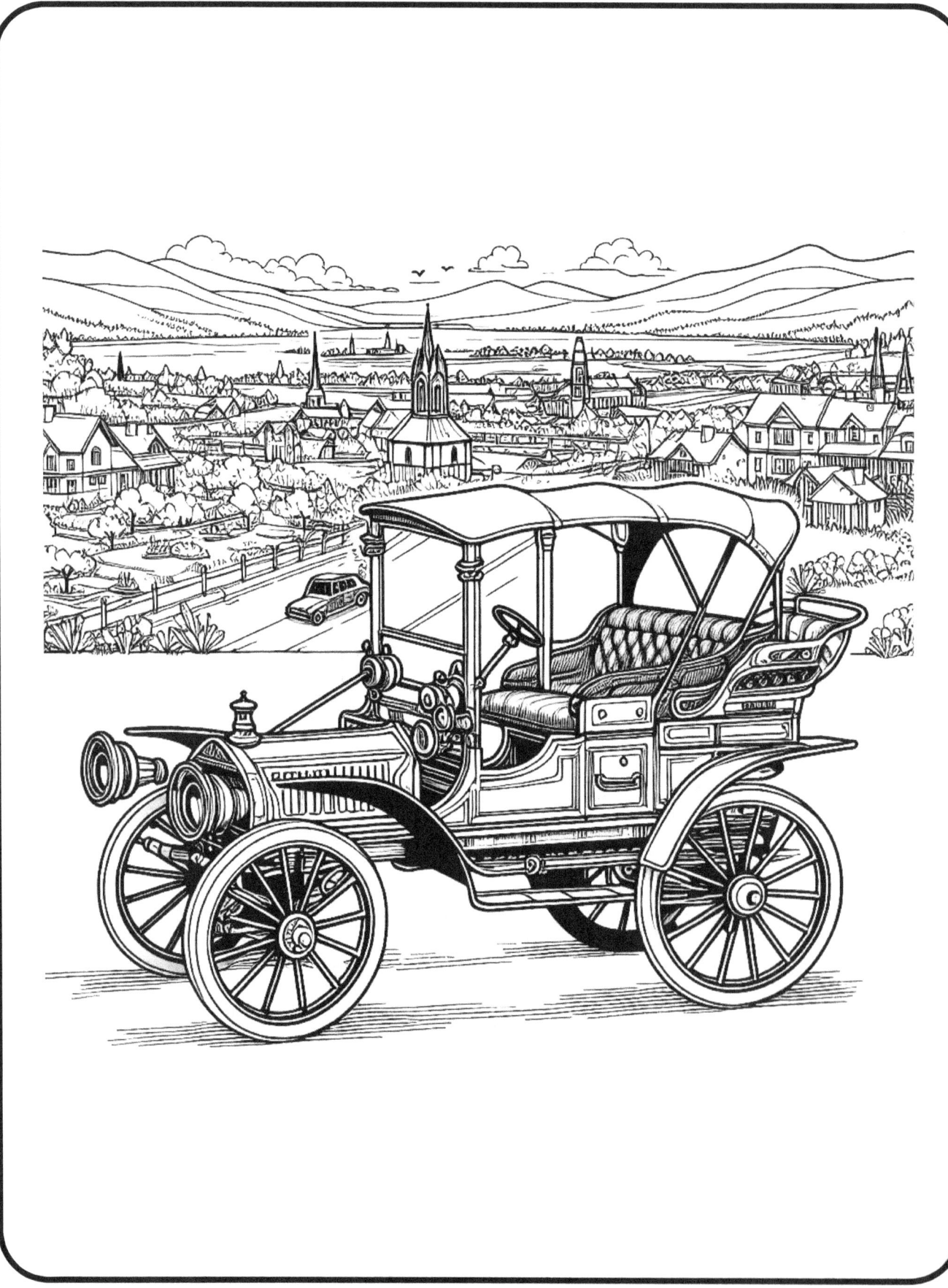

"CREATE YOUR DESIGN HERE"

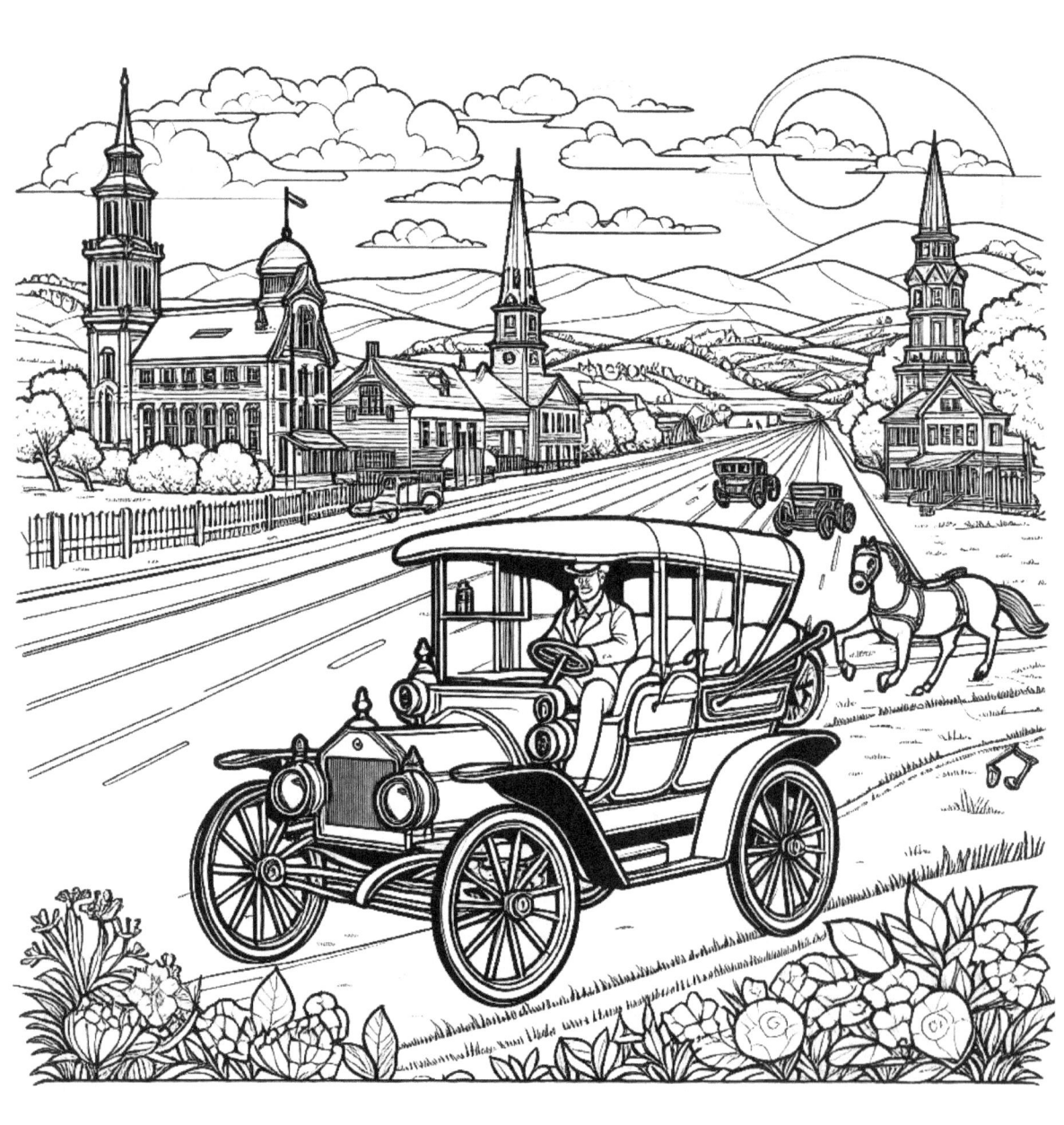

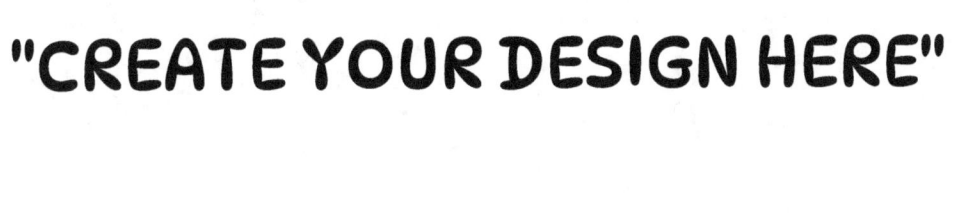
"CREATE YOUR DESIGN HERE"

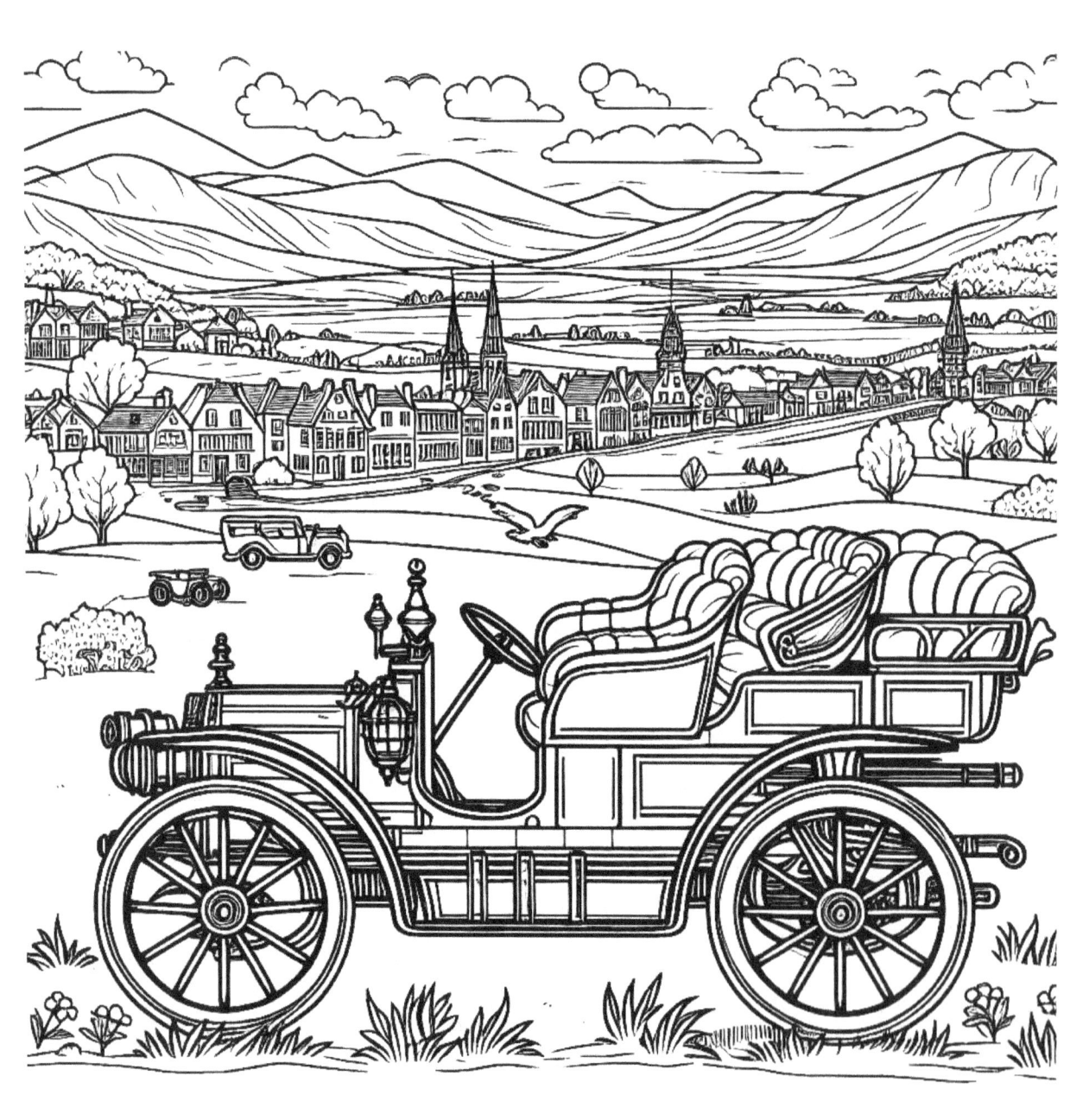

"CREATE YOUR DESIGN HERE"

www.ingramcontent.com/pod-product-compliance
Lightning Source LLC
Chambersburg PA
CBHW080945290526
45795CB00009B/2918